NEXUS TOEFL® iBT

Listening

2
Level

성공적인 학습을 위한 단계별 전략!
Development & Progress for Completion
NEXUS TOEFL *i*BT Listening Level 2

지은이 넥서스영어교육연구소, 박종현, Jacob Cho,
　　　Jeffrey S. Zeter, JoAnn Woods, Virginia Hanslien,
　　　Mary French, Yvonne Raub
펴낸이 임상진
펴낸곳 (주)넥서스

출판신고 1992년 4월 3일 제311-2002-2호 ⓡ
10880 경기도 파주시 지목로 5
Tel (02)330-5500 Fax (02)330-5555

ISBN 978-89-6000-627-0 54740

저자와 출판사의 허락없이 내용의 일부를 인용하거나
발췌하는 것을 금합니다.

가격은 뒤표지에 있습니다.
잘못 만들어진 책은 구입처에서 바꾸어 드립니다.

www.nexusEDU.kr

성공적인 학습을 위한 단계별 전략!
Development & Progress for Completion

NEXUS TOEFL® iBT

Listening

2

Level

NEXUS Edu

머리말

영어를 배우는 데 있어서, 네 가지 언어 영역을 균형 있게 학습해야 할 필요성은 오랫동안 인지되어 왔다. 하지만 국내 영어 학습 현실 속에서 그런 학습을 진행하기에는 현실적 여건이 따라 주질 못했다. 먼저 말하기나 쓰기 부분의 공인된 평가가 많지 않았던 탓도 있겠지만, 현실적으로 수업시간에 활용할 수 있는 다양한 학습 모델이 많지 않기 때문이기도 하다.

그러나 CBT 토플이 *i*BT로 바뀌어 speaking과 writing이 새롭게 추가되면서 여러 변화가 생겼다. 전반적인 문제 유형이 일차원적 문제 풀이 방식에서 벗어나 제공되는 정보를 잘 정리하여 이해하고, 이해한 내용을 다시 정리하여 표현할 수 있는 능력이 더 중요하게 되었다. 이런 능력 향상은 영어를 배울 때 암기와 반복에 의존하는 학습 방식보다는 절제된 문장 구조 속에서 "organized thoughts"를 할 수 있도록 유도하는 학습 방식을 통해 더 효과적으로 향상될 수 있다. 말하기나 쓰기의 통합적인 영역에서만 이런 능력이 필요한 것이 아니라, 독해 및 청취 영역에서도 마찬가지이다. 문제에 근거한 내용만을 맞히는 것이 아니라, 문단 간의 정보 관계를 전체적으로(global understanding) 훑을 수 있는 훈련이 되어야 한다. 따라서 토플을 단기간에 한 권으로 끝을 내려한다거나 한 학기의 강의 수업 방식으로 짧은 시간에 높은 성적을 올리기에 급급하기보다는 위와 같은 학습 방식에 초점을 맞춰 체계적인 계획을 가지고 접근하게 되면, 토플 성적 이외에도 전반적인 영어 실력을 키워갈 수 있으리라 생각된다.

넥서스 토플은 전반적으로 위와 같은 취지로 기획되었다. 다시 말해, 각 단원마다 주어진 스킬만 배우고 끝내는 것이 아니라 앞서 학습한 스킬을 다시 반복학습할 수 있게 하고, 지문을 통합적으로 활용하며, 짧은 시간 안에 정보의 구조를 파악하는 능력을 훈련할 수 있도록 구성하였다.

짧은 시간에 점수를 올리려는 전략적인 학습 방식을 선호하기보다는 체계적인 학습 계획과 그에 맞는 적절한 교재를 활용하여 토플 점수 향상 이외에도 영어로 생각하고 정리하는 표현 기술을 잘 연마할 수 있도록 학습하는 데 있어 이 교재가 많은 도움이 되기를 바란다.

| 넥서스영어교육연구소 |

이 책의 특징

1 단계별 기본 학습 훈련 장치 강조
- Second listening, note-taking practice를 통해 길어진 청취 지문을 효과적으로 들을 수 있게 도와 주는 기본 훈련 장치를 구성하였다.

2 다양한 테마의 강의와 대화 지문 구조의 체계적 분석
- 다양한 주제의 강의와 대화를 들려 주고, 그 구조를 체계적으로 분석할 수 있는 activity를 마련하였다.

3 체계적인 학습 스킬과 전략 구성
- 새롭게 바뀌는 iBT Listening Section에서 나오는 질문 유형을 철저히 분석하고, 질문 유형이 요구하는 기본적인 strategies를 바탕으로 listening skill을 체계적으로 습득할 수 있도록 구성하였다.

4 어휘력 확장의 학습
- 토플에 자주 쓰이는 테마와 관련된 기본 어휘 학습을 강조(동의어, 반의어, 영영 해석)하여, 어휘 능력 향상을 도모하였다.

5 iBT 실전에 맞춘 단계별 연습
- Skill Check-up, Exercise, Actual Test, Progress Test, Final Test로 이어지는 단계별 연습으로 iBT Listening을 완벽하게 대비할 수 있도록 구성하였다.

이 책의 구성

Overview

해당 Chapter에서 학습할 질문 유형을 미리 알아 두기 위하여 전체적인 개관, Question Types, 해결 전략 등을 소개했다.

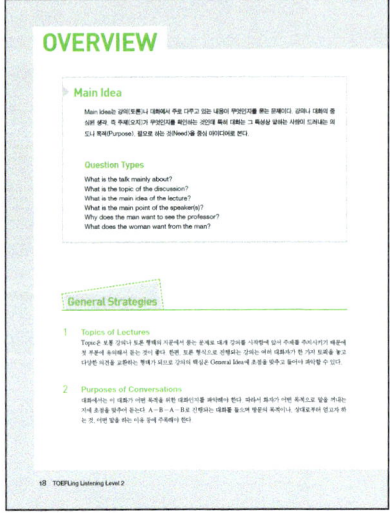

Sample

학습에 들어가기 전, 각 Chapter에서 다룰 문제 유형에 대한 샘플 테스트를 제시하였다.

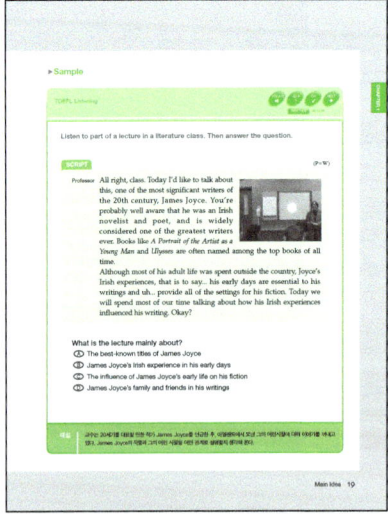

Vocabulary Preview

Skill Check-up에 들어가기 앞서 거기서 다룰 주요 어휘를 테스트 형식으로 제시하였다.

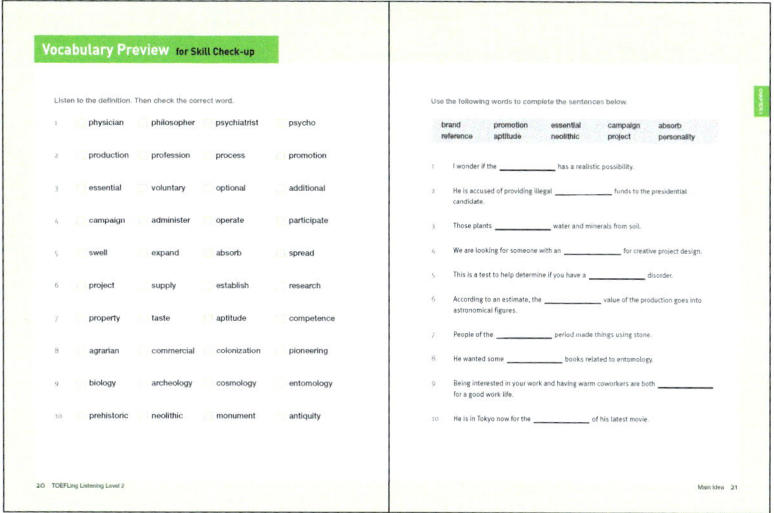

Skill Check-up

Overview에서 정리한 전략을 바탕으로 구체적인 문제유형에 맞는 Skill을 Dictation과 함께 단계별로 훈련할 수 있도록 구성하였다.

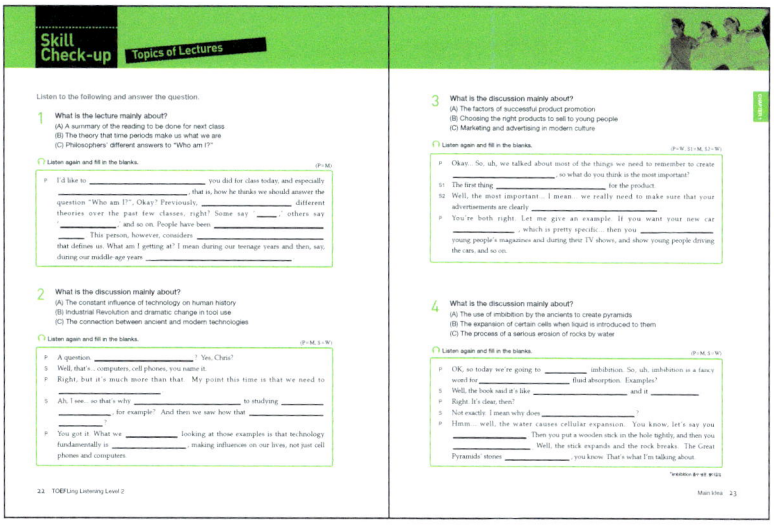

*주 S = Student, P = Professor, C = Counselor, L = Librarian or Lab worker

Exercise

해당 Chapter에서 학습한 질문 유형을 중점적으로 물어 본다. 다시 듣고 Note-taking을 완성하도록 하는 훈련을 통해 긴 지문을 효과적으로 정리하는 습관을 갖도록 구성하였다.

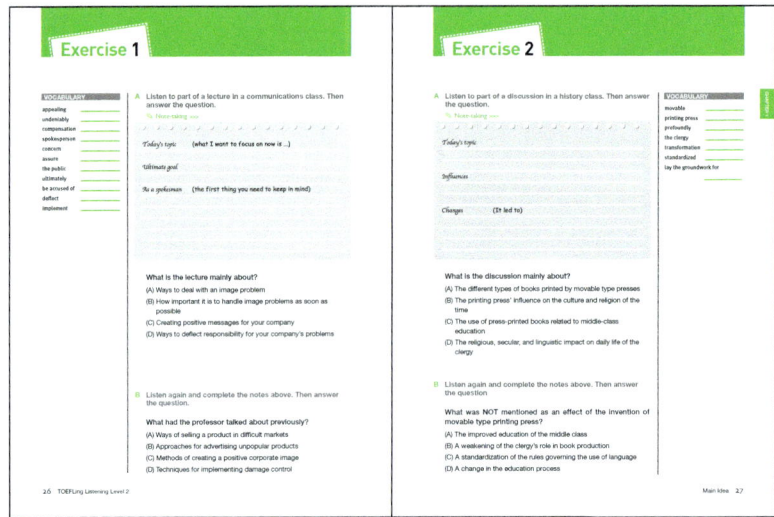

Actual Test

실전 감각을 높일 수 있도록 실제 테스트와 유사하게 구성하였다. Exercise와 마찬가지로, 다시 듣고 Note-taking할 수 있는 공간을 마련하였다.

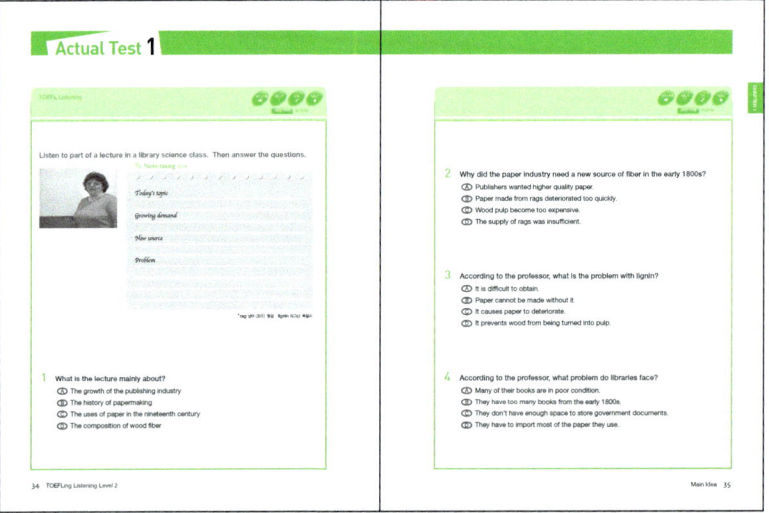

Progress Test

2개 Chapter가 끝날 때마다 앞에서 학습한 Skill들을 누적 출제하여 각각의 Skill들을 복습할 수 있도록 구성하였다.

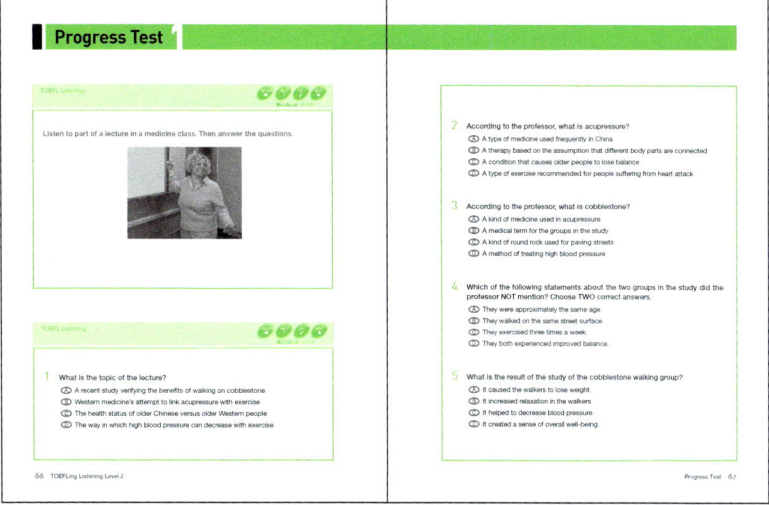

Dictation

Exercise와 Actual Test 및 Progress Test의 스크립트를 들으면서 Dictation 연습을 해 볼 수 있는 코너를 따로 마련해 두었다. 하단 부분에서는 지문 이해에 도움이 되도록 주요 구문을 정리하였다.

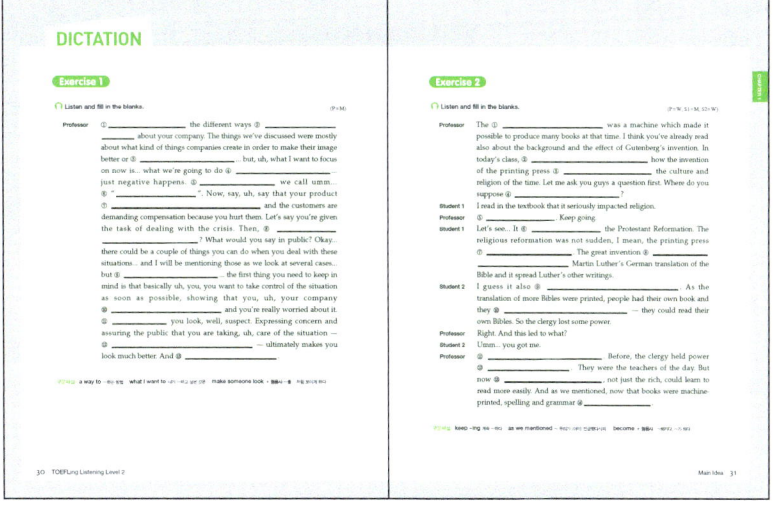

Vocabulary Review

앞에서 배운 단어들을 토대로, 어휘학습을 반복할 수 있도록 구성하였다.

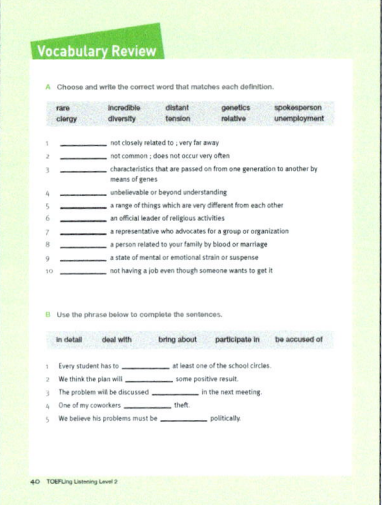

Final Test

Chapter 1~6를 아우르는 모든 Skill을 종합적으로 평가해 Skill을 마스터했는지 점검해 볼 수 있다.

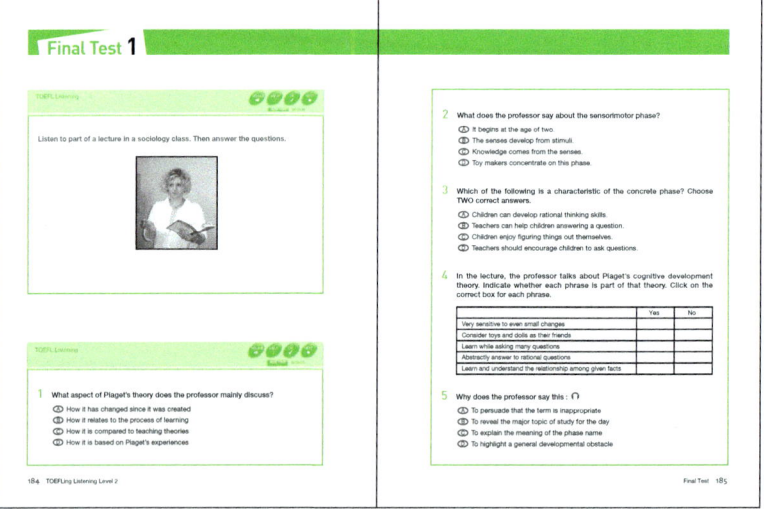

목차

■ **Introduction to *i*BT TOEFL**

CHAPTER 1 Main Idea
Topics of Lectures & Purposes of Conversations • 17

CHAPTER 2 Supporting Details
Important Information & True or False • 41

■ **Progress Test 1 · 2**

CHAPTER 3 Process / Classification
Identifying Process & Classifying Information • 73

CHAPTER 4 Organization
Organization of the Informaton Presented & Organization-Rhetorical Connection • 97

■ **Progress Test 3 · 4**

CHAPTER 5 Stance / Inference
Stance & Inference • 129

CHAPTER 6 Function
Function-Purpose • 153

■ **Progress Test 5 · 6**

■ **Final Test** • 183

Introduction to *i*BT TOEFL

*i*BT (Internet-based Test) TOEFL이란?

iBT는 Internet-based Test의 약자로 인터넷을 통해 시험을 치르게 하는 차세대 토플이다. 기존의 CBT가 미국으로 유학 오는 외국 학생들의 실제 영어구사능력을 제대로 측정하지 못한다는 비판에 대한 대안으로 새롭게 만들어졌으며 특히 말하기 능력에 대한 평가를 요구하는 미국 대학들의 요청에 따라 Speaking Section을 신설했다. 기존 CBT와는 달리 언어영역간의 통합을 접목시킨 것이 특징이며 학생들이 얼마나 빠르게, 제대로 미국 대학 생활에 적응해 갈 수 있을지에 대한 지표를 대학에 제공해 준다.

미국에서는 2005년 9월부터 시작되었고, 한국에서는 2006년 5월부터 실시되며, *i*BT가 실시되면 기존의 CBT 방식으로는 더 이상 시험이 치러지지 않는다.

CBT에서 *i*BT는 어떻게 달라졌나?

	CBT	*i*BT
Skills Test	Reading Listening Grammar * Writing은 별도	Reading Listening Writing Speaking
Test time	3.5 hours	4 hours
Reading	4~5 지문 (250~350 words) 각 지문당 11개 문제 (시간 70~90분)	3~5 지문 (700 words) 각 지문당 12~14개 문제 (시간 60~100분)

Listening	1. 11~17개 대화
	   (각 지문당 1개의 질문)
	2. 2~3개 짧은 대화
	   (각 지문당 2~3개의 질문)
	3. 4~6개 미니 강의와 토론
	   (각각 3~6개 문제)
	(시간 40~60분)
		1. 4~6개의 강의 및 교실토론
		   (각 지문당 5~6개의 질문)
		2. 2~3개의 대화
		   (각 5~6개의 질문)
		(시간 60~100분)

Speaking	없음	1. 2개의 independent tasks
		   일반 토픽에 대한 개인의 의견 발표
		2. 4개의 integrated tasks
		   읽고 들었던 것을 근거하여 말하기
		(시간 20분)

Writing	One independent task 토픽에 대한 의견을 개진하기 (시간 30분)	1. 1개의 integrated task 읽고 들은 내용에 근거하여 쓰기 (20분) 2. 1개의 independent task 토픽에 대한 의견을 개진하기 (30분)
Structure (Grammar)	20~25개의 문제 (시간 15~20분)	없음
전체 점수	300	120
피드백	점수만 제공	Section별 점수와 총점제공

*i*BT 시험 유형 세부 분석

*i*BT의 전체 시험 구성과 문항 수, 제한 시간은 다음과 같다.

Section	지문종류	지문	새로 추가된 특징
Reading		3~5 지문 (각 지문 당 12~14문제)	- 전문용어를 설명하는 Glossary - Multiple focus 정보를 분류하거나 summary를 완성 하는 문제 추가
Listening	Lecture	4~6 지문 (각 지문 당 6문제)	- Replay 문제 추가 - note-taking 허락
	Conversation	2~3 지문 (각 지문 당 5문제)	
Break		10분	
Speaking	Speaking	2문제	경험 또는 의견 말하기
	Reading → Listening → Speaking	2문제	- 제시된 안건을 읽고 그 안건에 대한 강의를 듣고 정리해서 말하기 - 제시된 안건을 읽고 안건에 대한 대화를 듣고 정리해서 말하기
	Listening → Speaking	2문제	- 강의를 듣고 요약하여 말하기 - 대화를 듣고 요약해서 말하기
Writing	Writing on topic	1개의 토픽	제시된 안건에 대한 의견 쓰기
	Reading → Listening → Writing	1개의 토픽	읽고 들은 내용에 근거하여 요점을 정리하여 논리적으로 쓰기

iBT Total Score Range Comparisons

Internet-based Total	Computer-based Total	Percentile Rank
111 - 120	273 - 300	97.6 - 100
96 - 110	243 - 270	85.9 - 96.8
79 - 95	213 - 240	64.8 - 85.0
65 - 78	183 - 210	45.6 - 63.6
53 - 64	153 - 180	29.9 - 44.3
41 - 52	123 - 150	16.7 - 28.6
30 - 40	93 - 120	7.4 - 15.8
19 - 29	63 - 90	1.7 - 6.5
9 - 18	33 - 60	0.1 - 1.2
0 - 8	0 - 30	0.04

iBT Listening Section의 구성

· 문제 유형으로 본 Listening Section에서 요하는 Listening Skills

1. Listening for basic comprehension
- 요지와 중요한 내용들, 요지와 관련된 핵심적인 세부 사항을 이해하는 능력

2. Listening for pragmatic understanding
- 화자의 태도나 확실성 정도를 인식하는 능력
- 화자의 목적 또는 역할, 기능을 인식하는 능력

3. Connecting and synthesizing information
- 정보가 어떻게 조직되어 제시되는지를 인식할 수 있는 능력
- 제공되는 아이디어 사이의 관계를 이해하는 능력(signal words를 파악할 필요가 있음)
- 듣기 지문에 암시되어 있는 내용에 의해 결론을 도출하거나 올바른 추론을 하는 능력
- 강의나 대화 안의 정보를 연결할 수 있는 능력
- 강의나 대화 안에서 화제가 어떻게 바뀌는지, 예시나 여담, 대화나 강의를 벗어난 이야기 등을 인식할 수 있는 능력

· Listening Section의 형식

듣기 자료	문제 개수	시간
4~6 강의, 강의 당 3~5분, 500~800 가량의 어휘로 구성	지문 당 5~6	60~90분
2~3 대화, 대화 당 약 3분 소요, 12~25번 정도의 대화의 교환이 이루어짐	지문 당 5~6	

Academic Lectures
- "a monologue by professor"인 유형이 있고, 학생의 질의·응답이 포함된 "talk in a class" 유형, 교수를 포함하는 학생들 사이의 "discussion", 세 가지 유형이 있다.

Conversations in an Academic Setting
- iBT에서 대화는 교수 또는 조교와의 면담 상황에서 벌어지는 경우가 많다. 또는 행정 직원이나 사서, 서점 직원 등과의 대화도 나온다.

· Listening Section의 특징

1 강의나 대화나 기본적으로 길어졌기 때문에 note-taking이 허용된다.
2 'well, uh, hmmm…'과 같이 실제로 말하듯이 자연스럽게 언어가 사용된다.
3 북미식 발음 이외의 엑센트가 나타날 수 있다.
4 기존 CBT의 Short Conversation이 사라졌다.
5 새로운 형태의 문제가 출제된다. 대화 및 강의의 일부를 다시 듣고 화자의 태도나 의도, 확실성 정도를 가늠하는 문제 형태로, 화자의 tone 또는 다른 힌트를 통해 화자가 논의되고 있는 화제나 주제에 대해 어떤 입장을 취하고 있는지 파악해야 한다.

Chapter 01
MAIN IDEA

OVERVIEW

▶ Main Idea

Main Idea는 강의〔토론〕나 대화에서 주로 다루고 있는 내용이 무엇인지를 묻는 문제이다. 강의나 대화의 중심된 생각, 즉 주제〔요지〕가 무엇인지를 확인하는 것인데 특히 대화는 그 특성상 말하는 사람이 드러내는 의도나 목적(Purpose), 필요로 하는 것(Need)을 중심 아이디어로 본다.

Question Types

What is the talk mainly about?
What is the topic of the discussion?
What is the main idea of the lecture?
What is the main point of the speaker(s)?
Why does the man want to see the professor?
What does the woman want from the man?

General Strategies

1 Topics of Lectures

Topic은 보통 강의나 토론 형태의 지문에서 묻는 문제로 대개 강의를 시작함에 앞서 주제를 주지시키기 때문에 첫 부분에 유의해서 듣는 것이 좋다. 한편, 토론 형식으로 진행되는 강의는 여러 대화자가 한 가지 토픽을 놓고 다양한 의견을 교환하는 형태가 되므로 강의의 핵심은 General Idea에 초점을 맞추고 들어야 파악할 수 있다.

2 Purposes of Conversations

대화에서는 이 대화가 어떤 목적을 위한 대화인지를 파악해야 한다. 따라서 화자가 어떤 목적으로 말을 꺼내는 지에 초점을 맞추어 듣는다. A−B−A−B로 진행되는 대화를 들으며 방문의 목적이나, 상대로부터 얻고자 하는 것, 어떤 말을 하는 이유 등에 주목해야 한다.

▶ Sample

TOEFL Listening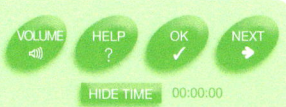

Listen to part of a lecture in a literature class. Then answer the question.

SCRIPT (P=W)

Professor All right, class. Today I'd like to talk about this, one of the most significant writers of the 20th century, James Joyce. You're probably well aware that he was an Irish novelist and poet, and is widely considered one of the greatest writers ever. Books like *A Portrait of the Artist as a Young Man* or *Ulysses* are often named among the top books of all time.
Although most of his adult life was spent outside the country, Joyce's Irish experiences, that is to say... his early days are essential to his writings and uh... provide all of the settings for his fiction. Today we will spend most of our time talking about how his Irish experiences influenced his writing. Okay?

What is the lecture mainly about?
Ⓐ The best-known titles of James Joyce
Ⓑ James Joyce's Irish experience in his early days
Ⓒ The influence of James Joyce's early life on his fiction
Ⓓ James Joyce's family and friends in his writings

해설 교수는 20세기를 대표할 만한 작가 James Joyce를 언급한 후, 아일랜드에서 보낸 그의 어린시절에 대해 이야기를 꺼내고 있다. James Joyce의 작품과 그의 어린 시절을 어떤 관계로 설명할지 생각해 본다.

Vocabulary Preview for Skill Check-up

Listen to the definition. Then check the correct word.

1. ☐ physician ☐ philosopher ☐ psychiatrist ☐ psycho
2. ☐ production ☐ profession ☐ process ☐ promotion
3. ☐ essential ☐ voluntary ☐ optional ☐ additional
4. ☐ campaign ☐ administer ☐ operate ☐ participate
5. ☐ swell ☐ expand ☐ absorb ☐ spread
6. ☐ project ☐ supply ☐ establish ☐ research
7. ☐ property ☐ taste ☐ aptitude ☐ competence
8. ☐ agrarian ☐ commercial ☐ colonization ☐ pioneering
9. ☐ biology ☐ archeology ☐ cosmology ☐ entomology
10. ☐ prehistoric ☐ neolithic ☐ monument ☐ antiquity

Use the following words to complete the sentences below.

| brand | promotion | essential | campaign | absorb |
| reference | aptitude | neolithic | project | personality |

1. I wonder if the _____ has a realistic possibility.

2. He is accused of providing illegal _____ funds to the presidential candidate.

3. Those plants _____ water and minerals from soil.

4. We are looking for someone with an _____ for creative project design.

5. This is a test to help determine if you have a _____ disorder.

6. According to an estimate, the _____ value of the production goes into astronomical figures.

7. People of the _____ period made things using stone.

8. He wanted some _____ books related to entomology.

9. Being interested in your work and having warm coworkers are both _____ for a good work life.

10. He is in Tokyo now for the _____ of his latest movie.

Skill Check-up — Topics of Lectures

Listen to the following and answer the question.

1 What is the lecture mainly about?
(A) A summary of the reading to be done for next class
(B) The theory that time periods make us what we are
(C) Philosophers' different answers to "Who am I?"

🎧 Listen again and fill in the blanks. (P=M)

P	I'd like to _____ you did for class today, and especially _____, that is, how he thinks we should answer the question "Who am I?", Okay? Previously, _____ different theories over the past few classes, right? Some say '_____,' others say '_____,' and so on. People have been _____ _____. This person, however, considers _____ that defines us. What am I getting at? I mean during our teenage years and then, say, during our middle-age years _____.

2 What is the discussion mainly about?
(A) The constant influence of technology on human history
(B) Industrial Revolution and dramatic change in tool use
(C) The connection between ancient and modern technologies

🎧 Listen again and fill in the blanks. (P=M, S=W)

P	A question. _____? Yes, Chris?
S	Well, that's... computers, cell phones, you name it.
P	Right, but it's much more than that. My point this time is that we need to _____.
S	Ah, I see... so that's why _____ to studying _____ _____, for example? And then we saw how that _____ _____?
P	You got it. What we _____ looking at those examples is that technology fundamentally is _____, making influences on our lives, not just cell phones and computers.

3 What is the discussion mainly about?
(A) The factors of successful product promotion
(B) Choosing the right products to sell to young people
(C) Marketing and advertising in modern culture

🎧 Listen again and fill in the blanks. (P=W, S1=M, S2=W)

P	Okay... So, uh, we talked about most of the things we need to remember to create _____ , so what do you think is the most important?
S1	The first thing _____ for the product.
S2	Well, the most important... I mean... we really need to make sure that your advertisements are clearly _____ .
P	You're both right. Let me give an example. If you want your new car _____ , which is pretty specific... then you _____ young people's magazines and during their TV shows, and show young people driving the cars, and so on.

4 What is the discussion mainly about?
(A) The use of imbibition by the ancients to create pyramids
(B) The expansion of certain cells when liquid is introduced to them
(C) The process of a serious erosion of rocks by water

🎧 Listen again and fill in the blanks. (P=M, S=W)

P	OK, so today we're going to _____ imbibition. So, uh, imbibition is a fancy word for _____ fluid absorption. Examples?
S	Well, the book said it's like _____ and it _____ .
P	Right. It's clear, then?
S	Not exactly. I mean why does _____ ?
P	Hmm... well, the water causes cellular expansion. You know, let's say you _____ . Then you put a wooden stick in the hole tightly, and then you _____ . Well, the stick expands and the rock breaks. The Great Pyramids' stones _____ , you know. That's what I'm talking about.

*imbibition 흡수 팽윤, 빨아들임

Skill Check-up: Purposes of Conversations

Listen to the following and answer the question.

1 Why does the woman talk to the professor?
(A) To cancel the project presentation schedule
(B) To put off the due date for her assignment
(C) To make an appointment with the professor next week

🎧 Listen again and fill in the blanks. (S=W, P=M)

S	Excuse me, Professor, I think I'll have some trouble _____. Actually, _____ what I'm going to do on it. I tried to keep the schedule as best as I can, but... I also have to do _____ .
P	Umm... what is the date to _____ ? Is it next Tuesday?
S	Yeah, right.
P	_____ , then?
S	Around three days, maybe _____ .
P	OK, I wish you luck!

2 What does the man want the woman to do?
(A) Get him organized material from a professor
(B) Give him useful information about honeybees' communication
(C) Find reference books about communication among insects

🎧 Listen again and fill in the blanks. (S1=M, S2=W)

S1	I decided to write about _____ .
S2	Did you study some _____ in the library?
S1	Oh, sure. But I was _____ because there's too much information printed there. I want to hear something from an expert. _____ !
S2	Well... about the communication, right. Honeybees are interesting, especially because they dance. It's _____ . They use body language to give _____ information about food, shelter, and other things.
S1	But _____ , like real language, is it?
S2	Actually, you'd be surprised. Bees can use this dance language to explain — within a few centimeters! — _____ .

24

3 Why does the woman go to see the professor?
(A) To get useful resources for a report she has to do
(B) To discuss the book with the professor in detail
(C) To ask where she can find more information

🎧 Listen again and fill in the blanks. (S=W, P=M)

S	Excuse me, Professor, I have _____ that you mentioned when we talked about the article today.
P	OK, which books in particular?
S	The one saying that men seem to have _____, while... umm... but women are _____.
P	Oh, yes. The name of the book is ... umm "To Communicate". It shows that this may be _____.
S	I was thinking maybe I want to _____ for my paper. And I was wondering if I could get _____ for other reference books.
P	Actually, I didn't _____, but I have a copy, the list of the books. Here it is.

4 What does the man want from the woman?
(A) The woman's class notes
(B) The handouts from the class
(C) Useful information for the paper

🎧 Listen again and fill in the blanks. (S1=M, S2=W)

S1	I'm _____ the Neolithic Agrarian Revolution. I'm really _____.
S2	Hmm... the big thing is that metal tools really _____ in human existence. This was around 8,000 B.C. You should _____ from the class.
S1	Actually, I have them. I mean... it would be better if I could get _____ _____ in the class.
S2	Well... I guess you'll have to _____.
S1	_____ that part and return it right after?
S2	Sure, no problem. And actually _____ until tomorrow anyway.

Main Idea 25

Exercise 1

VOCABULARY

appealing
undeniably
compensation
spokesperson
concern
assure
the public
ultimately
be accused of
deflect
implement

A Listen to part of a lecture in a communications class. Then answer the question.

✎ Note-taking >>>

Today's topic   (what I want to focus on now is ...)

Ultimate goal

As a spokesman   (the first thing you need to keep in mind)

What is the lecture mainly about?

(A) Ways to deal with an image problem
(B) How important it is to handle image problems as soon as possible
(C) Creating positive messages for your company
(D) Ways to deflect responsibility for your company's problems

B Listen again and complete the notes above. Then answer the question.

What had the professor talked about previously?

(A) Ways of selling a product in difficult markets
(B) Approaches for advertising unpopular products
(C) Methods of creating a positive corporate image
(D) Techniques for implementing damage control

Exercise 2

A Listen to part of a discussion in a history class. Then answer the question.

✎ Note-taking >>>

Today's topic

Influences

Changes   (It led to)

VOCABULARY

movable
printing press
profoundly
the clergy
transformation
standardized
lay the groundwork for

What is the discussion mainly about?

(A) The different types of books printed by movable type presses
(B) The printing press' influence on the culture and religion of the time
(C) The use of press-printed books related to middle-class education
(D) The religious, secular, and linguistic impact on daily life of the clergy

B Listen again and complete the notes above. Then answer the question

What was NOT mentioned as an effect of the invention of movable type printing press?

(A) The improved education of the middle class
(B) A weakening of the clergy's role in book production
(C) A standardization of the rules governing the use of language
(D) A change in the education process

Main Idea 27

Exercise 3

VOCABULARY

industrialization _____
perception _____
incredible _____
tension _____
accelerate _____
trigger _____
unemployment _____
an amount of _____
in terms of _____
be occupied with _____
keep house _____

A Listen to part of a lecture in a sociology class. Then answer the question.

✎ Note-taking >>>

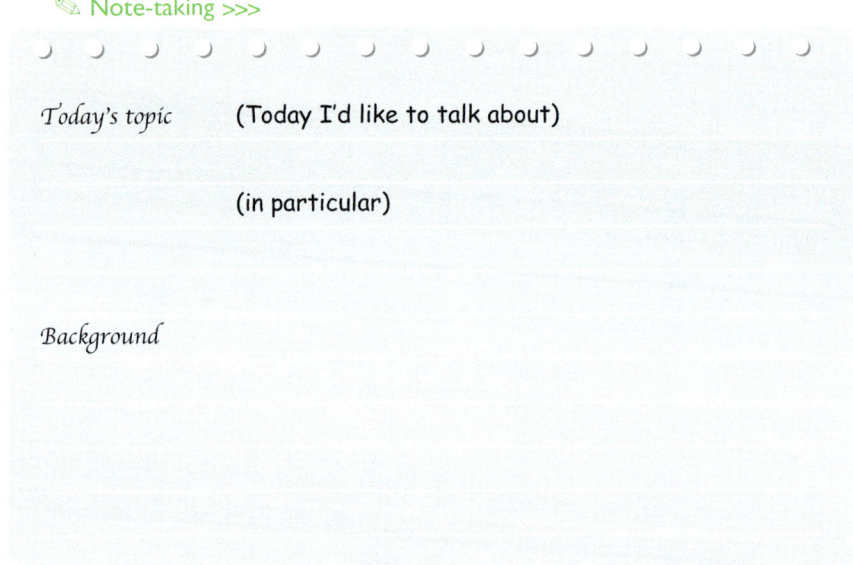

Today's topic   (Today I'd like to talk about)

                   (in particular)

Background

What will be the topic of the lecture?

(A) The kinds of tension and new technologies

(B) The 20th century as a turning point in economy

(C) The change in women's lifestyle by industrialization

(D) The comparison of women's roles in the 19th and 20th century

B Listen again and complete the notes above. Then answer the question.

What reason is given for women to work outside? Choose TWO correct answers.

(A) They were skilled at making the hand-made stuff.

(B) Employers wanted to save money by hiring them.

(C) Men could not be controlled by factory owners.

(D) Production was possible by less skilled workers.

Exercise 4

A Listen to part of a conversation between two students. Then answer the question.

✎ Note-taking >>>

Woman's problem

Man's suggestion

What woman wants

VOCABULARY

treatment _____
blood pressure _____
correlation _____
heart attack _____

*chronotherapy 시치료, 시간약물학

Why does the woman want to talk to the man?

(A) To get information on chronotherapy for the paper
(B) To get a copy of the notes from the man
(C) To ask where in the library she can find the articles
(D) To borrow the articles from a previous class

B Listen again and complete the notes above. Then answer the question.

What will the man probably do next?

(A) He will go to the library to find the article.
(B) He will attend the class.
(C) He will discuss the articles with the woman.
(D) He will go to the dorm to take the articles.

DICTATION

Exercise 1

🎧 Listen and fill in the blanks. (P=M)

Professor ① _____ the different ways ② _____ _____ about your company. The things we've discussed were mostly about what kind of things companies create in order to make their image better or ③ _____ ... but, uh, what I want to focus on now is... what we're going to do ④ _____ ... just negative happens. ⑤ _____ we call umm... ⑥ " _____ ". Now, say, uh, say that your product ⑦ _____ and the customers are demanding compensation because you hurt them. Let's say you're given the task of dealing with the crisis. Then, ⑧ _____ _____ ? What would you say in public? Okay... there could be a couple of things you can do when you deal with these situations... and I will be mentioning those as we look at several cases... but ⑨ _____ ... the first thing you need to keep in mind is that basically uh, you, you want to take control of the situation as soon as possible, showing that you, uh, your company ⑩ _____ and you're really worried about it. ⑪ _____ you look, well, suspect. Expressing concern and assuring the public that you are taking, uh, care of the situation — ⑫ _____ — ultimately makes you look much better. And ⑬ _____ .

|구문해설| **a way to** ~하는 방법   **what I want to** 내가 ~하고 싶은 것은   **make someone look** + 형용사 ~를 …처럼 보이게 하다

Exercise 2

🎧 **Listen and fill in the blanks.**

(P=W, S1=M, S2=W)

Professor The ① _____ was a machine which made it possible to produce many books at that time. I think you've already read also about the background and the effect of Gutenberg's invention. In today's class, ② _____ how the invention of the printing press ③ _____ the culture and religion of the time. Let me ask you guys a question first. Where do you suppose ④ _____ ?

Student 1 I read in the textbook that it seriously impacted religion.

Professor ⑤ _____ . Keep going.

Student 1 Let's see... It ⑥ _____ the Protestant Reformation. The religious reformation was not sudden, I mean, the printing press ⑦ _____ . The great invention ⑧ _____ _____ Martin Luther's German translation of the Bible and it spread Luther's other writings.

Student 2 I guess it also ⑨ _____ . As the translation of more Bibles were printed, people had their own book and they ⑩ _____ — they could read their own Bibles. So the clergy lost some power.

Professor Right. And this led to what?

Student 2 Umm... you got me.

Professor ⑪ _____ . Before, the clergy held power ⑫ _____ . They were the teachers of the day. But now ⑬ _____ , not just the rich, could learn to read more easily. And as we mentioned, now that books were machine-printed, spelling and grammar ⑭ _____ .

구문해설 **keep ~ing** 계속 ~하다   **as we mentioned** ~ 우리가 (이미) 언급했다시피   **become** + 형용사 : ~해지다, ~가 되다

DICTATION

Exercise 3

🎧 Listen and fill in the blanks.   (P=W)

Professor   Now remember that ① _____ that made industrialization happen? But today, I'd like to talk about ② _____ .

In particular, I want to talk about the ways in which industrialization not only changed ③ _____ — in the home and in society — but it also changed the ④ _____ , Okay? Basically, what we're gonna look at is how new technologies changed the country's job market and pushed women ⑤ _____ . And then how that change... ⑥ _____ tension in our culture... ⑦ _____ . For your understanding, I'll use some visual aids during the lecture. Okay... first let's look into how industrialization brought change to the job market. ⑧ _____ , it was possible to do most work without much time or effort. As a result, factory owners employed women, and sometimes children ⑨ _____ because women ⑩ _____ . A number of male laborers lost their jobs. In other words, women's social activities ⑪ _____ male unemployment. Now, let's glance over what was expected of women at that time. Traditionally women ⑫ _____ and caring for their children at home. Keeping house was their duty. From the old point of view, getting out of the home to work ⑬ _____ .

|구문해설| remember that ~ (that절 이하를) 기억하다   leave off ~을 그만두다   not only ~, but also ... ~뿐만 아니라 …도

Exercise 4

🎧 **Listen and fill in the blanks.** (S1=W, S2=M)

Student 1 Do you have a second? I need to talk to you about ① _____ _____ .

Student 2 Well, I have a class in 15 minutes. Make it short.

Student 1 Yeah… remember ② _____ about therapy… ③ _____ or something?

Student 2 Right… yeah… What about it?

Student 1 For some reason, ④ _____ the professor handed out.

Student 2 ⑤ _____ ? I remember there… um… two or three articles he gave us.

Student 1 That's… uh… The article talks about ⑥ _____ time, blood pressure and heart attacks. It says ⑦ _____ _____ when we wake up in the morning… and uh… heart attacks are um… ⑧ _____ , or something. That's what I'm looking for.

Student 2 I know what you mean.

Student 1 ⑨ _____ ?

Student 2 Actually, ⑩ _____ . Have you tried the library?

Student 1 ⑪ _____ the library now.

Student 2 All right… You want me to get them for you later?

Student 1 You think you could do that for me?

Student 2 ⑫ _____ after class.

Student 1 Oh, thanks.

|구문해설| **Make it short.** (시간이 없으므로) 얘기를 짧게 하라는 뜻이다.   **hand out** 내주다 (= give out)   **on one's way back from** ~로부터 돌아오는 중인

Main Idea

Actual Test 1

TOEFL Listening

Listen to part of a lecture in a library science class. Then answer the questions.

Note-taking >>>

Today's topic

Growing demand

New source

Problem

*rag 넝마 (조각), 헝겊   lignin 리그닌, 목질소

1 What is the lecture mainly about?
- Ⓐ The growth of the publishing industry
- Ⓑ The history of papermaking
- Ⓒ The uses of paper in the nineteenth century
- Ⓓ The composition of wood fiber

2. Why did the paper industry need a new source of fiber in the early 1800s?
   Ⓐ Publishers wanted higher quality paper.
   Ⓑ Paper made from rags deteriorated too quickly.
   Ⓒ Wood pulp became too expensive.
   Ⓓ The supply of rags was insufficient.

3. According to the professor, what is the problem with lignin?
   Ⓐ It is difficult to obtain.
   Ⓑ Paper cannot be made without it.
   Ⓒ It causes paper to deteriorate.
   Ⓓ It prevents wood from being turned into pulp.

4. According to the professor, what problem do libraries face?
   Ⓐ Many of their books are in poor condition.
   Ⓑ They have too many books from the early 1800s.
   Ⓒ They don't have enough space to store government documents.
   Ⓓ They have to import most of the paper they use.

Actual Test 2

TOEFL Listening

Listen to part of a conversation in a professor's office. Then answer the questions.

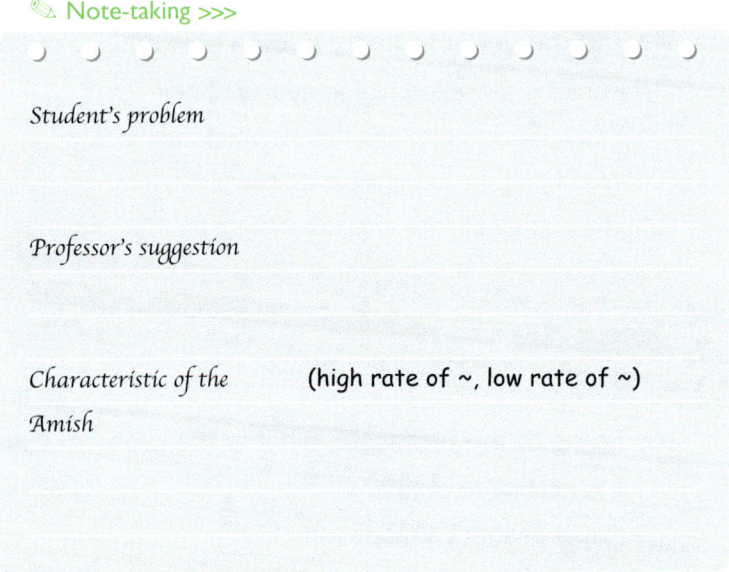

✎ Note-taking >>>

Student's problem

Professor's suggestion

Characteristic of the   (high rate of ~, low rate of ~)
Amish

1 Why does the man go to see the professor?
  Ⓐ To hear the professor's opinion on his topic
  Ⓑ To look for ways to meet the Amish people
  Ⓒ To consult the professor regarding the paper
  Ⓓ To confirm what the Amish have to do with genetics

2. What happens when distant relatives marry?
   - Ⓐ Many different genes are passed on to children.
   - Ⓑ It causes the birthrate to decline significantly.
   - Ⓒ The number of inheritable genes is limited.
   - Ⓓ The children are less likely to inherit parents' genes.

3. According to the professor, what is genetic diversity?
   - Ⓐ The tendency of families to intermarry
   - Ⓑ A problem caused by closed societies
   - Ⓒ The refusal to use advanced technology
   - Ⓓ The existence of many different genes

4. What is true about the relationship between genetics and the Amish?
   - Ⓐ They have stayed healthier because of lack of rare diseases.
   - Ⓑ Their society results in a higher incidence of rare diseases.
   - Ⓒ Their marriage patterns have resulted in new genes.
   - Ⓓ They seem to inherit the ability to form close-knit communities.

DICTATION

Actual Test 1

🎧 Listen and fill in the blanks. (P=W)

P   In the early 1800s, the paper industry was still using ① _____ _____ as it had for many centuries. However, the rag supply ② _____ for paper. The United States alone was using 250 thousand tons of rags each year. And ③ _____ had to be imported. It was clear that ④ _____ _____ to keep up with the demand for paper. The answer to this problem turned out to be paper made from wood pulp, something ⑤ _____ North America. In Canada, the first wood pulp mill ⑥ _____ 1866 and it was immediately successful. But while wood pulp ⑦ _____, it created a problem of quality. Wood contains a substance called lignin. ⑧ _____ of cheap paper involved leaving the lignin in the wood pulp. But lignin is acidic and ⑨ _____ _____ the life expectancy of paper from several centuries for rag paper ⑩ _____ for paper made from wood pulp. This means that books printed less than a hundred years ago ⑪ _____, even though books printed much earlier are in perfect condition. This is bad enough for the older books on your bookshelf ⑫ _____ for libraries and the collections of government documents.

|구문해설| **keep up with** ~을 따라가다, 쫓아가다   **a quarter of** ~의 1/4

38

Actual Test 2

🎧 **Listen and fill in the blanks.** (S=M, P=W)

Student   Professor... Can I come in for a minute?
Professor Sure. Have a seat.
Student   Well... ① _____ for my genetics paper, but... ② _____ ... so I sent you an email to get some help.
Professor Yeah... I got your email... and... well, I was thinking it might be good ③ _____ the Amish and their genetics... what do you think?
Student   The Amish? I think I've read about them and ④ _____ _____ about their community. They live ⑤ _____ _____, right? No cars or electric lights... But what does that have to do with genetics?
Professor Actually, you should ⑥ _____ in Amish communities. It occurs because, ⑦ _____, there is ⑧ _____.
Student   What do you mean by genetic diversity?
Professor Well, it's really ⑨ _____. What happens is that there is ⑩ _____ for marriage, and so people who marry in these societies are mostly distant relatives. ⑪ _____ _____ being passed on, ⑫ _____. And then, if there is a gene for a rare disease in a family, if both people are members of that, this can significantly increase ⑬ _____ getting the gene for the disease.
Student   Oh, I see. This topic ⑭ _____. I'd like to work on it as you recommended.

|구문해설| **such a closed community** the Amish를 가리킨다   **What do you mean by ~?** ~를 통해 (당신이) 말하려는 것은 무엇인가요? (상대방 말의 의미를 확인할 때 쓰는 표현이다.)   **What happens is that** ~ 일어난 일은 that절 이하이다 (What happens가 주어, is가 동사로 쓰였다.)   **And then ~** (앞에 언급한 내용에 이어) 그러면, 그 다음에는

Vocabulary Review

A Choose and write the correct word that matches each definition.

| rare | incredible | distant | genetics | spokesperson |
| clergy | diversity | tension | relative | unemployment |

1 _____ not closely related to ; very far away
2 _____ not common ; does not occur very often
3 _____ characteristics that are passed on from one generation to another by means of genes
4 _____ unbelievable or beyond understanding
5 _____ a range of things which are very different from each other
6 _____ an official leader of religious activities
7 _____ a representative who advocates for a group or organization
8 _____ a person related to your family by blood or marriage
9 _____ a state of mental or emotional strain or suspense
10 _____ not having a job even though someone wants to get it

B Use the phrase below to complete the sentences.

| in detail | deal with | bring about | participate in | be accused of |

1 Every student has to _____ at least one of the school circles.
2 We think the plan will _____ some positive result.
3 The problem will be discussed _____ in the next meeting.
4 One of my coworkers _____ theft.
5 We believe his problems must be _____ politically.

Chapter 02
SUPPORTING DETAILS

OVERVIEW

▶ Supporting Details

Detail 문제는 강의(토론)나 대화에서 언급한 구체적인 정보를 얼마나 잘 파악하고 있는지를 확인하는 유형이다. Speaker가 '직접 언급한 사실'을 토대로 답을 찾아야 하므로 짐작되거나 개인적인 추론을 바탕으로 답해서는 안 된다. 중요하다고 생각되는 정보는 Note-taking하여 문제 풀이 시 참고하는 것이 좋다.

Question Types

What does the professor say about ~?
What is mentioned as the reason why ~?
What is the man's suggestion for ~?
What is the best definition for ~?
What evidence was given by the professor?
According to the conversation, what does ~ mean?
Who / When / Where / Why / How ~?
What is (NOT) true about ~?

General Strategies

1 Important Information

강의의 지엽적인 부분보다는 요점과 직접적으로 관련된 중요 정보를 확인하는 문제 유형으로, 정의(Definition), 예(Example), 장점(Benefits), 이유(Reason), 원인(Cause), 결과(Result), 문제점(Problem), 증거(Evidence) 등으로 제시하는 정보들을 묻는다. 새로운 정보가 등장할 때마다 그것이 어떤 역할(정의, 문제점, 증거 등)을 하는지를 파악하고 성격을 부여하면서 듣도록 하자.

2 True or False

강의나 대화에서 언급된 내용을 토대로 선택지의 내용이 사실인지 거짓인지를 파악하는 문제이다. 오답의 경우에도 보통 Speaker가 언급한 내용을 조금씩 변경하여 제시하기 때문에 대개 partly right, but partly wrong이다.

▶ **Sample**

TOEFL Listening

Listen to part of a talk in a class about essay writing. Then answer the question.

SCRIPT (P=M, S=W)

Professor Okay, so... once you're done doing the quick outline for your writing... you should spare some time for 'free writing'... before you actually write your essay. What it does is... it helps you come up with fresh ideas. For successful free writing... well, there should be a time limit. First, you give yourself a set period of time to write — say 10 minutes. Then, just write down as much as you can. Anything that comes into your head is valid.

Student Well, it's not like I use everything that comes to my mind, though... I mean the writing might not be very focused...

Professor Well, I'll put it this way... by not thinking too much at first, your mind is clear to come up with new and interesting things. In other words, you can be more creative.

What does the professor say about free writing?
Ⓐ Some of the ideas should be ignored because they're probably invalid.
Ⓑ You shouldn't use everything that comes to mind.
Ⓒ It should take longer than 10 minutes.
Ⓓ Anything you come up with could be useful.

해설 교수는 free writing을 '머릿속에 떠오르는 생각들을 가감없이 그대로 적는 과정을 통해 보다 흥미롭고 창의적인 아이디어가 나오는 것'이라고 정의했다. Ⓑ는 학생의 의견이다.

Supporting Details

Vocabulary Preview for Skill Check-up

Listen to the definition. Then check the correct word.

1	☐ emerge	☐ extract	☐ decrease	☐ extinct
2	☐ foreigner	☐ neighbor	☐ inhabitant	☐ migrator
3	☐ physical	☐ sensory	☐ mental	☐ spiritual
4	☐ guarantee	☐ expand	☐ courage	☐ challenge
5	☐ incentive	☐ opportunity	☐ wages	☐ compensation
6	☐ retire	☐ enlist	☐ register	☐ recruit
7	☐ biography	☐ geometry	☐ physics	☐ geography
8	☐ history	☐ myth	☐ fable	☐ theory
9	☐ invade	☐ spread	☐ guard	☐ defend
10	☐ pronunciation	☐ alien	☐ accent	☐ dialect

Use the following words to complete the sentences below.

| extinct | guarantee | inhabitant | solar | recall |
| register | invade | dialect | translate | sensory |

1. It's said when we get older, our physical and _____ abilities decline.

2. US President George Bush had said that God had directed him to _____ Afghanistan and Iraq.

3. As too many students _____ for the course, the school increased the quorum.

4. The government promised to come up with a package of measures to _____ food safety.

5. There are several hypotheses about why dinosaurs became _____.

6. Publishers from many countries have tried to _____ *Harry Potter* into their own languages.

7. The use of _____ and different tones of voice made the listeners able to distinguish one person from another.

8. A typical _____ of these mountainous areas eats only vegetables.

9. He remodeled his house to be run on _____ energy.

10. The company made a policy to _____ all the defective cars produced after 2005. 9.

Supporting Details 45

Skill Check-up — Important Information

Listen to the following and answer the question.

1 According to the professor, what is Champ?
(A) A prehistoric fish that has been seen by explorers
(B) A large, common fish known to live in Lake Champlain
(C) An inhabitant of the lake that has not been proven to exist

🎧 Listen again and fill in the blanks. (P=W, S=M)

P	For some reason, the world's large lakes are _____. Any of you heard of the uh, Creature of Lake Champlain? Its name is Champ and _____ hundreds of times, even by explorer Samuel de Champlain in 1609.
S	So, what is it, then? I mean it's something, right?
P	It's uh… well… some say Champ is a plesiosaur, _____. Others claim that it's simply a large lake sturgeon, _____ Lake Champlain. But let's put it this way: until there is undeniable documentation of _____, he'll just be a mystery.

*plesiosaur 〔생물〕 장경룡 sturgeon 〔어류〕 철갑상어

2 What is the man's problem?
(A) He does not decide which book is proper for his assignment.
(B) The librarian says that she can't recall the book.
(C) The book is loaned out to another student.

🎧 Listen again and fill in the blanks. (S=M, L=W)

S	I desperately need this book for my paper, but it's _____.
L	How soon is your paper due?
S	_____.
L	Perfect. I can _____ for you. The person who has it now will _____ this Friday.
S	But what if he doesn't return it?
L	Umm, _____ he will, but _____ for not returning recalled books. It's _____!

46

3 Why do people taste the same food differently?
  (A) Because of difference in the number of taste buds
  (B) Because of difference in the sizes of taste sensors
  (C) Because of difference in the shapes of tongues

Listen again and fill in the blanks.
(P=M)

P	_____, we all don't taste things in the... in the same way. Some people, for example, love the taste of broccoli; I know _____ very often, am I right? Meanwhile other people like me might think _____ in the world. Why is that? Well, there's _____ for this. Some people just _____! Taste buds are those _____ _____ that let you know what you're eating. And so the bigger taste buds you have, the more you taste. It seems too simple, but what I can say is... it's true...

4 What is the woman's solution for the man's registration problem?
  (A) Ask the professor to allow him to take the class
  (B) Register an intermediate class not so many people take in
  (C) Try to register for the geography class next semester if possible

Listen again and fill in the blanks.
(S1=M, S2=W)

S1	Arg! I'm so frustrated! I keep trying to _____, but I can't get in! If I don't get in this semester, I'll be really behind.
S2	That's _____. They fill up so fast. The other thing is that there are _____ this semester.
S1	Maybe. Anyway, is there any way I can get in?
S2	Maybe you could ask the professor _____. You can usually get in when a professor _____ to join a class that's already full.
S1	Yeah, that might work.

Supporting Details 47

Skill Check-up — True or False

Listen to the following and check the correct answer. (T = True F = False)

1 What does the professor say about videos? T F
 (A) They were not smoothly produced. ☐ ☐
 (B) They had certain qualities of a Hollywood movie. ☐ ☐
 (C) They created support for the war among adults. ☐ ☐

🎧 Listen again and fill in the blanks. (P=W)

> P   OK, so we've been talking about the Vietnam War's effect on American youth. But today I want to expand that to a discussion of something that affected Americans in general – I mean all Americans – and _____. You see, video news stories seen nightly _____. Sounds crazy, huh? Well, it's not when you consider that night after night, Americans watched those horribly graphic, jerky, _____ on their TVs. The images often had _____ ... I mean they weren't your typical well-done Hollywood production. _____ to the viewers as if they were really there.

2 What does the professor say about English in earlier times? T F
 (A) The Germanic language split into two branches in 3 BC. ☐ ☐
 (B) The invasion of the British Isles slowed down the changes in English. ☐ ☐
 (C) Old English is a mix of West Germanic and the Angles' language. ☐ ☐

🎧 Listen again and fill in the blanks. (P=M)

> P   The English we speak today is the result of _____. Well, even the early history of English is _____. It began as a Germanic branch of the Indo-European language. In about 2 BC, this Germanic language _____ _____, one of which was called West Germanic. People who spoke this language _____, and then the language _____ _____ of the Angles, the inhabitants there. This became Anglo-Saxon, or what we know today as Old English. Now… mmm… why don't we _____ _____ 65… to see the process?

48

3 What do they say about wave-generated energy? T F
  (A) Wave-generated energy has rarely been successful.
  (B) Waves could possibly provide humankind with a lot of energy.
  (C) Tidal electric generators rely on rivers to make energy.

🎧 Listen again and fill in the blanks. (P=W, S1=M, S2=M)

P	The ocean seems to _____. Yet... well... it's difficult to harness its energy.
S1	Didn't you say that we could _____, or something?
S2	Yeah... but wave-generated energy is small-scale and _____.
P	Well, don't discount it just yet, OK? Lately, more success has come from using the power of tides to create energy. _____ use the rise and fall of water that occurs _____. They generate electricity much as hydroelectric dams do on rivers. _____ because tides are caused by _____ of the solar system. So tidal power is considered endless, well, as far as humans are concerned.

*hydroelectric 수력 발전의, 수력 전기의

4 What does the woman say about the Rosetta Stone? T F
  (A) The stone itself contained all the hieroglyphic forms known at the time.
  (B) Researchers could translate an unknown language with a known one.
  (C) Before the stone people didn't note the existence of any hieroglyphs.

🎧 Listen again and fill in the blanks. (S1=M, S2=W)

S1	When the professor said she'll talk about the Rosetta Stone next class, did she mention anything else? Like, why it is important, _____ or anything like that?
S2	Uh, yeah, she _____ on its importance. That's all. Nothing special.
S1	The importance?
S2	That's, umm, _____ to finally understand hieroglyphs. They hadn't been able to _____.
S1	How did this stone help them do that?
S2	Luckily, on the stone, there was a translation of the hieroglyphs _____. Because they understood ancient Greek, they were able to understand the hieroglyphs.

*hieroglyph 상형문자

Supporting Details 49

Exercise 1

VOCABULARY

obstruction
intentionally
flooding
divert
irrigate
hydroelectric
generate
block
resettlement
flood out

A   Listen to part of a lecture in an environmental class. Then answer the question.

Note-taking >>>

Dam

Purposes

Benefit   example

Problem   example

Which of the following is NOT mentioned as a benefit of dam building?

(A) Water can be used to help agriculture.

(B) Revenues from electric sales can be generated.

(C) Dam-created lakes benefit tourist industries.

(D) Control over the water flow prevents flooding.

B   Listen again and complete the notes above. Then answer the question.

What problem is caused by big-scale dam construction?

(A) It costs a lot of money to run the dams.

(B) Big-scale dams resulted in starvation among farmers.

(C) Some people have to relocate.

(D) Operating big-scale dams costs a lot of effort and time.

Exercise 2

A Listen to part of a talk in an English class. Then answer the question.

✎ Note-taking >>>

Question   (I guess you've had an experience like)

Examples   S1:
                    S2:

Dialect

Separate language

VOCABULARY	
pronounce	
New Yorker	
region	
identical	
so-called	
variation	
usage	
syntax	
fulfill	
peculiar to	

What does the professor say about vocabulary in a dialect?

(A) It is completely different from the standard language.
(B) It may vary slightly from region to region.
(C) It is always easy to understand when it is spoken.
(D) It is pronounced the same as standard vocabulary.

B Listen again and complete the notes above. Then answer the question.

What is mentioned as constituting a separate language? Choose TWO correct answers.

(A) Distinct vocabulary
(B) Familiar pronunciation
(C) Complicated syntax
(D) Different verb structures

Exercise 3

VOCABULARY

medication _____
barely _____
stay overnight _____
in a row _____
wrap up _____
respond to _____

A Listen to part of a conversation between two students. Then answer the question.

✎ Note-taking >>>

Last class   (we talked a lot about)

Placebo

Placebo Effect

According to the conversation, what does placebo mean?

(A) A type of medicine the mind is not familiar with

(B) A pill that does not contain active medicine

(C) A way of thinking that causes mental healing

(D) A theory that proposes the mind can heal the body

B Listen again and complete the notes above. Then answer the question.

What causes the placebo effect?

(A) Doctors secretly give medicine to the patient.

(B) Patients realize they are not really sick.

(C) The mind is tricked into believing the pill is real medicine.

(D) Doctors misunderstand the patient's symptoms.

Exercise 4

A Listen to part of a conversation between two students. Then answer the question.

✎ Note-taking >>>

Hockney's theory

Camera obscura (It worked like this.)

Evidence

VOCABULARY

transformation _____
Renaissance _____
flat _____
realistic _____
opposite _____
projection _____
device _____
figure out _____

*camera obscura 카메라 옵스큐라, 주름상자, 암실

What does the man say about a camera obscura?

(A) Hockney's ambition as an artist led to its development.
(B) Major artists proved it was used by Hockney.
(C) It contributed to the creation of more realistic paintings.
(D) Some photographers used it to try new artistic styles.

B Listen again and complete the notes above. Then answer the question.

What is mentioned as being proof that painters used a camera obscura? Choose TWO correct answers.

(A) The figures were left-handed.
(B) The transformation of the paintings was subtle.
(C) Some things were out of focus.
(D) There was written testimony.

Supporting Details   53

DICTATION

Exercise 1

🎧 **Listen and fill in the blanks.** (P=M)

Professor A dam is basically ① _____ a river for a couple of different reasons. OK, sometimes umm... they're constructed to ② _____, sometimes to ③ _____ ... and uh, at other times they're built to produce hydroelectric power — that is, electricity that is ④ _____. Now, these have been around for a long time, but ⑤ _____ that they really began being built ⑥ _____ that say, the Hoover or Aswan Dams were built on. Until this time, dams had little effect on the rivers. But ⑦ _____, we've seen a lot of problems that occur ⑧ _____ that dams give human societies. One problem is ⑨ _____. For example, in the West African country of Ghana, the Upper Volta River was dammed in the late 1970s in order to generate electricity for the people of the country, ⑩ _____ other countries. However, ⑪ _____, a huge lake of water was created. This completely flooded out land that people in the Upper Volta Region ⑫ _____ for hundreds, thousands, of years. So, ⑬ _____ by electricity, but the farmers ⑭ _____ for resettlement. At that time, around 78,000 people ⑮ _____ .

|구문해설| **sometimes ~, at other times** 가끔은 ~, 또 다른 때는   **a series of** 일련의 ~, 연속의 ~

54

Exercise 2

🎧 **Listen and fill in the blanks.**　　　　　　　　　　　　　　　　(P=W, S1=M, S2=W)

Professor	I guess you've had an experience like this… someone is speaking your language, but the words they use and ① _____ _____, make it seem like they are speaking another language.
Student 1	Oh, yes, ② _____, but sometimes when I talk with one of my club members, who is from another state, I feel that way.
Student 2	Even in my family gatherings, I notice it frequently. My mother ③ _____ _____ New York since her twenties and she's from a small village in a western state. ④ _____, but whenever she talks with her parents, she ⑤ _____ _____.
Professor	That's a typical case! Then why does this happen? I could say that's, it's because ⑥ _____. Yet, uh, for the most part, the structures and the vocabulary ⑦ _____ the so-called standard language. We call ⑧ _____.
Student 1	How's it different from a separate language? A separate language ⑨ _____, too.
Professor	Good question. To be a separate language, ⑩ _____ should be different from the standard version. Also, the grammar should be significantly different, such as ⑪ _____, or ⑫ _____ — that is ⑬ _____. If these conditions are fulfilled, we truly have a separate language.

|구문해설| **sound like** ~처럼 들리다　　**call A B** A를 B라고 부르다　　**that way** 그런 식으로, 그렇게

DICTATION

Exercise 3

🎧 Listen and fill in the blanks.   (S1=W, S2=M)

Student 1   Hello Ted, you ① _____ the other day. I was wondering if there was something wrong with you.

Student 2   I really wanted to get some sleep that morning 'cause ② _____ _____ two days ③ _____. I had to ④ _____ _____ with some graduate students. Anyway, what did I miss in the last class?

Student 1   We talked a lot about ⑤ _____ in affecting the body.

Student 2   Like ⑥ _____?

Student 1   Well... not in that way. One thing we looked at was the placebo effect.

Student 2   What is that?

Student 1   You know, a placebo is a sugar pill or something ⑦ _____.

Student 2   A sugar pill?

Student 1   Well, um... actually there's more than that. The other important thing about placebos is ⑧ _____. You see, they think that placebos really contain medication, not just sugar.

Student 2   So, what's ⑨ _____? And what's the placebo effect exactly?

Student 1   What they found out after all, ⑩ _____, is many people's bodies respond to the placebo, as though ⑪ _____ _____. If they think that they are getting medicine, ⑫ _____.

Student 2   That's amazing! It's just another example of ⑬ _____ we barely understand, I think.

구문해설 **as though** ~인 것처럼 (= as if)   **get better** 더 나아지다 (get + 형용사 비교급 : 점점 더 ~해지다)

Exercise 4

🎧 **Listen and fill in the blanks.**   (S1=M, S2=W)

Student 1 What's your paper about, Allie?

Student 2 I'm writing about the transformation of European painting in the early Renaissance, from ① _____ to ② _____ .

Student 1 Are you going to talk about Hockney's theory?

Student 2 Actually, I don't know about that. What is it?

Student 1 Hockney says that the great masters of those days actually used a camera obscura to help them ③ _____ .

Student 2 I think I can ④ _____ in my paper. Please tell me more about it.

Student 1 Well, Hockney, who's a painter himself, claims that there's all kinds of evidence to show that ⑤ _____ .

Student 2 A camera obscura? How does it work?

Student 1 Simple. It's like this. Cover the windows of your bedroom ⑥ _____ . Then make a small hole in the cover. ⑦ _____ makes an image ⑧ _____ , that is to say, you'll see ⑨ _____ , except the image is ⑩ _____ and ⑪ _____ .

Student 2 That's cool! How did he figure out that painters used the camera obscura?

Student 1 Because so many of the subjects in the paintings ⑫ _____ , the change was sudden, and ⑬ _____ . Hockney felt like he had good reason to think ⑭ _____ .

|구문해설| **feel like + that** 절 that 절 이하라고 느끼다 (cf. feel like ~ing : ~하고 싶다)

Actual Test 1

TOEFL Listening

Listen to part of a discussion in a biology class about symbiosis. Then answer the questions.

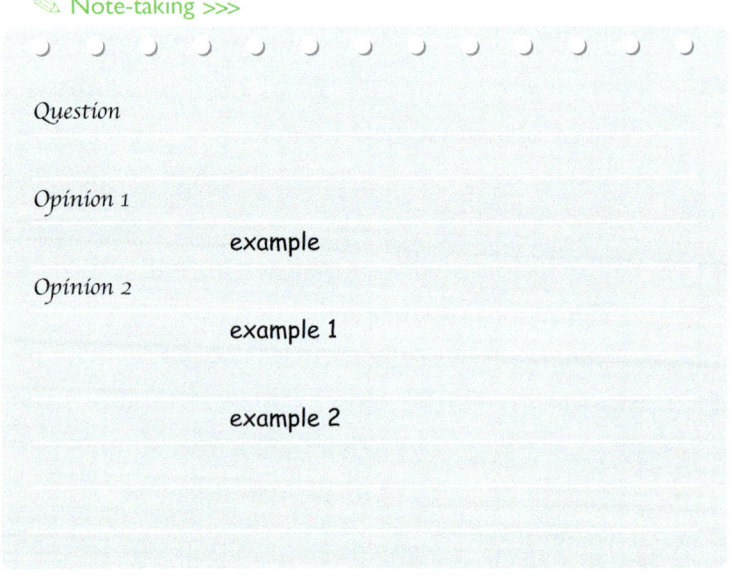

✎ Note-taking >>>

Question

Opinion 1
    example

Opinion 2
    example 1

    example 2

*tapeworm 〔동물〕 촌충 cattle egret 〔조류〕 황로, 붉은 백로 goby fish 망둥이

1 According to the discussion, what is symbiosis?

- Ⓐ A harmful condition that occurs in nature
- Ⓑ An interdependent relationship between two organisms
- Ⓒ An example of the result of parasitism
- Ⓓ An interrelationship between animals and environment

2 What does one of the speakers say about parasites?
- Ⓐ They exemplify a negative form of symbiosis.
- Ⓑ They have little effect on the host organism.
- Ⓒ It is unclear how parasites benefit from the host.
- Ⓓ They give the host organism nutrition to survive.

3 How can the cattle egret and cow's relationship be characterized?
- Ⓐ Beneficial for both organisms
- Ⓑ Neither beneficial nor harmful for either organism
- Ⓒ Beneficial for one organism, but harmful for the other
- Ⓓ Beneficial for one organism, but not effecting the other

4 How does the goby fish help the shrimp to survive?
- Ⓐ It digs a deep burrow for the shrimp.
- Ⓑ It feeds food to the shrimp to keep it healthy.
- Ⓒ It fights with predators for the shrimp.
- Ⓓ It gives a signal for the shrimp to escape a predator.

Actual Test 2

TOEFL Listening

Listen to part of a conversation between a professor and a student. Then answer the questions.

✎ Note-taking >>>

Electroshock treatment

First stage

Reason for the reuse

*schizophrenia (정신의학) 정신분열증 muscle relaxant 근육 이완제 psychotherapeutic 정신치료학의

1 **What does the student want to know?**
- Ⓐ What the professor discussed in lecture yesterday
- Ⓑ The definition of electroshock therapy
- Ⓒ Why the use of shock treatment has revived
- Ⓓ The professor's opinion on shock treatment

2. What reason is NOT true for stopping use of shock treatment?
   - Ⓐ It was a negative experience for the patients.
   - Ⓑ It was too expensive though it worked for everyone.
   - Ⓒ Medicines came to be seen as more effective.
   - Ⓓ It was seen as barbaric and ineffective.

3. What reason is given for beginning to use shock treatment again?
   - Ⓐ Medicines for mental disorders were toxic.
   - Ⓑ Mental patients demanded it be used again.
   - Ⓒ It was the only option doctors could think of.
   - Ⓓ It seemed to be effective when medicine wasn't.

4. According to the professor, how does modern shock treatment differ from past shock treatment?
   - Ⓐ It is more painful for patients, but more effective.
   - Ⓑ It is administered in a more humane way.
   - Ⓒ Less electricity is used in modern shock therapy.
   - Ⓓ Psychiatrists found that newer techniques do not work as well as the old treatment for some patients.

DICTATION

Actual Test 1

🎧 Listen and fill in the blanks. (P=W, S1=M, S2=W)

Professor There's a variety of ways ① _____ in an environment. One common way is called symbiosis. This means that one organism interacts with another organism and that they ② _____. The question I'd like to discuss now is whether symbiotic relations ③ _____ or harmful for participants.

Student 1 Symbiotic relationships ④ _____ rather than beneficial. I'm talking about parasites. For instance, a tapeworm lives inside the intestines of another animal, uh, to survive, and ⑤ _____ that the other animal takes in. So what happens to the other animal? ⑥ _____ malnutrition.

Student 2 Not all symbiotic relationships are harmful. ⑦ _____; they ⑧ _____ the organism. And ⑨ _____.

Professor Yeah, right. Can you give me an example of beneficial symbiosis?

Student 2 Umm… we can look at the example of the cattle egret and the cow. Cows are covered with small insects, ⑩ _____. If they transmit disease, potentially, the cow could die, or at least get really sick. The egret, a uh… small bird, ⑪ _____, eats the insects and well, this keeps the cow healthy. The egret needs the cow to survive, but both organisms benefit from the relationship.

Professor Another example is the goby fish and the shrimp. The goby fish sometimes lives together with a shrimp. The shrimp, almost blind ⑫ _____ when above the ground, ⑬ _____ in which it lives with the goby fish. In case of danger, the goby fish touches the shrimp ⑭ _____. When that happens, they ⑮ _____. That's what we call mutualism, a form of symbiosis.

|구문해설| **A rather than B** B보다는 오히려 A   **Not all ~** 전부 ~한 것은 아니다 (= not everything(everyone))

Actual Test 2

🎧 **Listen and fill in the blanks.**   (S=W, P=M)

Student	Professor, I have a question.
Professor	Sure. Go on.
Student	Well, I think ① _____ is really ② _____ , but it is still being used in psychiatry, right?
Professor	Yes, that's true. Though at first it seemed to do a good job at ③ _____ like ④ _____ and schizophrenia, there were many, ⑤ _____ . Especially when it was first used, treatment was performed without the use of anesthesia or muscle relaxants. It was ⑥ _____ people. Later, when effective medication ⑦ _____ was developed a half-century ago, ⑧ _____ the electroshock treatment ⑨ _____ .
Student	So why would psychiatrists start using it again?
Professor	Well, one of the things that we've found is that ⑩ _____ _____ didn't work for everybody. In some cases, shock treatment really was much more effective ⑪ _____ like schizophrenia.
Student	Even though it is a horrible experience?
Professor	Well, these days, it isn't nearly so bad. ⑫ _____ before treatment and treated much better than ⑬ _____ _____ . But still, as you mentioned, electroshock treatment ⑭ _____ in both psychology and among the general public.

|구문해설| **start ~ing** ~하기 시작하다 (= start to ~)

Vocabulary Review

A Choose and write the correct word that matches each definition.

| hydroelectric | generate | medication | experiment | pill |
| transformation | theory | divert | interact | organism |

1. _____ scientific test of something
2. _____ an idea to explain something
3. _____ make something go a different way from which it was first intended
4. _____ two things affect each other's behavior or condition
5. _____ produce a form of energy or power
6. _____ medicine that is used to treat or prevent the symptoms of disease
7. _____ a dose of medicine that you swallow without chewing
8. _____ a function that changes or converts something into another
9. _____ a creature that has the ability to function independently
10. _____ relating to or used in the production of electricity made from the energy of running water

B Use the phrase below to complete the sentences.

| in general | peculiar to | identical to | respond to | effect on |

1. _____ , people suffering from heart attacks are overweight.
2. Uncharacteristically, she _____ his remark with sensitivity.
3. Some Chinese products nearly _____ those of Korean brands are receiving public criticism.
4. The hanbok is _____ Korean culture.
5. People believe movies have an _____ children's behavior both in positive and negative ways.

PROGRESS TEST

Listening Comprehension Section Directions

This section measures your ability to understand conversations and lectures in English. You will hear each conversation or lecture only one time. After each conversation or lecture, you will answer some questions about it. The questions typically ask about the main idea and supporting details. Some questions ask about a speaker's purpose or attitude. Answer the questions based on what is stated or implied by the speakers.

You may take notes while you listen. You may use your notes to help you answer the questions. Your notes will not be scored. If you need to change the **volume** while you listen, click on the Volume icon at the top of the screen. In some questions, you will see this icon: 🎧 This means that you will hear, but not see part of the question.

Some of the questions have special directions. These directions appear in a gray box on the screen. Most questions are worth one point. If a question is worth more than one point, it will have special directions that indicate how many points you can receive. You must answer each question. After you answer, click on **Next**. Then click on **OK** to confirm your answer and go on to the next question. After you click on **OK**, you cannot return to previous questions.

You will have 20 minutes to answer the questions in this section. A clock at the top of the screen will show you how much time is remaining. The clock will not count down while you are listening to test material.

Progress Test 1

TOEFL Listening

Listen to part of a lecture in a medicine class. Then answer the questions.

TOEFL Listening

1 What is the topic of the lecture?
- Ⓐ A recent study verifying the benefits of walking on cobblestone
- Ⓑ Western medicine's attempt to link acupressure with exercise
- Ⓒ The health status of older Chinese versus older Western people
- Ⓓ The way in which high blood pressure can decrease with exercise

2   According to the professor, what is acupressure?
    Ⓐ A type of medicine used frequently in China
    Ⓑ A therapy based on the assumption that different body parts are connected
    Ⓒ A condition that causes older people to lose balance
    Ⓓ A type of exercise recommended for people suffering from heart attack

3   According to the professor, what is cobblestone?
    Ⓐ A kind of medicine used in acupressure
    Ⓑ A medical term for the groups in the study
    Ⓒ A kind of round rock used for paving streets
    Ⓓ A method of treating high blood pressure

4   Which of the following statements about the two groups in the study did the professor NOT mention? Choose TWO correct answers.
    Ⓐ They were approximately the same age.
    Ⓑ They walked on the same street surface.
    Ⓒ They exercised three times a week.
    Ⓓ They both experienced improved balance.

5   What is the result of the study of the cobblestone walking group?
    Ⓐ It caused the walkers to lose weight.
    Ⓑ It increased relaxation in the walkers.
    Ⓒ It helped to decrease blood pressure.
    Ⓓ It created a sense of overall well-being.

Progress Test 2

TOEFL Listening

Listen to part of a conversation between two students. Then answer the questions.

TOEFL Listening

1. According to the woman, which of the following is NOT true about getting a part time job?
   - Ⓐ He would be able to pay some of this academic expenses.
   - Ⓑ The amount of the money for the tuition can be earned.
   - Ⓒ The job experience will be helpful when getting a job.
   - Ⓓ Various job choices are available for him to choose.

2 What does the man say about working on campus?
- Ⓐ He doesn't think he is qualified to work in the library.
- Ⓑ He isn't aware of any jobs on campus that are open.
- Ⓒ He thinks that an on-campus job wouldn't be interesting.
- Ⓓ He believes that on-campus jobs aren't good resume builders.

3 According to the conversation, where does the woman work now?
- Ⓐ At on campus library
- Ⓑ At a bank
- Ⓒ At a law firm
- Ⓓ At a computer lab

4 What does the man say about the woman's job?
- Ⓐ He thinks it must be boring for her.
- Ⓑ He considers it good experience for her.
- Ⓒ He isn't sure how it relates to her career goals.
- Ⓓ He is upset that she got the job he wants.

5 Which of the following is mentioned as a reason the man wants to find a job in finance?
- Ⓐ He believes it will benefit his future job search.
- Ⓑ He wants to see if he should major in finance.
- Ⓒ He thinks of entering graduate school.
- Ⓓ He doesn't think that the job would be helpful.

DICTATION

Progress Test 1

🎧 **Listen and fill in the blanks.** (P=W)

Professor   Over the last few classes, we've discussed how western medicine has attempted to ① _____. Western practitioners have made efforts to incorporate two of the world's major medical schools of thought. What I'd like to look at today is ② _____ that uh, basically... shows that ③ _____ can help old people remain healthy. Now, acupressure, a therapy, claims that various, distant, and ④ _____ of the body are connected. It involves placing physical pressure on different ⑤ _____, by hand, with the elbow, or with ⑥ _____. Thus, acupressurists will ⑦ _____ in order to treat a headache and so on. Now, interestingly, a study looked at the Chinese practice of older people ⑧ _____ for exercise. Cobblestones are those rounded rocks and ⑨ _____, right? Not only does the practice exercise the body, but ⑩ _____ seems to benefit overall health. The effect of walking on cobblestones ⑪ _____. It ⑫ _____ who just walked for an hour a day three days a week, while another group walked ⑬ _____ three days a week but on cobblestones. The results were pretty fantastic. In the ⑭ _____, people's blood pressure dropped significantly and ⑮ _____. However, the regular walking group didn't see these benefits at all.

|구문해설| **Over the last few classes** 지난 몇 시간에 걸쳐 (over ~ 하는 동안)   **Not only ~, but ...** ~ 뿐만 아니라 …도 (=... as well as ~)
not ~ at all 전혀 ~ 아니다

Progress Test 2

🎧 **Listen and fill in the blanks.** (S1=M, S2=W)

Student 1 I can't believe ① _____ . I don't know how I'm going to ② _____ .

Student 2 Well, I ③ _____ campus employment services. It's only part-time, but ④ _____ textbooks and even ⑤ _____ _____ a bit. It's actually not a bad job, either.

Student 1 So, ⑥ _____ ? Like working in the library? Those jobs are so boring.

Student 2 No, actually, private employers in town ⑦ _____ with campus employment services. So, there are a lot of different choices. ⑧ _____ a group of lawyers downtown.

Student 1 Cool. That'll come in handy when you apply to law school. I wonder if there are ⑨ _____ ... that'd be really good for my résumé... I'm graduating soon.

Student 2 Well, you should just go to the office and check it out. ⑩ _____ _____ ... all you have to do is go in and ⑪ _____ . They list the openings by field.

Student 1 It's that simple, huh? Well, in addition to providing some extra cash, it'd make my parents happy. ⑫ _____ to get a part-time job for months.

Student 2 It really does help you out when you graduate to have some experience.

|구문해설| **all you have to do is ~** ~ 하기만 하면 된다(is 다음에는 동사원형이 온다.) **They've been bugging me** 그들이 계속 나를 괴롭히고 있다.(have been ~ing : 계속 ~해오고 있다)

Vocabulary Review for Progress Test

A Choose and write the correct word that matches each definition.

| incorporate | acupressure | stimulate | verify | pressure |
| tuition | offset | afford | opening | résumé |

1. _____ a brief account of your academic and work history
2. _____ money paid for being taught in a university or college
3. _____ have enough money to pay for something
4. _____ make into a whole
5. _____ force made by pressing hard on something
6. _____ treatment of pain by pressing particular places on the body
7. _____ cause something to act further
8. _____ compensate for the other
9. _____ a good opportunity for a job
10. _____ confirm that something is true

B Use the phrase below to complete the sentences.

| come in handy | into practice | in order to | in addition to | run an errand |

1. My doctor suggested that I jog regularly _____ lose weight.
2. As soon as Jim put his ideas _____ , the company began making a little progress.
3. _____ exercise, many ways of dieting can help in weight loss.
4. I am working in an international context and my languages _____ .
5. She often makes her sister _____ for her such as buying snacks or bringing things to her.

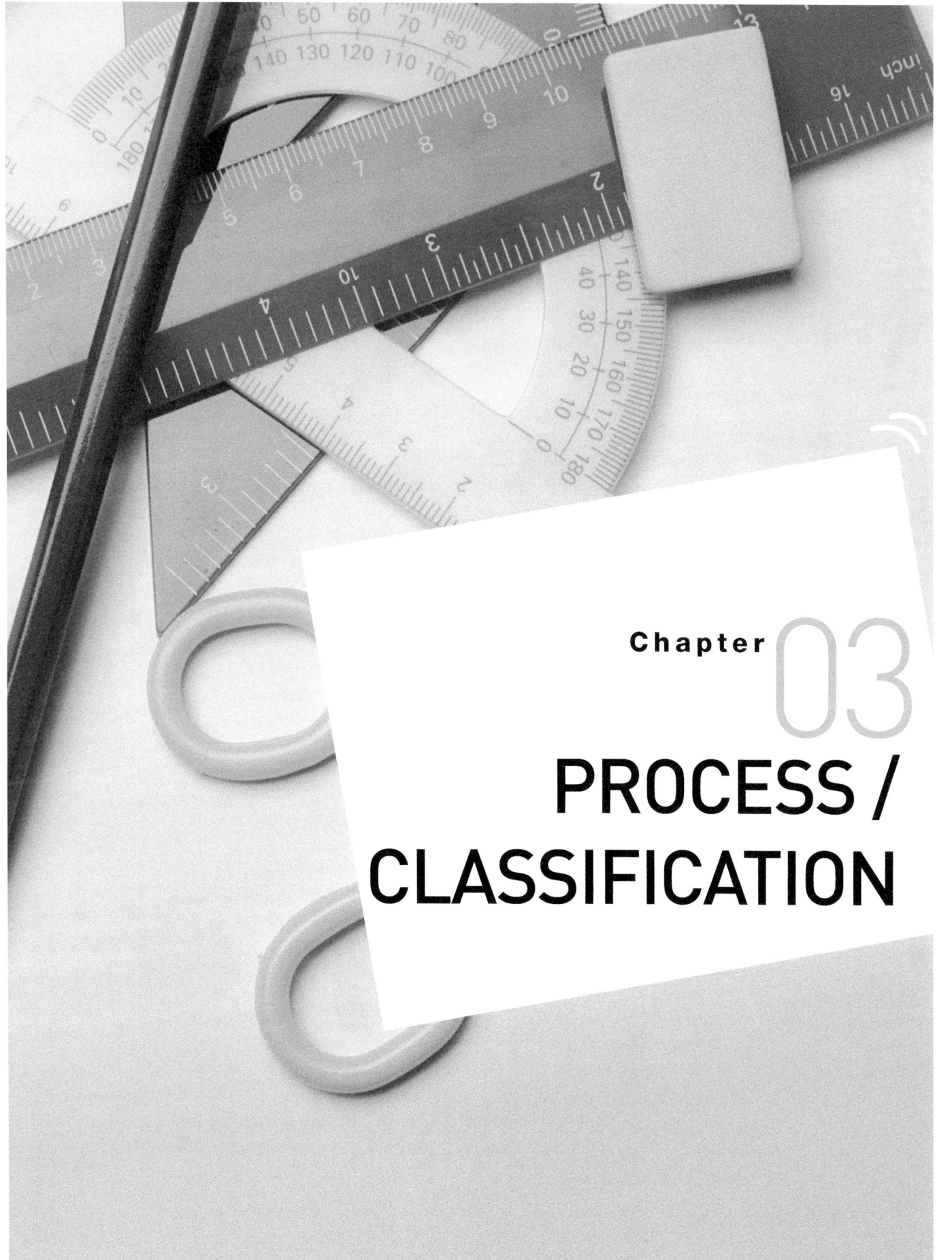

Chapter 03
PROCESS / CLASSIFICATION

OVERVIEW

Process / Classification

Process는 강의나 대화에서 드러나는 단계·절차·시간상의 순서를, Classification은 전체 내용을 일정 기준에 따라 분류하는 것을 말한다. Speaker는 자신이 말하려고 하는 것을 쉽고 명확하게 설명하기 위해서 이런 방법들을 동원하기 때문에 이런 형식 자체가 전체 내용을 이끌어가는 중요 정보라고 볼 수 있다.

Question Types

Which of the following are the steps of ~?
In what order, does the professor talk about ~?
Indicate whether each of the following is a step in the process. Click on the correct box for each phrase.
Which of the following can be an example of ~?
Classify the phrases below. Click on the correct box for each phrase.
According to the conversation, how does A differ from B?

General Strategies

1 Identifying Process

주요 정보를 특정 순서나 절차, 또는 연대순으로 나열한 것을 말한다. Speaker가 자신이 언급할 내용을 한꺼번에 얘기한 다음 하나씩 풀어서 설명하는 경우도 있고, 하나의 절차나 순서를 언급하고 그것에 관한 구체적 설명까지 말한 다음 다시 다른 절차나 순서로 넘어가는 경우가 있다. 예를 들어, 실험 과정이나 역사적 사건을 설명할 때, 또는 어떤 인물의 전기를 다룰 때 Process가 두드러진다. Speaker가 제시하는 절차나 순서에 맞게 Note-taking하도록 한다.

2 Classifying Information

어떤 것의 특징을 Speaker가 정한 기준에 따라 분류하여 비교·대조한 것을 말한다. 예를 들어, 조기 유학의 좋은 점과 나쁜 점이라든가, 문학 사조의 구분 같은 것들이다. 비교의 기준(크기, 범위, 시기, 특징 등)이 무엇인지, 비교 대상(서로 다른 이론, 연구 방법, 연구 목적 등)이 무엇인지를 알고 공통점과 차이점을 파악해야 한다. Speaker가 비교하고 있는 대상에 대한 세부적인 설명을 메모하거나 비교하면서 예로 든 내용에 주목하자.

▶Sample

TOEFL Listening

HIDE TIME 00:00:00

Listen to part of a lecture in a movie class. Then answer the question.

SCRIPT (P=W)

Professor: Okay... as I said earlier, the whole point of cel animation is to make the animating process, more, er... well, efficient. But how do animators put this method into practice, anyway? When they are doing cel animation, each character is drawn on a separate piece of transparent paper.  Remember... a separate paper for each character... Okay? A background is also drawn on a separate piece of opaque paper. Then, when it comes to shooting the animation, the different characters are overlaid on top of the background in each frame. It makes the work much easier for the animators.

Which of the following are the steps of cel animation? Check the correct box for each phrase.

	Yes	No
Frames are drawn by head artists.		
A character is drawn on a see-through paper.		
Sketches are scanned into the computer.		
A background is drawn on a opaque paper.		
Characters are laid on top of the background.		

해설 교수는 셀 애니메이션의 가장 중요한 특징이 작업 과정의 효율성에 있다고 말한다. 작업 과정의 효율성을 어떻게 설명하고 있는지 강의 내용을 잘 따라가보자.

Vocabulary Preview for Skill Check-up

Listen to the definition. Then check the correct word.

1. ☐ tuition ☐ course ☐ diploma ☐ scholarship

2. ☐ extrovert ☐ introject ☐ introvert ☐ extraordinary

3. ☐ protestant ☐ bourgeoisie ☐ proletarian ☐ nobleman

4. ☐ disperse ☐ maintain ☐ advance ☐ converge

5. ☐ volcano ☐ flood ☐ drought ☐ explosion

6. ☐ fresco ☐ croquis ☐ watercolor ☐ sculpture

7. ☐ square ☐ complex ☐ chamber ☐ container

8. ☐ interest ☐ career ☐ talent ☐ mission

9. ☐ record ☐ résumé ☐ application ☐ recommendation

10. ☐ doom ☐ prediction ☐ prospect ☐ forecast

Use the following words to complete the sentences below.

| converge | introvert | scholarship | challenging | authorize |
| career | application | ecosystem | transcript | commitment |

1. A classmate of his got the _____ due to excellent grades.

2. People usually think that an _____ may be shy, but not all shy people are.

3. As the discussion went on, their opinions began to _____ even though at first the participants of the meeting seemed to be in disagreement.

4. With his _____ almost finished, he expected to receive a lifetime achievement award at the Film Festival.

5. I filled out an _____ form for a credit card.

6. The President is _____ to use the Armed Forces in order to defend the national security of the United States.

7. A _____ is a comprehensive record of an individual's academic progress.

8. The director of the film says he'd love to star in his own film again and like to keep trying _____ roles in the movie.

9. The company made a strong _____ to innovation, high quality product, and service standards.

10. The experiment resulted in environmental destruction of the local marine _____.

Process / Classification

Skill Check-up — Identifying Process

Listen to the following and answer the question.

1 Write Yes or No to indicate whether each phrase is mentioned as a stage of successful photographic capture.

Camera collects the light in the body.　　　　_____
Grains on the film reacts to the light.　　　　_____
Aperture opens to control the amount of light.　_____

🎧 Listen again and fill in the blanks.　　　　　　　　　　　　　　　　　　(P=M)

P　To successfully _____, first... light has to be _____ _____ by the camera body. This is called _____. Then, in convergence, _____ to slow and bend, then _____. Finally, in registration, tiny, light-sensitive grains on the film _____ and record the image in front of the camera lens.

2 Check the correct box to indicate whether each of the following is a step in the process of volcanic eruption.

	Yes	No
Formation of magma	☐	☐
Cooling of magma	☐	☐
Appearance of cone	☐	☐
Magma forming mountain	☐	☐

🎧 Listen again and fill in the blanks.　　　　　　　　　　　　　　　　　　(P=M)

P　Volcanoes begin underground, then _____, finally bursting through the crust. The first stage is birth. _____ is made _____ by high temperature. It's called magma. It rises and _____. Because it is so hot, it rises easily. Then, comes collection. The magma _____ near the surface of the earth. Often, _____ will appear on the surface, signaling an imminent eruption. Last, the magma _____ the surface or the cone, _____. This is the explosion.

3 Which of the following is NOT a step in painting frescos? Check TWO answers.

Plaster is spread on the wall. ☐
Images of painting are carved into dry plaster.` ☐
Pigment is mixed with water. ☐
Pigment is applied to dried plaster wall. ☐

🎧 Listen again and fill in the blanks.

(P=W)

> P Frescoes are, uh, paintings _____. How is it done? The painter would _____, or colors, with water. And then he'd, he'd _____ _____. Then, he would put the pigment on his brush, and, uh, paint it directly on the wet plaster. _____, the color would, uh, _____. This is why these paintings have lasted so long.

4 Write Yes or No to indicate whether each phrase is mentioned as a step in getting a financial aid.

Prove the amount of money your parents spend   _____
Have an interview with a financial aid officer   _____
Pick up the check for an approved grant at the cashier _____
Send your transcript to Financial Aid   _____

🎧 Listen again and fill in the blanks.

(S1=W, S2=M)

> S1 John, did you have to _____ your high school transcripts _____?
> S2 _____ you're applying for an academic scholarship. What I have, a _____ scholarship is more, uh, well... _____.
> S1 Yeah? How do you apply?
> S2 Well, first drop by Financial Aid and _____.
> S1 I can do that online, right?
> S2 For the initial application, no— _____. So you fill that in. Oh, and ask your parents for their _____. The school needs to know how much money they made. Then _____. About two weeks later, you'll be _____ _____ with the financial aid officer. If you qualify, _____ and you can _____ and pick up your check.

Skill Check-up — Classifying Information

Listen to the following and answer the question.

1 How does the professor contrast a job and a career?
(A) How much of commitment you are willing to put in
(B) How many skills are required to have
(C) How much time you spend working

🎧 Listen again and fill in the blanks. (P=M)

P	Okay. When we talk about _____, there are two types; _____. A job doesn't _____. This is negative if you _____. However, if you just _____ make money, a job can be a good thing. On the other hand, a career is something _____, interests, and experience. It's positive if you can focus and spend a lot of time on your work. However, if you are not prepared to... uh, _____, a career will not be your best choice.

2 Which of the following is an example of the doom model?
(A) The world's oil supply will run out within our lifetime.
(B) Minerals and ores are already beginning to run out.
(C) The rate of population growth is beginning to decline.

🎧 Listen again and fill in the blanks. (S1=M, S2=W, P=M)

S1	_____ of population growth really _____, did it?
S2	No. I guess in the 70s researchers predicted that the earth _____ _____ within the next few decades because the population would increase so much. As a result, _____.
P	Yeah. _____ seems more realistic. _____ the fact that in most developed countries the population rate is actually declining. _____ all over the world.

3 Who does each phrase describe?

<Bourgeoisie> <Proletariat>

Decides how much to pay ☐ ☐
Uses the machines in the factories ☐ ☐
Makes profit from the products ☐ ☐

🎧 Listen again and fill in the blanks.

(P=W, S1=M, S2=W)

P	Okay, so as we look at Marx, _____. One is bourgeoisie. Anyone know what it means?
S1	It's French for "someone who came from the city", or the "burg."
S2	Yeah, _____ Marx, the bourgeoisie _____.
P	Right. _____, the machines etc. They _____. And then there is the proletariat. They work in the factories, use the machines to _____. They _____ the bourgeoisie.

4 What does each phrase describe?

<Extroverts> <Introverts>

Have better planning skills ☐ ☐
Less enthusiastic about starting a businesses ☐ ☐
Generally leaders in a company ☐ ☐
Can rise to a high level in the field of sales ☐ ☐

🎧 Listen again and fill in the blanks.

(S1=M, S2=W)

S1	I learned something interesting in my business management class today _____. Well, get this. There was a major university study _____. And _____ would you guess most business leaders have?
S2	Extroverted, for sure. Right?
S1	Actually, _____. Most of the, uh, the top brass, you know _____ _____ are not extroverts. They're usually quiet, _____ who can plan well.
S2	Oh, come on — to lead, say, a sales department, you have to be outgoing.
S1	Oh, right, right. That's true. _____ within a company where extroverts generally _____ was _____ sales and marketing. Interesting, huh? Oh, and by the way, _____ start their own companies, too.

Process / Classification

Exercise 1

VOCABULARY

puzzle _____
heavy-duty _____
pollutant _____
show up _____
pristine _____
Arctic Circle _____
migrating _____
plankton _____

*fulmar 〔조류〕 풀마갈매기

A Listen to part of a talk in an environment class. Then answer the question.

✎ Note-taking >>>

Class' topic   (researchers have been puzzled by)

Cause of pollution

Check Yes or No to indicate whether each phrase describes one of the steps of pollution in the Arctic or not.

	Yes	No
Sea creatures are contaminated by pollution.		
Boats from Canada pollute Arctic waters.		
Water becomes polluted by industry.		
Birds carry pollution in their bodies to Arctic.		

B Listen again and complete the notes above. Then answer the question.

Which of the following are true? Choose TWO correct answers.

(A) Scientists suspected the northern fulmar immediately.

(B) Plankton is contaminated by industrial pollutants.

(C) It is not clear how the birds get the pollutants to the Arctic.

(D) Migration patterns of birds account for the pollution.

Exercise 2

A Listen to part of a lecture in zoology class. Then answer the question.

✎ Note-taking >>>

Topic

Similarity   (look a lot like one another)

Difference   1. Cooper's hawk

                 2. Sharp-shinned hawk

                 3. Northern goshawk

VOCABULARY

distinguish _____
recognizable _____
plumage _____
identification _____
mature _____
goshawk _____
beat _____
snappy _____
tend to _____

*accipiter 매, 맹금
*hawk [조류] 매

What comparison does the professor make between western accipiters?

(A) The feather of the bird
(B) Their mating call
(C) The size and shape of their wings
(D) The beat of their wings

B Listen again and complete the notes above. Then answer the question.

When distinguishing a goshawk from a Cooper's Hawk what do you have to remember?

(A) The cooper's hawk is larger than the northern goshawk in size.
(B) The wing beat of a goshawk is stiff and fast.
(C) The mature northern goshawk is the only hawk identifiable by feathers.
(D) The Cooper's hawk has long, narrow wings.

Exercise 3

VOCABULARY

potential
hire
prospective
candidate
multiple
devise
interpret
impression
indicator

A Listen to part of a discussion in a sociology class. Then answer the question.

✎ Note-taking >>>

Class' topic   (Two ways)

Interview

            (problem is)

Psychological Test

            (problem is)

Check Yes or No to indicate whether each sentence is one of the steps of the psychological test or not.

	Yes	No
Candidates answer a series of multiple choice questions.		
Answers are reviewed by a testing company.		
Candidates must pass a physical exam.		
Employers watch candidate's facial expressions closely.		

B Listen again and complete the notes above. Then answer the question.

Which of the following is NOT an example of an interview?

(A) The candidate must answer questions face-to-face.

(B) Psychologists interpret the answers the candidate gives.

(C) The interviewer listens carefully as the candidate responds to questions.

(D) The hiring person decides if the candidate's answers are good ones.

84

Exercise 4

A Listen to part of a conversation between two students. Then answer the question.

✎ Note-taking >>>

Man's goal

Things to do

Man's pledge

VOCABULARY	
petition	
statement	
platform	
rehab	
funding	
fit for	

Which of the following are the steps of running for student president? Check True or False.

	True	False
Have fellow students sign a petition		
Pay the application fee at the Student Government office		
Submit a declaration of your platform		
Seek funding from approved sources		
Campaign on campus		

B Listen again and complete the notes above. Then answer the question.

What does the man promise to do if he is elected?

(A) Obtain money for tennis court renovation

(B) Listen to the students' needs

(C) Get funding for the tennis championship

(D) Offer prize money to the winners

Process / Classification

DICTATION

Exercise 1

🎧 **Listen and fill in the blanks.** (P=W, S=M)

Professor So researchers ① _____ that really heavy-duty pollutants have been ② _____ in the otherwise pristine Arctic. Now, the Arctic Circle is really isolated from the rest of the world, so how ③ _____ appeared there was at first ④ _____ . Anyone have any ideas?

Student ⑤ _____ , right? Birds, for instance. Anything that spends time in the industrialized regions, but then later spends time in the Arctic.

Professor You've done your homework. First we've got the birds — ⑥ _____ _____ migrate very long distances. The most common pattern being for birds is ⑦ _____ the temperate or arctic northern zone and winter ⑧ _____ . All right, in this case, let's take a look at the northern fulmar. Northern fulmar, almost looks gull-like, ⑨ _____ . These birds winter in the southern parts of Canada and the northern U.S. They're eating plankton, ⑩ _____ _____ . Then, they're summering in the Arctic, and their waste and their young contain this pollution which ⑪ _____ _____ .

|구문해설| **puzzled by the fact (that)** ~라는 사실에 놀라다   **show up** 나타나다   **be isolated from** ~로부터 고립되다

Exercise 2

🎧 **Listen and fill in the blanks.**

(P=M)

Professor ① _____ any of the three western accipiters, or hawks from one another can be somewhat difficult. They are ② _____, but tend to look a lot like one another. Accipiters or true hawks have short, ③ _____ to produce quick flight. These hawks have long shines and long, ④ _____. And in size, the female accipiter is often much larger than the male. The cooper's hawk is ⑤ _____. Of its relatives, the sharp-shinned hawk is smaller and the northern goshawk is larger. What about the plumage? The plumage of an accipiter ⑥ _____, the way it can be with other birds. Only the mature northern goshawk has distinct plumage. Thus, the best thing to look at to make a positive identification is ⑦ _____ _____. The Cooper's hawk has stiff wing beats ⑧ _____. The Cooper's hawk flies with several quick wing beats and a glide. The sharp-shinned hawk, however, flies with rapid, snappy wing beats. ⑨ _____ than other accipiters. Their wing beat is quick, deep strokes and a flapping motion at the "wrist." And the northern goshawk has long, slow wing beats as ⑩ _____. It flies with several flaps and a short glide. By noting these details ⑪ _____ make a correct identification.

|구문해설| **be recognizable as** ~로 인식되다   **tend to** ~하는 경향이 있다   **Accipiters or true hawks** 동격을 나타내는 or
By noting these details 이런 세부 사항에 주목함으로써   **be more likely to** 좀더 ~할 것 같다

DICTATION

Exercise 3

🎧 Listen and fill in the blanks. (P=W, S1=M, S2=W)

Professor Two ways employers ① _____ is the interview or the psychological test. The interview is the most common. An interview is a conversation between two or more people where questions are asked ② _____. The hiring person meets with ③ _____ and asks him or her a series of questions. And the employer tries to see if the candidate has the social skills and intelligence ④ _____. The answers the candidate gives really allow the employers to decide. ⑤ _____ is becoming more common. Psychological testing ⑥ _____ larger generalizations about the individual being tested. Candidates are given a multiple-choice test ⑦ _____ psychologists. They answer the questions and then ⑧ _____ by the test company. By those answers of the individual, ⑨ _____ the behavior of the person to the responses of a normal group.

Student 1 But an interview just ⑩ _____. Within the first few seconds, he ⑪ _____ people, which are often wrong... and once the first impression is made, ⑫ _____. It seems like the psychological test is a much better indicator.

Student 2 How can a multiple-choice test really say what kind of person you are, though?

Professor Well, exactly. Both of your points really ⑬ _____ _____.

구문해설 a series of 일련의 ~, 연속의 ~   suitable for ~에 적합한   devised by ~가 고안한   compare A to B A를 B에 비교하다
it seems like (그것은) ~ 인 것 같다   both of ~ 둘 다, ~ 모두

Exercise 4

🎧 Listen and fill in the blanks.

(S1=M, S2=W)

Student 1	Did you hear about the student presidential election?
Student 2	Well, not yet. What is ① _____ student president?
Student 1	Well, it's very simple. Candidates for the president must have a 2.5 ② _____ and maintain a 2.4 GPA during their terms. I'm going to ③ _____ .
Student 2	Oh, really? But you know, uh, to represent students' views within the university will be somewhat tough. You must be ④ _____ _____ to students.
Student 1	I know, but I'd like to try.
Student 2	Oh, you are serious.
Student 1	See, you never take me seriously. But it's true. ⑤ _____ _____ .
Student 2	I see. Well, no wonder you look so busy these days! So what do you have to do, anyway?
Student 1	Lots! I must have 100 students ⑥ _____ _____ . Next, I hand in the petition, ⑦ _____ _____ to the Student Government Office. After that, ⑧ _____ .
Student 2	So what will you change if you're elected, anyway?
Student 1	If I win, you can bet ⑨ _____ !
Student 2	That sounds great! These tennis courts are falling apart. ⑩ _____ _____ .
Student 1	Hey, thanks. And guess what? ⑪ _____ right here in my backpack. I'll get it now!

|구문해설| **run for** ~에 출마하다 **be responsible for** ~에 책임을 지다 **go for it** 시도하다, 해보다 **no wonder (that)** ~하는 것도 당연하다 **sign a petition saying** ~라고 써 있는 청원서에 서명하다 **fit for** + 직위(임무) ~에 적합한, ~에 적당한 **be free to** ~하는 것이 자유롭다, 자유롭게 ~하다 **happen to** (우연히) ~ 하게 되다

Process / Classification

Actual Test 1

TOEFL Listening

Listen to part of a talk in an education class. Then answer the questions.

Note-taking >>>

Variable category

        (dualism)

        (gray stage)

        (relativistic stage)

Static category   (post-21 year period)

1 Classify the statements according to the stages below. Check the correct box for each phrase.

	Dualism	Gray stage	Relativism
Black-and-white perspective			
It's not easy to decide who's right.			
Both sides can be right.			
The issue is complex.			
Only one person can be right.			

2. Which of the following are the stages of the variable category? Click on TWO answer choices.

Make choices based on settled upon values.	
Decide based on old habits and biases.	
See the world as composed of clear-cut choices.	
Begin to doubt that anyone is truly ever right.	
Change one's position based on societal expectations.	

3. Which of the following can be an example of the dualistic stage?
   A. Suspecting that no one around you is telling the truth
   B. Not acknowledging there are two sides to every story
   C. Being unsure about a controversial issue
   D. Making a choice based on your moral values

4. Which of the following is NOT an example of variable stage behavior?
   A. No decision is made in a dispute because both sides are right.
   B. The details of the world are simplified, seen as right or wrong.
   C. It is difficult to make a decision because both sides have merit.
   D. A decision comes about based on a stable pattern of values.

Actual Test 2

TOEFL Listening

Listen to part of a conversation between a student and a professor. Then answer the questions.

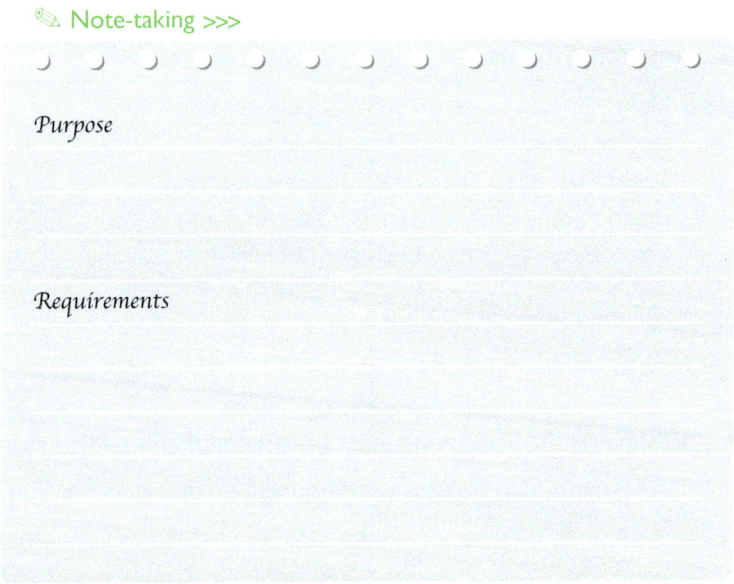

✎ Note-taking >>>

Purpose

Requirements

1 Why does the student call the professor?
 Ⓐ He is unable to attend the class.
 Ⓑ He wants to deliver something to her office.
 Ⓒ He wants to hand in a late assignment.
 Ⓓ He wants to drop her course.

2. Which of the following statements are true or false about the course on landscape painters? Check True or False.

	True	False
For juniors and seniors		
Study several painters		
Examine painters' political thoughts		
Learn painters' personal history		
For non-majors		
Give several presentations		

3. What will the students be required to do in the course the professor describes? Choose TWO correct answers.
   A) Paint a landscape.
   B) Give an oral report.
   C) Take a final exam.
   D) Buy a book.

4. What does the professor suggest the student do?
   A) Come to her office before her meeting
   B) Change his major
   C) Meet with her tomorrow
   D) Discuss the class with his roommate

DICTATION

Actual Test 1

🎧 **Listen and fill in the blanks.** (P=W, S=M)

Professor Between about 13 and 21, young people ① _____ _____. During this time, humans are ② _____ _____ ethical behavior.

Student What's the name again?

Professor ③ _____. In other words, ④ _____. There are a lot of changes taking place. ⑤ _____ _____, which is known as static. What's involved with the variable category? ⑥ _____ we call dualism. In general, the idea is that there are ⑦ _____. In theology, for example a 'dualist' is someone who ⑧ _____ _____. That is to say, the perception of the world is that ⑨ _____. Then this gets ⑩ _____ _____, where young people begin to realize it's not so simple. Near the 17th year, we... ⑪ _____ ... where we question all judgments and think what we believe now can change later ⑫ _____. That is to say, uh, we think the truth is not always the same but varies according to circumstance, so one can be right on one hand, and wrong on the other hand. But by 21 we begin to move back to a place ⑬ _____. That is, we enter ⑭ _____.

|구문해설| **undergo** (변화 등을) 겪다, (고난 등을) 견디다 (= go through, experience, endure) **variable category of** ~의 다양한 범주 **on one hand ~, on the other hand** 한편으로는 ~, 다른 한편으로는 **move back to** ~로 되돌아가다

Actual Test 2

🎧 **Listen and fill in the blanks.**   (P=W, S=M)

Professor	Susan Smith speaking.
Student	Dr. Smith, my name is Jason Anderson. My roommate, Peter O'neil, ① _____ . Uh-m... Art History 502.
Professor	Yes.
Student	Well, he is sick and ② _____ today. He asked me to bring his term paper to your office.
Professor	OK. The paper is due by three o'clock.
Student	I have a class from one to two. ③ _____ after my class.
Professor	Well, I have a meeting this afternoon. So ④ _____ _____ of the art history department.
Student	OK. Oh, I almost forgot. I'm a Biology major. But my advisor told me that I need one more humanities course to graduate. ⑤ _____ that you are teaching a course on landscape painters next semester. Could you tell me a little bit about it?
Professor	Sure. Well, ⑥ _____ . We'll be looking at several different painters and examining their works. We'll also look at the history and politics ⑦ _____ .
Student	That sounds interesting. ⑧ _____ ?
Professor	There is no final exam. And there is only one required book. But each student ⑨ _____ on an individual painter at the end of the course.
Student	Hmm. It sounds good. Will you be in your office later today? I'd like to talk to you some more about it.
Professor	Well, ⑩ _____ all afternoon. Why don't you stop by tomorrow? ⑪ _____ would be fine. My office is in the fine arts building right next to the library.
Student	Thanks. I'll do that.

|구문해설| **be scheduled to** ~하기로 예정되어 있다

Vocabulary Review

A Choose and write the correct word that matches each definition.

| require | migrating | potential | petition | distinguish |
| variable | relativism | undergo | pollutant | identification |

1. _____ changing quite often
2. _____ differentiate one thing from another
3. _____ the belief that the truth varies according to circumstances
4. _____ moving at a particular season from one part of the world to another, usually to breed or to find new feeding grounds
5. _____ waste matter that pollutes the environment
6. _____ the act of recognition that something exists; the close association with the other
7. _____ go through a change
8. _____ having possibility of something
9. _____ a document signed by a lot of people which asks an official group to do a particular thing
10. _____ request and expect someone to do

B Use the phrase below to complete the sentences.

| when it comes to | fill in | apply for | drop by | make a commitment to |

1. You need to _____ the application first if you want to apply for membership.
2. We know that he _____ reform the educational system.
3. Although there's little possibility of being hired, she _____ the position.
4. He asked if I would _____ later to meet him.
5. _____ chemical industry, I know your company ranks as one of the top companies.

Chapter 04
ORGANIZATION

OVERVIEW

Organization

Speaker는 자신이 말하고자 하는 내용(중심 주제)을 가장 효과적으로 전달하기 위한 방법으로 배경 설명, 비교, 예, 이유 제시 등을 이용하여 강의를 준비하게 되는데, 이를 Organization(강의나 이야기가 진행되는 구조)이라고 한다. 중심 주제와 그에 대한 설명이 어떤 관계로 어떻게 배열되고 있는지, Speaker가 그와 같은 구조를 사용하는 이유가 무엇인지를 파악하는 것이 목적이다.

Question Types

How does the professor explain ~?
How does the professor clarify his/her point about ~?
How does the man develop the topic?
Why does the woman say about ~?
Why does the professor mention ~?

General Strategies

1 Organization of the Information Presented

이야기의 구조를 파악하기 위해서는 먼저 Topic이나 Main Idea를 인지하여야 한다. 그리고 Speaker가 그것을 뒷받침하기 위해 어떤 설명 구조를 사용하고 있는지를 살펴 본다. Speaker가 자신의 의견을 Supporting하는 방식은 다음과 같다.

- By giving examples
- By comparing & contrasting or classifying
- By showing sequence or process
- By showing cause & effect
- By providing evidence or possible explanation
- By defining or describing characteristics

2 Organization-Rhetorical Connection

Speaker가 어떤 정보를 주는 이유(Why)가 무엇인지를 염두에 두고 듣는다. 전체 내용과 어떤 식으로 연결되어 있는지는 다음 사항들을 인식함으로써 보다 쉽게 이해할 수 있다.

- To change the topic
- To give an example of ~
- To support the speaker's point
- To suggest / explain or describe / introduce or conclude

▶Sample

TOEFL Listening

Listen to part of a lecture in a biology class. Then answer the question.

SCRIPT (P=M)

Professor Migrating animals seek ideal conditions for survival. So... um... for example, your African antelopes migrate annually following the supply of green grass. Weather patterns and other conditions change, so the migratory path varies. But... uh... it's all about the food, right? On  the other hand, Pacific trout will migrate for reproductive reasons. This fish migrates only once in its life, traveling from the small streams of its birth to the open sea to mate, finally returning to the small streams to lay its eggs and then die.

How does the professor explain why animals migrate?
Ⓐ By explaining the pattern of rainfall and grass growth in Africa
Ⓑ By illustrating the life cycle of a trout as it lives in the ocean
Ⓒ By exemplifying the motives for African antelope and Pacific trout migration
Ⓓ By comparing the life of a migrating animal to a non-migrating one

해설 교수는 이주하는 이유를 크게 두 가지, 즉 먹이와 번식에 두고 각각의 대표 동물(영양과 송어)을 예로 들며 구체적으로 설명하고 있다.

Vocabulary Preview for Skill Check-up

Listen to the definition. Then check the correct word.

1. ☐ govern ☐ invade ☐ attack ☐ colonize
2. ☐ audience ☐ composers ☐ colony ☐ organization
3. ☐ architect ☐ contractor ☐ plumber ☐ projector
4. ☐ sextant ☐ space ☐ plane ☐ meteorite
5. ☐ translate ☐ interpret ☐ transform ☐ recognize
6. ☐ abstract ☐ practical ☐ inferential ☐ deductive
7. ☐ zoology ☐ cultivation ☐ wildlife ☐ ecosystem
8. ☐ residence ☐ range ☐ chamber ☐ refuge
9. ☐ route ☐ passage ☐ navigate ☐ cosmos
10. ☐ adept ☐ incompetent ☐ eliminated ☐ genuine

Use the following words to complete the sentences below.

| colonize | adept | fascinated | interpret | audience |
| master | suspicious | celebrate | desirable | voluntary |

1. He believes _____ Africa and enslaving millions of its people is a historical sin of the West.

2. A speaker needs to keep the _____ awake, alert, and involved in his address.

3. People have been _____ for centuries by the fact that the building leans at such a strange angle.

4. Once you learn a word or phrase, you need to try to become _____ at using it.

5. He couldn't _____ half of what the man said.

6. All the students of this school are expected to _____ one or two foreign languages.

7. He'd been working at a home for the aged on a _____ basis.

8. We all gathered to _____ his eightieth birthday on Sunday.

9. Everybody was _____ of the new idea that Stephen suggested.

10. The new projects are not _____ because they usually don't produce many things easy to sell to people.

Skill Check-up: Organization of the Information Presented

Listen to the following and answer the question.

1 How does the professor explain changing perceptions?
(A) By contrasting past and present movies
(B) By describing the special effects used
(C) By defining its status as interesting

Listen again and fill in the blanks. (P=W, S1=M, S2=W)

P	So... right... today, we're going to talk about _____ ... well, at movies today, _____ by special effects and action, I mean a lot of people... for sure... but _____? Anyone seen a Lumiere brothers' film from around 1895?
S1	Yeah, it just showed _____! It was so boring!
S2	You're _____ modern eyes. I'm sure at the time it seemed really amazing.
P	Indeed. After all, just the fact that _____ was interesting _____.

2 How does the professor explain Gehry's sculptural architecture?
(A) By listing the cities in which his skyscrapers were built
(B) By providing evidence that shows his style
(C) By emphasizing his inspiration from other architects

Listen again and fill in the blanks. (P=M)

P	Most of us probably don't think too much about the buildings _____ every day. _____ like Frank Gehry, a building has the potential to be _____ – it can be _____. He is known for his sculptural approach to building design and building curvaceous structures. His most famous work, which _____, is the Guggenheim Museum — I mean the one in Bilbao, Spain — which is an extraordinary combination of interconnecting shapes; _____ contrast with _____ titanium. And because of its complexity, some curved forms were designed _____ computers. He, in fact, _____ than other architects as his major influences.

*curvaceous 곡선미의

3 How does the professor show that meteorites were used by ancient cultures?
(A) By giving an example of an ancient knife found in a tomb
(B) By comparing different types of metals used in Egypt
(C) By describing ancient myths of rocks falling from the sky

🎧 Listen again and fill in the blanks. (P=W, S=M)

P	Man has always been fascinated with _____, what do we call these?
S	Um, meteorites?
P	Correct. In ancient times, meteorites were usually _____ and people prayed to them for rain or things like that. But _____ _____, so people began to use them _____. At some point, ancient cultures realized that there was metal in them and began to use them in their technology. Take a dagger for example... this one in particular was made of iron from meteorites and was found in King Tut's _____! So we can see that though these rocks _____ a message from the Gods, they _____ very practical purposes.

4 How does the professor emphasize the importance of the field trip?
(A) By explaining that the trip is a mandatory part of class
(B) By illustrating what can be seen there
(C) By suggesting that the refuge is made primarily of concrete

🎧 Listen again and fill in the blanks. (S=W, P=M)

S	Professor, I wanted to get some more information about _____ _____.
P	Sure... what do you need to know?
S	_____?
P	On the contrary, _____. But it will help, I think, _____ we've been talking about more concrete. For example, we just read about _____ _____, but we'll hopefully be able to see those birds _____ _____.

Skill Check-up — Organization–Rhetorical Connection

Listen to the following and answer the question.

1 Why does the professor mention the colonization of Easter Island?
(A) To support his point regarding the Polynesians' ability to navigate
(B) To give an example of the Polynesians' colonization
(C) To provide background of the Polynesians

🎧 **Listen again and fill in the blanks.** (P=M)

P	_____ must be tough, right? Well, the Polynesians _____ _____ navigating the sea. They were so adept at navigation, in fact, that they could do it _____ . The Polynesians were able to _____ hundreds of years before Europeans mastered long-distance sailing. They were actually able to reach and _____ , which is _____ from their original homes. They did it without sextants or compasses.

*sextant 육분의(위도 · 경도를 재는 도구)

2 Why does the professor mention the causes of the Harlem Renaissance?
(A) To give examples of famous writers at the time
(B) To provide background for the topic of the lecture
(C) To change the topic of the lecture

🎧 **Listen again and fill in the blanks.** (P=W, S=M)

P	The years between 1920 and 1930 marked _____ African-American culture. What do we call this period of time?
S	Wasn't it the 'Harlem Renaissance'?
P	Exactly. But _____ we really have to focus on today, umm... why would this have occurred then? Well... the economy was pretty good, for one. And African-Americans _____ their heritage and make more demands _____ . This ultimately turned into a cultural movement. But _____ , it was the good economy that _____ _____ . All right? Now take a look at the influences of the 'Harlem Renaissance' on American arts.

3 Why does the professor mention the poll?
(A) To reach a conclusion about what most people think of newspapers
(B) To suggest that polls are not very reliable
(C) To introduce the reasons why people trust their local newspapers

🎧 Listen again and fill in the blanks. (P=M, S1=W, S2=W)

P	_____ showed that most people, _____ that they "don't trust" what they _____ national newspapers, also said that _____.
S1	Well, that doesn't make any sense!
S2	_____ ... the farther away the news source gets, _____ _____.
P	Yeah, that's pretty much what we can conclude from this. The other thing that we can conclude is that people don't realize _____. You know what I mean?... They don't see that they are affected _____. Then, why do most people trust their local news sources? I'd like to discuss a couple of reasons. First of all, we should carefully look at the materials _____ their newspapers... what do these newspapers usually talk about?

4 Why does the professor mention gold?
(A) To describe the lands the Cherokees occupied
(B) To note the causes of Native Americans being pushed out of their home
(C) To explain the background of US-Indian treaties

🎧 Listen again and fill in the blanks. (P=W)

P	Let's look at _____ of the Cherokees, a nation of Native Americans that _____ Georgia for centuries. The population of that state began to increase rapidly _____ — there were six times the number of people there in 1830 than in 1790. In order to have room to build and farm there, _____ began taking what had been native lands, and forcing the Cherokee and other native people _____. The path upon which the native Americans trod as they were forced from their homes was _____. The second thing that led to the Trail of Tears was _____. Land that had not been seen as valuable was _____, and again the natives were displaced.

Exercise 1

VOCABULARY

narrow
herald
nude
acceptable
notable
enthusiasm
clad
convention
innovative
draw one's attention

A Listen to part of a lecture in an art history class. Then answer the question.

✎ Note-taking >>>

Topic

Manet's painting   (controversial among critics)

                    (distinguished from realism)

How does the professor explain Manet's paintings?

(A) By defining the link between Manet and modernity
(B) By providing a description of Manet's painting by a critic
(C) By listing things that were innovative in his paintings
(D) By contrasting his paintings with the paintings of the 19th century

B Listen again and complete the notes above. Then answer the question.

In what aspects are Manet's works distinct from realistic paintings?

(A) Manet considered view important.
(B) Realistic painters did a black outlining of figures, but Manet didn't.
(C) Manet described figures and objects less distinctly.
(D) Manet chose controversial subjects for his paintings.

Exercise 2

A Listen to part of a discussion in a business economics class. Then answer the question.

✎ Note-taking >>>

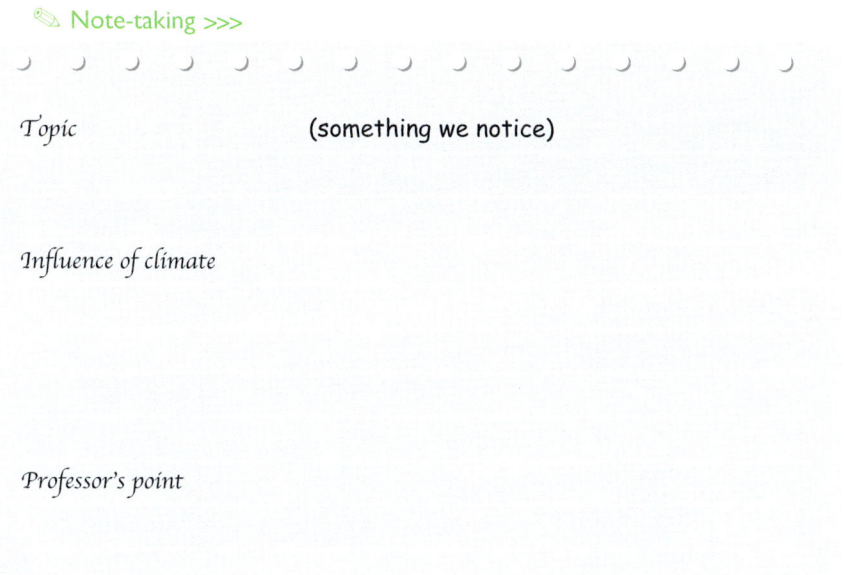

Topic   (something we notice)

Influence of climate

Professor's point

VOCABULARY	
boost	
stagnation	
facility	
tropical	
stagnate	
tendency	
prosperity	
exposure	
parasite	
interfere with	

Why does the professor mention tropical regions?

(A) To illustrate their negative impact on building stable structures

(B) To compare tropical climates to those of European nations

(C) To introduce a case study on climate into the lecture

(D) To give reasons why the climate could have a huge impact on economies

B Listen again and complete the notes above. Then answer the question.

What does the professor say about tropical cultures?

(A) The more tropical a society is, the slower its economy develops.

(B) The climates could prevent the activity of people from engaging in economic activities.

(C) People in tropical regions have a tendency to die of disease.

(D) Technological development is most influenced by climate.

Organization   107

Exercise 3

VOCABULARY

locust
interval
devour
harvest
plague
scrub
swarm
insecticide
dose
aerial
in search of

*fungus 균, 호모균

A Listen to part of a talk in an agriculture class. Then answer the question.

✎ Note-taking >>>

Topic
Damage

Effort to control   1.
                    2.

Effect

How does the professor explain the methods of controlling the locust plague?

(A) By listing the benefits of the methods
(B) By comparing the effects of the methods on the environment and animals
(C) By exemplifying the successful use of pesticides
(D) By introducing how the methods work on the locust population

B Listen again and complete the notes above. Then answer the question.

Which of the following is mentioned about desert locusts? Choose TWO correct answers.

(A) They lurk in the western part of Asia.
(B) The desert locusts do not travel.
(C) A certain climate causes them to increase in number.
(D) They are killed less than a week after fungus is applied.

108

Exercise 4

A Listen to part of a talk between a student and a librarian. Then answer the question.

✎ Note-taking >>>

Problem   (I want to ~, but...)

Ways to get through

Result

How does the librarian help the student understand the problem?

(A) By directing her to describe the problem to someone at the IT desk

(B) By asking her to write her problem down and submit it in the morning

(C) By indicating that she does not have the proper information

(D) By suggesting that her computer needs to be updated

VOCABULARY

authorize _____

issue _____

log on _____

B Listen again and complete the notes above. Then answer the question.

What is the woman most likely going to do now?

(A) She will wait until the IT desk opens tomorrow.

(B) She will try again with a new password and user name.

(C) She will use the computer in the library.

(D) She will tell the man what information she wants from the database.

DICTATION

Exercise 1

🎧 Listen and fill in the blanks. (P=M)

Professor Today's lecture is going to really ① _____ Edouard Manet, and in particular the way ② _____ modern painting. At first, we'll have a quick look at his life and at some aspects of his paintings that made his work different from ③ _____. Okay, so Manet painted in the 1860s through the 1880s. Manet's work was very ④ _____ because he chose subjects ⑤ _____ the old style. One of his famous paintings *Luncheon on the Grass* is an example. The painting of ⑥ _____ was not commonly acceptable at the time. Another of Manet's notable works is *Olympia*, a semi nude woman is wearing a few items of clothing and ⑦ _____. The effect ⑧ _____ *Luncheon on the Grass*. Despite such criticisms from older artists, a group of young painters expressed enthusiasm for Manet's work. In addition to ⑨ _____, Manet used an innovative technique, a rough sketch-like style, that further distinguished his work from realism. He also did ⑩ _____ to draw viewers' attention to the surface of the picture plane. This is considered modern, too.

|구문해설| **fully-dressed men** 정장 차림을 한 신사들 **in those times** 여기서는 1860 ~ 1880년대를 가리킨다.
One of his famous paintings ~. Another of ~ ~ 중 하나는 ~, 다른 하나는
despite + 명사(구) ~에도 불구하고 **draw one's attention to** ~에 …의 주목을 끌다

Exercise 2

🎧 **Listen and fill in the blanks.**

(P=W, S1=M, S2=W)

Professor   As we look at ① _____ ... uh... like I said earlier... something we notice is that ② _____ economies. I mean the climate has an influence on economic growth and its stagnation. ③ _____ ?

Student 1   I can ④ _____ happenings in the rainy season. Hurricanes, floods, storms... there are some factors ⑤ _____. Roads are sometimes ⑥ _____ or communication facilities ⑦ _____ by hurricanes. Roads and communication networks are basically key elements of a country's economy. Consequently, natural disasters ⑧ _____ paralyzing of the country, and then influence other aspects of economy.

Student 2   ⑨ _____ ... I don't have any exact source... but I've heard that ⑩ _____ economies.

Professor   Well, yes and no. Umm, we may say that there is a tendency of tropical cultures to have depressed or stagnated economies. The climate could interfere with growth, technological development and ⑪ _____ . However, there's no reason that climate should, ⑫ _____ , prevent societies from developing ⑬ _____ . But the fact is that the climate, for example in the tropical region as you mentioned, is part of the problem, in that ⑭ _____ certain diseases to exist and thrive in tropical places. Even if people ⑮ _____ parasites and viruses, they are ⑯ _____ where they cannot work, which has a massive and negative impact on the economy of these regions.

|구문해설| **have an influence on** ~에 영향을 미치다   **impact on** ~에 대한 (강한) 영향력, 효과   **blow away** 날려버리다, 날리다, 휩쓸어 버리다
              result in ~의 결과가 되다

DICTATION

Exercise 3

🎧 Listen and fill in the blanks   (P=M, S1=W, S2=M)

Professor   ① _____ that, in large numbers, and ② _____
             _____ , destroys huge areas of farmland, ③ _____ .
             The locust plague is a worldwide issue now. It has occurred ④ _____
             _____ . It originated in Africa and ⑤ _____
             _____ western Asian countries such as India, Nepal, and China.
             The, um, the desert locusts normally increase in number when climate
             conditions are favorable… and as adults, ⑥ _____ and
             travel great distances ⑦ _____ . They harm the crops in this
             way.

Student 1   What has been done to control the problem?

Professor   Uh… for the method of controlling the desert locust swarms, at present,
             some specialized insecticides ⑧ _____ . They are
             sprayed directly to the insects by vehicle-mounted and aerial sprayers.

Student 2   The use of chemicals, I think, possibly, ⑨ _____ , and even
             animals or birds.

Professor   Yes, many people have been concerned about it. This is why
             ⑩ _____ since the late nineties. The biological
             product… ⑪ _____ . It doesn't kill locusts quickly. The
             fungus typically takes ⑫ _____ ninety percent of
             the locusts. But the advantage is very evident, though. It affects only
             locusts, ⑬ _____ to continue their work.

|구문해설| **as far as** ~만큼 멀리   **in search of** ~을 찾아   **at present** 현재에, 현재는   **be concerned about** ~에 관해 염려하다, 걱정하다
              This is why (이것이) ~한 이유이다   **take (time) to** ~하는 데 … 의 시간이 걸리다   **allow ~ to …** ~가 … 하는 것을 허락[허용]하다

Exercise 4

🎧 **Listen and fill in the blanks** (S =W, L =M)

Student	Excuse me.
Librarian	How can I help you?
Student	I want to ① _____ from my computer in my dorm room. But ② _____ . Can you help me?
Librarian	Is this a new problem or have you experienced it before?
Student	Actually, this is the first time I have tried to access the database.
Librarian	Did you ③ _____ ?
Student	Yes, but it kept telling me ④ _____ .
Librarian	Ah… well, I think I know what has to be done with it… Did you ⑤ _____ from the Information Technology desk to use when you log on?
Student	Oh, ⑥ _____ . I thought I could just use my e-mail name and password.
Librarian	⑦ _____ a new user name and password for you.
Student	Is the IT desk open now?
Librarian	Well, its hours ⑧ _____ . Sorry, but ⑨ _____ tomorrow morning. But you are welcome to use the library computers for the time being.
Student	⑩ _____ . Thanks.

|구문해설| **be authorized to** ~하는 것이 허용되다   **log on** ~에 접속하다 (= log in)   **for the time being** 한동안, 얼마간 (= for a while)

Actual Test 1

TOEFL Listening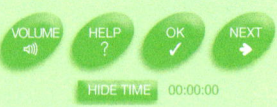

Listen to part of a discussion in a music history class. Then answer the questions.

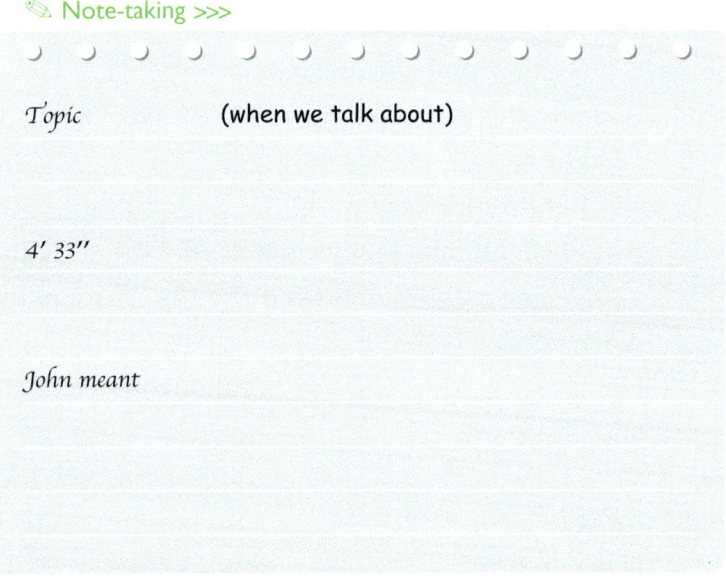

✎ Note-taking >>>

Topic　　　　　(when we talk about)

4' 33"

John meant

1　Why does the professor mention 4'33"?
  Ⓐ To support her point that silence is valuable as music
  Ⓑ To introduce John Cage's concept that listening is important part of music
  Ⓒ To provide the evidence that music is closely related to time
  Ⓓ To give an example of the important music compositions in the 1950s

2. What is the main point of the professor?
   - Ⓐ Cage's work should not be classified as music.
   - Ⓑ Cage's experimentation is a model for young musicians.
   - Ⓒ Music involves much more than just the playing.
   - Ⓓ Music can only be defined by those hearing it.

3. What does the professor say about John Cage?
   - Ⓐ Cage is perhaps best known as a piano player.
   - Ⓑ He didn't played a single note for his piece 4' 33" on stage.
   - Ⓒ Cage used a notebook when he composed his work.
   - Ⓓ He tried to show that there are various definitions of music.

4. What is the professor's opinion of Cage's work?
   - Ⓐ She is positive because it made audience consider music differently.
   - Ⓑ She is neutral and wants to hear the students' ideas.
   - Ⓒ She is negative due to the composer's use of deception.
   - Ⓓ She is changing her mind on account of the students' opinions.

Actual Test 2

TOEFL Listening

Listen to part of a conversation between two students. Then answer the questions.

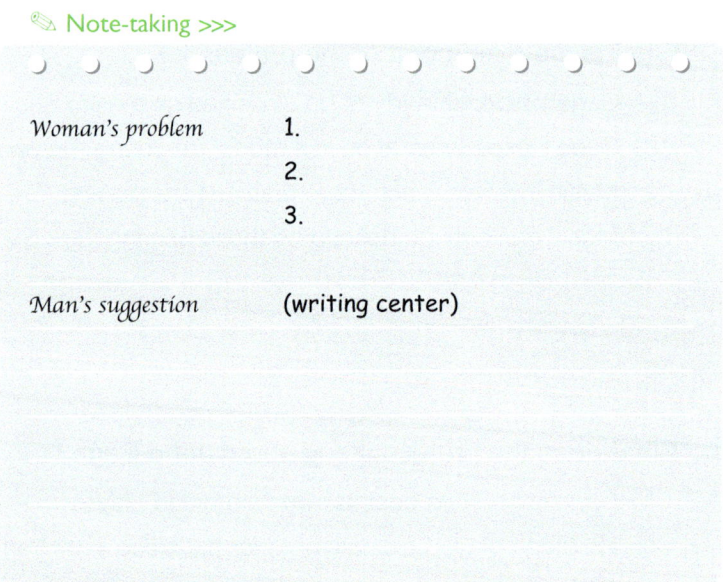

Note-taking >>>

Woman's problem   1.
                   2.
                   3.

Man's suggestion   (writing center)

1 How does the man explain his suggestion?
- Ⓐ By suggesting that his friend work harder with the thesis of the essay
- Ⓑ By comparing the benefits of the writing center and his help
- Ⓒ By persuading her that they know the topic she is writing on
- Ⓓ By describing the result of her last essay

2   Why does the woman go to talk to the man?
   Ⓐ To complain about the comments on her paper
   Ⓑ To discuss the thesis statement on her paper
   Ⓒ To ask if the man can help her with the paper
   Ⓓ To check if the man had the similar problems

3   Which of the following was NOT a problem, as stated by the professor?
   Ⓐ The thesis statement wasn't easy to understand.
   Ⓑ There were grammatical errors throughout.
   Ⓒ Basic assertions weren't backed up well enough.
   Ⓓ Much of the paper included erroneous claims.

4   According to the talk, what are the writing center tutors like?
   Ⓐ They can help research sources for a paper.
   Ⓑ They can suggest several good grammar books.
   Ⓒ They have all had a lot of experience in writing.
   Ⓓ They are adept at pointing out structural problems.

DICTATION

Actual Test 1

🎧 Listen and fill in the blanks.   (P=W, S1=M, S2=W)

Professor When we talk about ① _____, we often recall John Cage, one of the most important and controversial musicians of the 20th century. He is possibly best known for his piece 4′33″. He ② _____. All the audience ③ _____ sit at the piano and lift the lid of the piano. Some time later, ④ _____, he closed the lid. ⑤ _____, again he lifted the lid. And then again, having played nothing, ⑥ _____. The piece was finished without a note being played.

Student 1 Wait a second… he didn't play a single note?

Professor Nope. ⑦ _____. Now what do you suppose he was doing?

Student 1 Maybe he was trying to prove that he thought his audience ⑧ _____ tickets for a concert that had no music?

Professor *(laughing)* Not exactly, but…

Student 2 Well, to me, he was making an important point. The audience ⑨ _____ and listen to ⑩ _____. It really made them think about listening, which is an important part of music.

Professor Exactly. For Cage, listening was the important part of music. That is to say, John ⑪ _____ expect unexpected sounds. He regarded that ⑫ _____ in silence. That was how John Cage defined music. He was a person who ⑬ _____.

|구문해설| **be known for** ~으로 유명하다, ~으로 알려지다   **all the audience** 모든 청중 (audience 는 집합 명사로 복수 취급한다.)
be forced to ~하는 것을 강요당하다   **put ~ into practice** ~을 실천하다, ~을 실행에 옮기다

Actual Test 2

🎧 **Listen and fill in the blanks.** (S1=M, S2=W)

Student 1	Hey Marie, come in, how can I help you?
Student 2	I just got ① _____ from my professor and she basically said ② _____ the whole thing!
Student 1	That's pretty stressful, huh? What did she say the problem was?
Student 2	Almost everything! She said I didn't use enough sources to support my claims, that ③ _____, and that my writing had ④ _____. I don't know how I'm going to ⑤ _____ next Friday. Would you help me?
Student 1	Well, if you want I could help you on the weekend, but I think the writing center is a better option because you ⑥ _____.
Student 2	What can I get from the writing center, then?
Student 1	Umm, they can show you the places where you need more evidence, and uh, help you ⑦ _____. The center's tutors can ⑧ _____ and grammar problems, too. They're really fast and extremely professional.
Student 2	⑨ _____ anything about my paper's topic?
Student 1	Well, I think your problem is not the information; it's more ⑩ _____. I guarantee they can help.
Student 2	Umm... I've got to visit the center to get help from them. The center, let's see, ⑪ _____?
Student 1	It's in the humanities building.

|구문해설| get ~ back from ~을 …로부터 되돌려받다

She said (that) I didn't use ~, (she said) that my thesis ~, and (she said) that my writing ~

that 절을 서로 연결할 때는 that 을 생략하지 않는다.

Vocabulary Review

A Choose and write the correct word that matches each definition.

| authorize | criticism | distinct | climate | rapid |
| negative | evident | destroy | controversial | guarantee |

1 _____ arousing public argument
2 _____ different in nature or quality from something
3 _____ an evaluation or Judgement
4 _____ the weather condition at a place over some long period of time
5 _____ done in a brief period of time
6 _____ disapproving, denying or refusing
7 _____ ruin or cause irreparable damage to something
8 _____ clearly noticeable
9 _____ give a right to do
10 _____ make a promise or assurance about something

B Use the phrase below to complete the sentences.

| be forced to | that is to say | try to | in time | figure out |

1 He works at the orphanage voluntarily, _____ , he works without being paid.
2 Although it was very difficult, she _____ complete the project by herself.
3 He grumbled that he couldn't _____ what the professor was saying.
4 The two companies came up with solutions just _____ .
5 A large number of people in the countryside _____ migrate to cities due to lack of jobs.

PROGRESS TEST

Listening Comprehension Section Directions

This section measures your ability to understand conversations and lectures in English. You will hear each conversation or lecture only one time. After each conversation or lecture, you will answer some questions about it. The questions typically ask about the main idea and supporting details. Some questions ask about a speaker's purpose or attitude. Answer the questions based on what is stated or implied by the speakers.

You may take notes while you listen. You may use your notes to help you answer the questions. Your notes will not be scored. If you need to change the **volume** while you listen, click on the Volume icon at the top of the screen. In some questions, you will see this icon: 🎧 This means that you will hear, but not see part of the question.

Some of the questions have special directions. These directions appear in a gray box on the screen. Most questions are worth one point. If a question is worth more than one point, it will have special directions that indicate how many points you can receive. You must answer each question. After you answer, click on **Next**. Then click on **OK** to confirm your answer and go on to the next question. After you click on **OK**, you cannot return to previous questions.

You will have 20 minutes to answer the questions in this section. A clock at the top of the screen will show you how much time is remaining. The clock will not count down while you are listening to test material.

Progress Test 3

TOEFL Listening

Listen to part of a talk in a biology class. Then answer the questions.

*cataclysmic 격변하는 iridium (화학) 이리듐

TOEFL Listening

1. What is the main topic of the talk?
   - (A) The controversy surrounding the extinction of the dinosaurs
   - (B) The role of mammals in causing the extinction of dinosaurs
   - (C) The influence of objects from space in mass extinctions
   - (D) The impact of climate change on the survival of dinosaurs

2 Why does the professor discuss meteors?

- Ⓐ To suggest that it had nothing to do with dinosaurs
- Ⓑ To indicate that the meteor theory has been disproved
- Ⓒ To propose that a meteor impact caused disease
- Ⓓ To describe the meteor theory as the most plausible so far

3 How does the professor emphasize the influence of the meteor theory?

- Ⓐ By summarizing the opinions of various scientists
- Ⓑ By describing how a change in climate could kill off dinosaurs
- Ⓒ By indicating that he is most convinced by the theory
- Ⓓ By discounting the validity of the other theories

4 Which is NOT a possible reason for the dinosaur's extinction as outlined by the professor?

- Ⓐ The onset of a widespread ice age
- Ⓑ The increased role of mammals as predators
- Ⓒ The effects of extraterrestrial rocks
- Ⓓ A major epidemic affecting the dinosaurs

5 In the talk, the professor describes the cataclysm theory. Indicate whether each of the following is related to that theory.

	Yes	No
The iridium layer is offered as proof.		
Extinction was brought about by the impact of an outer space object.		
The dinosaurs couldn't survive because of radiation.		
Climate change resulted in the end of the dinosaurs.		
Meteorites brought viruses that killed off the dinosaurs.		

Progress Test 4

TOEFL Listening

Listen to part of a conversation between a student and a counselor. Then answer the questions.

TOEFL Listening

1 Why does the student come to the office?
  Ⓐ To complain about his current living situation off campus
  Ⓑ To express concern over not meeting other college students
  Ⓒ To find housing on campus
  Ⓓ To indicate that he will not have enough money for a meal plan

2 How does the counselor explain the second option, co-op?

- Ⓐ By suggesting the student remain with his cousin for now
- Ⓑ By showing how it is different from the dorm
- Ⓒ By pointing out what is not available compared to the dorm
- Ⓓ By listing the benefits the student could get living in a co-op

3 What does the dormitory NOT offer the student?

- Ⓐ A common kitchen
- Ⓑ A shared TV room
- Ⓒ A laundry room
- Ⓓ A common bathroom

4 Why does the student not want to live in the dorms?

- Ⓐ He does not want to have a roommate.
- Ⓑ He is concerned it will be too noisy.
- Ⓒ He wants to be able to prepare his own meals.
- Ⓓ He is worried it is too far from campus.

5 Which of the following is NOT offered by the co-op?

- Ⓐ A single room
- Ⓑ A common kitchen
- Ⓒ Shared tasks
- Ⓓ A laundry room

DICTATION

Progress Test 3

🎧 Listen and fill in the blanks. (P=M, S=W)

Professor Let's pick up today ① _____ the dinosaurs. This has been ② _____ the scientific community. What caused this extinction? Now, as you might guess, millions upon millions of animals died. But I want you to keep in mind the concepts, not so much the numbers. In trying to find answers, scientists have proposed ③ _____. One type of theory suggests that there was a cataclysmic event ④ _____. Another type holds disease accountable. And a third type suggests that it was ⑤ _____ that ⑥ _____ dinosaur eggs that led to their demise. The meteor or cataclysm theory ⑦ _____ by the discovery of the iridium layer. The presence of this chemical element in the soil ⑧ _____ from space, which would have caused a major, though temporary, ⑨ _____. This ⑩ _____ the dinosaurs.

Student But why would other species have survived? They needed a stable climate and sunlight too, right?

Professor Right! And let me tell you, ⑪ _____. Some suggest that because other animals were smaller ⑫ _____. Others feel that this is not a convincing explanation and are ⑬ _____ to explain their disappearance. So ⑭ _____ what happened.

|구문해설| **a number of** 많은 (cf. the number of: ~의 수)   **the presence of** ~의 존재, 실재   **point to** 지적하다, 암시하다

126

Progress Test 4

🎧 **Listen and fill in the blanks.** (S=M, C=W)

Student Hi. ① _____ Germany. I was told that I should come to this office ② _____ campus housing.

Counselor Yes, ③ _____ the right place. Where are you staying right now?

Student With a cousin who ④ _____ the college. But I'd like to be on campus.

Counselor ⑤ _____! And you have a couple of options. One is to live in the dormitory. ⑥ _____ with another student and there is a common bathroom, laundry room, and TV room.

Student Is there a kitchen?

Counselor If you live in the dorm, you have to ⑦ _____ at the cafeteria.

Student ⑧ _____ to save money, actually.

Counselor Okay, well then another on-campus housing option ⑨ _____. You would have a roommate, and a laundry room, just like the dorm, but there is a common kitchen. Residents sign up to cook, clean, and ⑩ _____ around the house. ⑪ _____ _____.

Student And I still get to live with and meet other students, right?

Counselor Yep! Should I ⑫ _____?

|구문해설| **exchange student from** ~ 출신의 교환 학생   **get information about** ~에 관한 정보를 얻다   **come to the right place** 적당한 장소에 오다, 제대로 찾아오다   **prefer A to B** A 보다 B 를 더 좋아하다 (prefer *to cook for myself* to *save money*)

Vocabulary Review for Progress Test

A Choose and write the correct word that matches each definition.

| mass | extinction | cataclysmic | meteor | mammal |
| demise | flaw | plausible | dormitory | resident |

1. _____ defect or weakness in something or undesirable quality of someone
2. _____ likely to be true but not certain
3. _____ a place for students to live offered by a college or university
4. _____ living in a particular place or someone who lives at a particular place
5. _____ a large number of things that are grouped together
6. _____ no longer in existence
7. _____ end or death of something
8. _____ a small particle that burns brightly when it enters the earth's atmosphere from space
9. _____ changing in a severely destructive way
10. _____ animals, especially female, which give birth to babies rather than laying eggs

B Use the phrase below to complete the sentences.

| point out | prey on | kill off | be searching for | prefer to |

1. The organization said, "We don't have enough money to _____ the beetle eggs in the trees."
2. Cats _____ mice and beetles on mites.
3. He _____ my mistake in the essay.
4. When you _____ information through the Internet, using various kinds of portals is helpful.
5. Please let me know if this is OK with you or if you _____ cancel the meeting.

Chapter 05
INFERENCE / STANCE

OVERVIEW

Inference / Stance

Inference는 말한 내용을 토대로 또 다른 사실이나 결론을 추론해 내는 것을 말하며 Stance는 내용에 대한 Speaker의 생각이나 입장을 유추하는 것이다. 특히, Replay Question으로 전체의 일부를 들려주고, 그 중 다시 특정 부분에 나타난 화자의 입장이나 태도를 묻는다.

Question Types

What can be inferred from the lecture[conversation]?
What does the professor imply when she says this ~?
What will the man probably do next?
What is the professor's attitude toward ~?
How does the man feel about ~?
What is the woman's opinion of ~?

General Strategies

1 Inference

Speaker가 한 말에 근거하여 어떤 것을 추론할 수 있는가(Inference), Speaker는 무엇을 암시하는가(Implication), 또 어떤 것을 예상할 수 있는가(Prediction)를 질문한다. 자신의 생각이나 이론으로 재해석한 지나친 억측은 피해야 하며, 본문에 근거가 확실히 드러나지 않거나 반박 가능한 것은 추론이라고 볼 수 없다.

2 Stance

Speaker의 말이나 표현에 드러난 느낌이나 입장을 판단하는 문제로, 언급한 내용 자체는 물론이고, 그 말을 하게 된 이유나 배경까지 파악하고 있어야 보다 정확한 답을 찾을 수 있다. 같은 말이나 표현이라도 그 말을 한 상황에 따라 긍정적인지 부정적인지, 신뢰하는지 의심하는지, 회의적인지 적극적인지가 달라질 수 있다.

- positive / negative / neutral
- amused / upset
- respectful / defiant
- favorable / critical / objective
- pleased / worried
- humorous / outraged

▶ Sample

TOEFL Listening

Listen to part of a conversation between a professor and a student. Then answer the question.

SCRIPT (S=W, P=M)

Student	Your Psych 101 class is a prerequisite for 102, which I have to take next semester, but it's full. Can't I get in somehow?
Professor	Have you tried Professor Kim's section? It should be open by now.
Student	I've thought about that... But there are some scheduling conflicts with Professor Kim's class.
Professor	Or, and it's a long shot... but you could petition to open another section. If 50 people do this, the college is required by law to open a class.
Student	50 people... hmm...(*sounds skeptical, like it's impossible to get that many people to sign*)
Professor	Say, you're attending classes full-time this semester, right? Then... just get on the registrar's standby list. I think you have a much better chance.
Student	(*excited*) Oh... how do I do that?

What can be inferred from the conversation?

Ⓐ The student is not going to take the class.
Ⓑ The professor will open up another section.
Ⓒ The student is considering taking Professor Kim's class.
Ⓓ The student will put her name on the standby list.

해설 학생이 수강하려는 심리학 101 수업이 정원 마감되어 교수에게 도움을 구하고 있다. 교수는 분반 개설과 대기자 등록이라는 두 가지 안을 제시한다. 학생이 어떤 안에 긍정적인지를 살펴보자.

Vocabulary Preview for Skill Check-up

Listen to the definition. Then check the correct word.

1. ☐ innate ☐ brilliant ☐ heritable ☐ immature

2. ☐ gene ☐ breed ☐ habitat ☐ seed

3. ☐ senior ☐ alumni ☐ faculty ☐ undergraduate

4. ☐ vacation ☐ tuition ☐ term ☐ diploma

5. ☐ interfere ☐ soak ☐ absorb ☐ insulate

6. ☐ opaque ☐ frozen ☐ repressed ☐ transparent

7. ☐ interest ☐ deposit ☐ stock ☐ share

8. ☐ amnesia ☐ insomnia ☐ anorexia ☐ acrophobia

9. ☐ injury ☐ casualty ☐ traumatic ☐ disaster

10. ☐ supplement ☐ command ☐ appendix ☐ instruction

Use the following words to complete the sentences below.

| amnesia | traumatic | instruction | innate | transfer |
| deposit | transparent | repress | susceptible | telescope |

1. I've heard that you're going to be _____ to London.

2. After you sign a lease for the house, you have to _____ some money.

3. In particular, the old are _____ to those diseases.

4. To watch the moon or stars through a _____ is one of her hobbies.

5. The death of his beloved dog was a _____ experience at his age.

6. A dragonfly's wings are almost _____.

7. The guy had _____ his feelings for so long that he seemed to almost forget how to express himself.

8. You can easily learn how to use this oven with these _____!

9. Some people believe in the ethical doctrine of _____ goodness, but I don't.

10. The victim of the car accident has _____ and can't remember his childhood.

Skill Check-up: Inference

Listen to the following and answer the question.

1. What can be inferred from the lecture?
(A) Lacunar amnesia is more serious than retrograde amnesia.
(B) The mind may protect trauma victims by "erasing" certain memories.
(C) Amnesia can be treated relatively easily through psychotherapy.

🎧 Listen again and fill in the blanks. (P=W)

P	You know, in the movies, it seems amnesia _____, right? Well, this kind of amnesia _____ and _____ retrograde amnesia; you just don't remember anything in the past… right? _____ the most common form of amnesia is called lacunar amnesia, the… uh… it's, _____ _____, it's like you can't remember a specific moment or sometimes a traumatic event. You know what's interesting, though? _____! Amazing, isn't it? Anyway, if a person recognizes this has happened, he should get help through _____ .

*retrograde amnesia 역행성 건망증　lacunar amnesia 일부기억상실

2. What can be inferred from the conversation?
(A) The woman is taking a different class.
(B) The professor typically misses her office hours.
(C) The man didn't know when to visit the professor.

🎧 Listen again and fill in the blanks. (S1=M, S2=W)

S1	Man, I'm really worried about _____ tomorrow.
S2	What do you mean? You don't understand the instructions?
S1	_____ . I heard she explained what she wanted in class… uh, but I was sick on that day, so _____ .
S2	Hmm… well, why don't you go talk to the professor?
S1	That's what I did several times, but _____ .
S2	Check out the syllabus, _____ . Or… isn't Cindy Preston in your class? _____ and talk to her.
S1	Cindy is nice… but, I think _____ .

3 What does the man mean when he says this: 🎧
  (A) He believes dogs are intelligent.
  (B) He feels that Rico is exceptionally bright.
  (C) He thinks too few dogs were studied.

🎧 Listen again and fill in the blanks.

(P=W, S=M)

P	Well... we think now that _____ to learn human language. As you know this dog, Rico, a border collie in Germany, _____ _____ a large number of words. Rico, in fact, knows over 200, and seems to be able to understand what his owner means... even if he doesn't know the word!
S	Maybe Rico is _____ !
P	But, while Rico had the biggest vocabulary of dogs studied in this research project so far, _____ large vocabularies, too. Dogs _____ to communicate well with humans.

4 What does the woman probably do next?
  (A) She is going to leave some money to reserve a room.
  (B) She will discuss paying the money to rent the place with her professor.
  (C) She will ask the man for another available room.

🎧 Listen again and fill in the blanks.

(S1=W, S2=M)

S1	Hi there. Who do I talk to about _____ a student group meeting?
S2	I can help you with that here. What's the group?
S1	_____ .
S2	All right... and I'm assuming you're all students?
S1	Umm... well, we have _____ ...
S2	Well, the majority of participants need to be students _____ you the room.
S1	That's no problem, then.
S2	Okay. _____ . I just need you to fill out this form and the group _____ . And is this a one-time thing or ...?
S1	We'll need it Monday nights, between 7 and 9 p.m.

Inference / Stance

Skill Check-up — Stance

Listen to the following and answer the question.

1 What is the man's attitude toward registration?
(A) He is frustrated because he couldn't get into the classes that he wanted.
(B) He is displeased because of the large number of the students.
(C) He is upset and cynical about the slow network system.

🎧 Listen again and fill in the blanks. (S1=W, S2=M)

S1 _____?
S2 Trying! Every class I try and _____. I don't know what I'm going to do.
S1 _____ about being a freshman. We have to register last. But _____ _____. Just keep trying.
S2 _____?
S1 People change their schedules around a lot and _____.
S2 Great… so basically, I have to _____ my computer trying to _____ _____?
S1 As I said, it's hard being a freshman. But it shouldn't be that bad.

2 What does the man mean when he says this: 🎧
(A) He knows that all the credit shouldn't be transferred.
(B) He is sure that there will be no problem with the number of the credits.
(C) He is not sure whether he can get the official transcript from the school.

🎧 Listen again and fill in the blanks. (S=M, C=W)

S Hi. I wanted to try and get _____ my previous school.
C Okay, sure. But _____ thirty six credit hours from other colleges.
S _____, so…
C All, right, then. I have to see an official transcript from your old school so we _____ that the classes _____, and … that should be provided by five o'clock tomorrow. Then it takes about _____.
S I'll have my old school send my transcripts right away.
C Okay… anything else you want me to do for you?

3 What is the professor's attitude toward Eden Project?
(A) She thinks it is a very important environmental cleanup site.
(B) She feels that it is a place everyone will want to visit.
(C) She is excited about the project for its size and the materials used.

🎧 Listen again and fill in the blanks.

(P=W)

| P | Okay... now let's talk about the Eden Project. This project we originally _____ _____ . Although relatively new, the project _____ _____ one of the most popular visitor attractions in the United Kingdom. Well... like I said... it's distinctive _____ . The complex includes two giant, transparent domes and it covers over 124 acres. The project _____ _____ to construct and it's ongoing. Additionally, as we'll, uh, see from this film, rather than using glass, _____ greenhouse construction, project architects used this special material... I mean... foil, _____ _____ , instead. It has excellent insulating properties, and is a, uh, a lot lighter, and is not as, uh, _____ damage by the sun. |

4 What does the man mean when he says this: 🎧
(A) He is not sure that he heard the professor right.
(B) He is curious about how the image would look like.
(C) He cannot believe what the professor is saying.

🎧 Listen again and fill in the blanks.

(P=W, S=M)

P	You may have looked _____ at the... moon, for example... But sometimes radio telescopes... _____ the naturally occurring radio signals... coming from distant galaxies.
S	Why use a radio telescope instead of a reflecting one?
P	Well, we use this kind of telescope to measure the... the thermal radiation _____ , which is not visible with a reflecting scope.
S	You mean _____ the thermal radiation? I never used _____ _____ .
P	Here... let's take a look at _____ radio telescopes to see what I mean.

*thermal radiation 열복사

Inference / Stance

Exercise 1

VOCABULARY

intake _____
restricted _____
sufficient _____
nutrients _____
ingest _____
life expectancy _____
mortality _____
be applied to _____

A Listen to part of a discussion about calories and longevity. Then answer the question.

✎ Note-taking >>>

Topic   (rats in the lab)

Condition

Result of Experiment   1.
                       2.
                       3.

Next class

What can be inferred from the discussion?

(A) The students disagree with the professor's opinion.

(B) The different results were seen in other animals.

(C) The same test was not done on humans.

(D) The professor agrees that the experiment would increase mortality.

B Listen again and complete the notes above. Then answer the question.

Which is NOT true about taking fewer calories?

(A) Increased longevity is seen.

(B) Fewer diseases are present.

(C) Different animals show similar results.

(D) Higher motivation was documented.

Exercise 2

A Listen to part of a lecture about bananas. Then answer the question.

✎ Note-taking >>>

First Topic

Route of movement   (its origin in Malaysia)

Second Topic   (having looked ~, let's focus)

Listen to part of the lecture again. 🎧

What does the professor mean when he says this: 🎧

(A) Banana is another term used by experts to discuss trade.
(B) The spread of the banana coincided with cultural and trade expansion.
(C) The banana is responsible for causing a trade war.
(D) Bananas were the result of Indian and Mediterranean botany.

VOCABULARY

plantain
exotic
herb
ivory
plantation
societal
consumption
trace back
spring up

B Listen again and complete the notes above. Then answer the question.

What will the professor discuss next?

(A) The acceptance of the banana into North American cuisine.
(B) The ways in which the banana have affected South America.
(C) Other types of herbs which are mistakenly called trees.
(D) How bananas originally came to North America.

Exercise 3

VOCABULARY

integrate _____
plagiarize _____
citation _____
paraphrase _____
quote _____

*plagiarism 표절, 도용

A Listen to part of a conversation between two students. Then answer the question.

✎ Note-taking >>>

Problem   (having a hard time)

Avoiding plagiarism

What can be inferred about the woman?

(A) Her advice should be met with skepticism.
(B) She has taken a workshop to help her with the same problem.
(C) She isn't sure she can help the man with his paper.
(D) Her suggestions are probably valid ones.

B Listen again and complete the notes above. Then answer the question.

Listen to part of the conversation again. 🎧

What does the woman mean when she says this: 🎧

(A) She is confident that she could help.
(B) The man can get some help if he comes to the workshop.
(C) She thinks it's better to go to the writing center.
(D) The man shouldn't expect much help from her.

140

Exercise 4

A Listen to part of a conversation between a professor and a student. Then answer the question.

✎ Note-taking >>>

Problem   (I've missed two weeks of class)
                   (Reason)_

What she wants

Solution

VOCABULARY

extension   _____
deadline   _____
be in the hospital
                     _____

Listen to part of the conversation again. 🎧

What does the professor mean when he says this: 🎧

(A) He never gave an extension on projects in the past.
(B) He is not sure what problems the extension of the project will cause.
(C) He is not sure if it's long enough for the student to finish the project.
(D) He doesn't know whether it's fair for other students.

B Listen again and complete the notes above. Then answer the question.

What can be inferred from the conversation?

(A) The student is not going to get an extension on the project.
(B) The professor will allow her to hand in the project whenever she is done.
(C) The professor will not ask her to come to class during the last week.
(D) The student will be able to work on the project even after the semester is over.

Inference / Stance

DICTATION

Exercise 1

🎧 Listen and fill in the blanks. (P=W, S1=M, S2=W)

Professor For a certain period of time, ① _____ had their caloric intake ② _____ ... in other words, they didn't eat much! The important thing here, however, is ③ _____, but sufficient quantities of minerals, vitamins, and ④ _____. Anyway, we got a result from the experiment, that ⑤ _____ increased by 33 percent when their caloric intake was restricted. Obviously weighing less... ⑥ _____ and fewer diseases appeared compared to a group of rats with a normal diet. More research was done and it showed ⑦ _____ other animals, too.

Student 1 I'm sure it's probably the same thing with humans! Being overweight increases ⑧ _____ and health conditions.

Student 2 No way. Our bodies ⑨ _____. We get the energy from food, so without enough food ⑩ _____ a healthy life. Worse than that, not eating enough would cause health problems and ⑪ _____, if anything.

Professor Well, the result of the experiment might be applied to other animals, too. Actually there are those who claim that as long as humans ingest ⑫ _____, they can live longer. Well, next class we'll look at those studies, ⑬ _____. Come and pick up your exams on your way out.

|구문해설| **increased by 33 percent** 33 퍼센트가 증가하다 **compared to** ~과 비교하여 **enough food** '충분한' 음식 (cf. not eating enough : '충분히' 먹지 않는 것) **run out of** ~을 다 쓰다, 소진하다

Exercise 2

🎧 **Listen and fill in the blanks.**

(P=M)

Professor   Modern bananas and plantains ① _____ the south-east Asian and western Pacific regions. But ② _____ Malaysia. So the, uh, the history of the banana is... the history of global exploration and trade, in a sense. The movement of people and ③ _____, the uh, fact that the world has uh, become smaller, helps explain how ④ _____ has come to be a common part of the Western diet. The tree... which is actually the world's biggest, uh, biggest herb plant... ⑤ _____ Malaysia, and ⑥ _____. From there, ⑦ _____ other parts of Asia and then, uh, on to the Mediterranean. Eventually, this tropical fruit reached Africa. Traders of slaves, ivory, and spices then introduced the banana to Africa, ⑧ _____. The banana trade followed the slave trade to the new world, then, and banana plantations ⑨ _____ South and Central America. And so by the 1800s, bananas had come to North America.

So, uh, having looked at the uh, history, let's uh, ⑩ _____ on the economic and societal impact in South America of this fruit. More specifically, I mean, we will take a look at the importance of bananas production for export, and developments in banana trade, ⑪ _____ _____.

|구문해설| **the origin of** ~의 기원, 시초   **in a sense** 어떤 면에서는   **by the 1800s** 1800년대 경에 이르러서는

DICTATION

Exercise 3

🎧 **Listen and fill in the blanks.** (S1=M, S2=W)

Student 1 I'm having a hard time ① _____. I want to make sure I do it right. Well, actually, I'm worried about plagiarism. To develop my idea, ② _____ some articles, but I don't know what the rules are about using them.

Student 2 I've actually been ③ _____ plagiarism at the writing center.

Student 1 Great! I'm trying to use this article ④ _____ that college tuition is too expensive, Okay? But I'm not sure ⑤ _____ _____ I got the info from an article, that it's not my idea.

Student 2 Hmmm… let me take a look at it… Okay, yeah, I see your point. ⑥ _____. In fact, if I read this, ⑦ _____ _____.

Student 1 Well, how can I make it clearer? I don't want to plagiarize!

Student 2 Well, you must give citations when using other's ideas and ⑧ _____ _____. Even if you paraphrased ⑨ _____, it's certain that they are not your own ideas. For example, ⑩ _____ _____, I would use ⑪ _____ the article. The quote marks will make it very clear that it's someone else's idea.

Student 1 Okay, that makes sense.

|구문해설| **have a hard time ~ing** ~ 하는 데 어려움을 겪다, ~하느라 애쓰다   **make sure** 확인(다짐)하다   **make sense** 말이 되다, 이치에 맞다

Exercise 4

🎧 Listen and fill in the blanks. (S=W, P=M)

Student Professor, I've missed two weeks of class, but I've been in the hospital.

Professor I knew you must have been sick, since you never missed a class before. Sounds serious. Are you feeling all right?

Student I'm still a little weak, but I'm going to be back in class this week… but… um… I know ① _____ , so…

Professor Yeah. ② _____ for the final. Are you worried about the final exam?

Student Well, not exactly… I mean… there was a homework assignment that I had to hand in, ③ _____ . I know each student is allowed ④ _____ if there is a medical reason ⑤ _____ . I'd like to get an extension on the project. I'm really ⑥ _____ and I don't think there's any way I can get everything done in two weeks.

Professor Hmm, I don't know about the extension, ⑦ _____ _____ .

Student I don't think I can complain about that.

Professor You know, finishing the project is one important thing but what grade you're getting is another thing you should consider… hmm… well… why don't we do this? ⑧ _____ … and in addition… I think I could allow a few more days even after the final exam to hand in the project. How does that sound? And you ⑨ _____ _____ .

Student Sure, I shouldn't have a problem. And I can't tell you how much I appreciate this.

|구문해설| **in addition** 게다가, 그 외에 (= besides)   **how the work goes** 작업(일)이 진행되어 가는 상태

Inference / Stance

Actual Test 1

TOEFL Listening

Listen to part of a talk in an economics class. Then answer the questions.

Note-taking >>>

Topic

Negative effect

Positive effect

1. What can be inferred about obesity?
   Ⓐ It is mainly ignored by the press and public.
   Ⓑ The trend toward being overweight is slowly reversing.
   Ⓒ It has been studied extensively these days.
   Ⓓ Its relation to health problems has been overstated.

2 What does the student imply about health problems and obesity?

- Ⓐ They are not taken seriously enough by doctors.
- Ⓑ They result in a major loss to the economy.
- Ⓒ They have little impact on people's productivity.
- Ⓓ They are only part of the country's overall economic decline.

3 Listen to part of the talk again.

What does the professor mean when he says this:

- Ⓐ He doesn't want to give another example.
- Ⓑ He is sure everyone understands what these markets are.
- Ⓒ He is not sure whether he has to give another example.
- Ⓓ He wants to know if everyone understands what the markets are.

4 What does the professor say about the weight-loss industry?

- Ⓐ It is having a negative economic impact on the country.
- Ⓑ It considers the health-care industry as its primary business model.
- Ⓒ It has helped limit the health problems and lost productivity of the obese.
- Ⓓ It generates at least as much money as is lost by obesity-related problems.

Actual Test 2

TOEFL Listening

Listen to part of a conversation in the computer lab. Then answer the questions.

Note-taking >>>

Porblem   (I'm just having problems)

Possible Reasons

Solution

1 What can be inferred about the lab worker?
   Ⓐ He is adept at writing difficult computer code.
   Ⓑ He offers a solution, which isn't useful at this point.
   Ⓒ He has only been working in the lab for a few days.
   Ⓓ He has helped the student download articles before.

2. What can be inferred about the student?
   - Ⓐ She is not a novice computer user.
   - Ⓑ She was not sure she had the correct website address.
   - Ⓒ She had never tried to access the website before.
   - Ⓓ She is uncomfortable using the computer for her homework.

3. What does the lab worker mean when he says this:
   - Ⓐ He thinks the student may have not been paying attention.
   - Ⓑ He believes that the problem may be an ongoing one.
   - Ⓒ He is confused about why the student needs the article.
   - Ⓓ He doesn't think he will be able to help the student.

4. What will the student probably do next?
   - Ⓐ Attempt to access the article on another computer
   - Ⓑ Get the article in printed form at the library
   - Ⓒ Find the necessary material in hard copy form
   - Ⓓ Ask the professor for a direct web address for the article

DICTATION

Actual Test 1

🎧 Listen and fill in the blanks. (P=M, S=W)

P ① _____ over the past several years as ② _____ continues to increase. There're some real economic implications here. Anyone want to throw some out?

S Well, being overweight causes a lot of health problems. So there's more money ③ _____ , right? And people miss work because of those health problems. I think I read somewhere that ④ _____ .

P It's true. According to a recent study, the impact of obesity on health ⑤ _____ smoking or drinking. Some diseases such as diabetes, heart diseases, and high cholesterol ⑥ _____ . So it is sure that those diseases caused by obesity are recognized as one of the major health problems nowadays. However, one economist recently suggested that there are some positive economic benefits to the obesity epidemic, too. He claims that we're missing the fact that our economy ⑦ _____ to dominate the global weight-loss market. This is what we call a niche economy. ⑧ _____ , remember? You need another example of these markets?... I guess not...
In response to the obesity problem, ⑨ _____ new businesses such as clinics and gyms have been generated. And these can be exported to other countries, ⑩ _____ the economy.

|구문해설| **continue to** 계속 ~하다 **Anyone want to throw some out?** 상대방에게 어떤 의견을 끌어내고자 할 때 묻는 표현(throw out : 제안하다) **be poised to** ~할 준비가 되다 **in response to** ~에 응하여, ~에 답하여

Actual Test 2

🎧 **Listen and fill in the blanks.** (S=W, L=M)

Student	Excuse me. Can you help me?
Lab worker	① _____ ?
Student	Well, I'm just having problems ② _____ .
Lab worker	I'm sorry.
Student	It worked yesterday! I think I've got the address right, ③ _____ other websites... I even shut down the computer and tried again. But ④ _____ that I'm supposed to download and summarize for class on Monday.
Lab worker	Hmm... yeah. I see that. ⑤ _____ having problems getting to the articles before?
Student	I don't think so...
Lab worker	Well, sometimes a homepage server ⑥ _____ _____ or the articles you wanted have so many images that ⑦ _____ . In both cases, all you have to do is wait and try again, I guess.
Student	But actually, all the other articles that the professor handed out have been photocopied.
Lab worker	Ah, I see. Then ⑧ _____ . Look, all you have to do is just ⑨ _____ in the address box. Links often don't work, but you can usually ⑩ _____ _____ .
Student	Uh oh! I'm not sure of the exact address, but I'll try to find it. I really need to get this article for class.
Lab worker	Well, I've done all I can. ⑪ _____ your professor? That's all the advice I can give at this point.

|구문해설| **link to** ~에 연결하다, 링크하다   **all you have to do is** + 동사원형 (당신은) ~하기만 하면 된다, 할 일은 ~ 뿐이다

wait and try 기다렸다가 해보다 (cf. wait and see : 일의 진행을 두고보다, 관망하다)   **get in touch with** ~와 접촉하다, 연락하다 (cf. keep in touch with : ~와 계속 연락하다)

Vocabulary Review

A Choose and write the correct word that matches each definition.

exotic	consumption	restricted	sufficient	nutrients
mortality	plagiarism	cite	extension	obesity

1 _____ more than average weight
2 _____ substances needed for animals to grow well
3 _____ coming from another place or part of the world
4 _____ quite small or limited in scope, quantity, degree, etc.
5 _____ enough to do something as it is purposed
6 _____ using someone else's idea or work and pretending that it is yours
7 _____ refer to something
8 _____ an additional period of time
9 _____ the act of buying goods to satisfy needs
10 _____ the ratio of death in an area or situation

B Use the phrase below to complete the sentences.

get through	trace back	be poised to	have a hard time	in response to

1 The government _____ lower oil import tariffs.
2 The kids are _____ doing a crossword puzzle.
3 I am sending you an e-mail _____ your suggestion.
4 I could _____ everything except writing.
5 Some phobias can _____ to childhood experiences.

Chapter 06
FUNCTION

OVERVIEW

Function

Function은 Speaker가 어떤 말을 하는 이유나 목적, 즉 그 말이 하는 기능을 말한다. 앞뒤 문맥을 파악하여 Speaker가 그 말을 하게 된 배경을 알고, 말에 나타나는 억양이나 어조를 통해 속에 담긴 의미까지 파악해야 제대로 이해할 수 있다.

Question Types

Why does the professor say this?
Why does the professor mention ~?
Why does the man say this?
What does the advisor mean when he says this?
What does the professor mean when she says this?

General Strategies

Function-Purpose

Speaker가 왜 이 말을 했는가, 즉 그 말의 기능을 파악하는 것으로 Speaker의 목적과 동기를 생각하도록 한다. 예를 들어, Speaker가 특정 말을 한 것이 사과를 하려는 것인지, 불평을 하려는 것인지, 제안을 하려는 것인지를 파악하는 것이다. Speaker의 Tone과 Intonation을 듣고 의도된 의미를 파악하도록 한다. 예를 들어, "Cool, huh?"와 같은 말은 상황에 따라 긍정일 수도 있고 비꼬는 것일 수 있으니 그 말의 뉘앙스를 파악하는 것이다.

- To give direction or instruction
- To recommend, suggest, advice or persuade
- To complain, apologize or forgive
- To give opinion, agree or disagree
- To request, invite

▶ Sample

TOEFL Listening

Listen to part of a conversation between two students. Then answer the question.

SCRIPT (S1=W, S2=M)

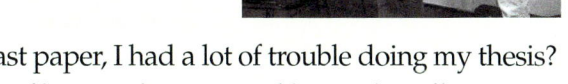

Student 1 Isn't Professor McEwan's class great?
Student 2 Well, I'm not so sure about that. I'm really not getting very much out of the lectures.
Student 1 Really? I think his lectures are fascinating. I especially like the slide presentations.
Student 2 That's the problem. I really can't take good notes on that stuff.
Student 1 Hmmm... remember the last paper, I had a lot of trouble doing my thesis? He helped me for a couple of hours when I visited him in his office.
Student 2 Yeah, right!
Student 1 Seriously, I bet he'd be willing to show you how to take good notes. He's really nice.

Listen to part of the conversation again.

S1 Hmmm... remember the last paper, I had a lot of trouble doing my thesis? He helped me for a couple of hours when I visited him in his office.
S2 Yeah, right!

Why does the woman say this:

S1 Hmmm... remember the last paper, I had a lot of trouble doing my thesis?

Ⓐ To indicate that notes are very important for papers
Ⓑ To encourage the man to ask the professor for help
Ⓒ To emphasize the low quality of her last paper
Ⓓ To ask the man not to do the same mistake as her

해설 여자는 McEwan 교수가 자신의 논문을 도와줬다고 말함으로써 교수의 적극적인 도움을 칭찬하고 있다. 남자의 문제점 역시 교수와 상의함으로써 해결할 수 있다는 암시이다. 즉, 궁극적으로 여자는 남자가 이 수업을 계속 들을 것을 권유하고 있다.

Vocabulary Preview for Skill Check-up

Listen to the definition. Then check the correct word.

1. ☐ undesirable ☐ correspondent ☐ incompatible ☐ accordant

2. ☐ inhabit ☐ obey ☐ permit ☐ disapprove

3. ☐ regular ☐ ordinary ☐ always ☐ irregular

4. ☐ discomfort ☐ benefit ☐ moderation ☐ convenience

5. ☐ preside ☐ ancient ☐ beforehand ☐ latest

6. ☐ sewage ☐ waste ☐ pollutant ☐ dirt

7. ☐ therapy ☐ medicine ☐ gene ☐ germ

8. ☐ ancestor ☐ offspring ☐ relative ☐ brotherhood

9. ☐ depict ☐ subscribe ☐ interpret ☐ embody

10. ☐ disappear ☐ replace ☐ revive ☐ survive

Use the following words to complete the sentences below.

| propose | survive | prevent | common | permit |
| regular | sewage | ancient | public | provide |

1. Our company offers _____ bus services to every worker.

2. My brother would never _____ me to use his digital camera.

3. This river was polluted with industrial _____.

4. Everybody agrees that English is a _____ language in the international society.

5. The committee _____ buying out Jefferson Industries to us, and they assured us that the price of our company's stock will go up after the sale goes through.

6. They found out several burial chambers of the great leaders of _____ China.

7. Police have strengthened security in Seoul to _____ possible terror attacks.

8. This new museum will be open to the _____ next month.

9. The priest is well-known to _____ food for the poor and needy.

10. I don't understand how she can _____ eating a meal once a day.

Skill Check-up — Function-Purpose

Listen to the following and answer the question.

1 Why does the woman say this: 🎧
  (A) To ask how much the man has to pay for each ticket
  (B) To advise the man on how to avoid getting more tickets
  (C) To suggest another way to commute to campus

🎧 Listen again and fill in the blanks.   (S1=M, S2=W)

S1	I can't believe _____ !
S2	Oof! Again? Isn't this your third time getting the ticket?
S1	Fourth, actually. I tried to _____ at the parking service… but they only have a limited number.
S2	How much do you have to pay for the tickets? I mean, _____ this semester, you should do something. Well how about a campus bus? It's free.
S1	Hmm… _____ . Does it run regularly?
S2	Yeah, like every 10 minutes. And _____ .
S1	Well, maybe I'll try it. _____ all these tickets!

2 Why does the man say this: 🎧
  (A) To express his doubt
  (B) To correct something that he just heard
  (C) To explain that the facts are common knowledge

🎧 Listen again and fill in the blanks.   (P=W, S1=M, S2=W)

P	We think that indoor plumbing is just a modern convenience. But the Romans _____ .
S1	_____ ! They had indoor toilets?
P	Yep. In fact, public lavatories and the homes of the rich had constantly running water _____ .
S2	Yeah, I heard that Rome today still uses _____ .
P	That's right. The Cloaca Maxima was the main drainage tank _____ and is still in use.

*plumbing 수도관 시설

3 Why does the man say this: 🎧
(A) To suggest what the woman can do to solve the problem
(B) To imply that the woman should address the problem to her roommate
(C) To show his understanding of most of the dorm problems

🎧 Listen again and fill in the blanks.   (A=M, S=W)

A	Can I help?
S	Yeah, it's my roommate. _____ , making tons of noise, but _____ _____ . So I'm not getting any sleep. And she brings her friends all the time... I mean.. we're, like, _____ . I just _____ or something..
A	_____ . You really have to talk to her first.
S	I tried several times and... that's not the only thing.
A	Well?
S	_____ on the housing form. But she smokes! I mean... that's something I can't really stand.
A	Hmm... the housing form _____ these problems. There must have been a mix-up. _____ .

4 Why does the professor say this: 🎧
(A) To express her approval of the theory
(B) To encourage students to enter the discussion
(C) To confirm that memes and genes are connected

🎧 Listen again and fill in the blanks.   (P=W, S=M)

P	When animals procreate, _____ , right? Well, interestingly, science writer Richard Dawkins proposed that cultural ideas do the same thing. He called these ideas memes.
S	It kinda sounds like the word "gene."
P	Yeah, right. That was Dawkins' point. Just like, er... _____ strong characteristics for the next generation, so _____ , like religion, rights, and so on, that make a culture stronger. _____ ? But just like all genes don't survive, _____ .

*meme 밈, 문화구성요소

Function 159

Exercise 1

VOCABULARY

disrupt _____
frequency _____
spectrum _____
whoosh _____
proven _____
incorporate _____

A Listen to part of a talk in a class about White Noise. Then answer the question.

✎ Note-taking >>>

Noise

White Noise   (what is white noise?)

                       (benefits)

Why is the light spectrum mentioned in the talk?

(A) To compare what makes white noise similar to white color in light

(B) To encourage the students to think of similar examples

(C) To explain why the word white is used in noise and color

(D) To provide an example of one type of common white noise

B Listen again and complete the notes above. Then answer the question.

Listen to part of the talk again. 🎧

Why does the professor ask this? 🎧

(A) To confirm that the students did the reading

(B) To introduce a definition of white noise

(C) To give his opinion on sleep disturbances

(D) To describe the sound that white noise makes

Exercise 2

A Listen to part of a talk in a history class. Then answer the question.

✎ Note-taking >>>

Huichol Indian   (migrated)

                          (unique arts)

Peyote flower

                          (hallucinogenic)

VOCABULARY

migrate
artwork
bead
yarn
sacred
fertility
renewal
divine
intricate

* peyote (멕시코산) 선인장의 일종, 이것으로 만든 환각제
* hallucinogenic 환각성의, 환각을 유발하는

Listen to part of the talk again. 🎧

What does the professor mean when he says this: 🎧

(A) To encourage the student to continue explaining
(B) To imply that it's what most people mistakenly think
(C) To express that the student's answer is correct
(D) To imply that he wants everyone to understand that

B Listen again and complete the notes above. Then answer the question

Why does the professor mention immigrants to Mexican cities?

(A) To imply that the city was the closest from
(B) To show that the artwork had some value at that time
(C) To give a primary reason why the artwork is widely known
(D) To express concern about the erosion of Huichol culture

Exercise 3

VOCABULARY

killer
nonstop
prediction
TA
relieve

A Listen to part of a conversation between two students. Then answer the question.

✎ Note-taking >>>

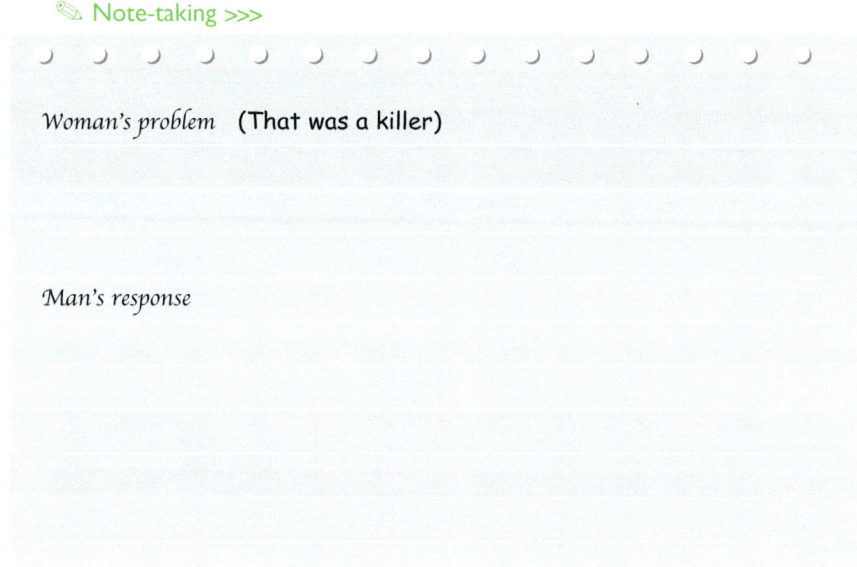

Woman's problem (That was a killer)

Man's response

Why does the woman say the number of the questions she didn't have the answers to?

(A) To emphasize how bad she did on the exam
(B) To complain that the exam was too hard
(C) To indicate that there were not many questions
(D) To imply that the exam was not that bad

B Listen again and complete the notes above. Then answer the question.

Listen to part of the conversation again. 🎧

What does the man mean when he says this: 🎧

(A) To contrast its difficulty level to this exam's
(B) To describe the similarities in both exams
(C) To complain about the number of tests in class
(D) To predict that the woman will do just as well

Exercise 4

A Listen to part of a conversation between a student and a counselor. Then answer the question.

✎ Note-taking >>>

What man wants	(I want to)
Requirements	1.
	2.
	3.

VOCABULARY

- committee
- measure
- graduate school
- transcript
- recommendation
- faculty
- field
- extracurricular

Why does the woman mention extracurricular activities?

(A) To persuade the man to do some extracurricular activities
(B) To indicate that it is important when applying for grad school
(C) To find out if the man has done any extracurricular activities
(D) To see whether the man is qualified enough to get accepted

B Listen again and complete the notes above. Then answer the question.

Listen to part of the conversation again. 🎧

Why does the woman say this: 🎧

(A) To ask if there are any other activities he has done
(B) To tell the man that he didn't answer her question
(C) To affirm that the activities he has done are enough
(D) To express that she is disappointed about his answer

Function 163

DICTATION

Exercise 1

🎧 **Listen and fill in the blanks.** (P=M, S=W)

Professor So, ① _____ . Cars, neighbors, barking dogs. But noise can also solve many people's sleep problems. ② _____ . So... what is white noise? Is it ③ _____ ? Actually, white noise is a combination of ④ _____ . If you took all kinds of sounds that you can hear around you and combined them together, you would have white noise. Why do we use ⑤ _____ ? It's because it works in the same way white light works. Just like the color white is made up of all the colors in the light spectrum.

Student I know that it sounds kinda like a "whoosh", like ⑥ _____ .

Professor Good... so, the result of the sound combination is... this whooshing sound. And then, how does it work? Here is one way to think about it. Suppose there are two kinds of sound, for example, a man is singing a song while listening to music. You may ⑦ _____ . And now, there are a hundred kinds of sound ⑧ _____ , and you may not distinguish one from the others. So when you try to sleep, it would be better if there is white noise, that is, a combination of all the sound frequencies than just two or three different kinds of sounds, not to make you distinguish one from others. Now, this sound has ⑨ _____ people relax. Because ⑩ _____ all sound frequencies, ⑪ _____ , it cancels out a lot of other noises, making people sleep easier.

|구문해설| **Suppose (that)** ~을 가정해 보라 (cf. Let us suppose : ~을 가정해 봅시다)　**not to make you** (네가) ~하지 않도록 하기 위해 (to 부정사의 부정문은 to 앞에 not을 쓴다.)

Exercise 2

🎧 **Listen and fill in the blanks.**

(P=M, S=W)

Professor   Over, uh, over the past 30 years, the Huichol Indians of Mexico ① _____ _____ Mexican cities in order to make money. And.. and... that's... how their, uh, ② _____ the rest of the world. The most common artworks that we see are um, are ③ _____ , depicting, which uh, ④ _____ Huichol culture. The uh, most common themes in these paintings are creation — we see deer and corn, ⑤ _____ for the Huichol — and the spirit world, which is, uh, often ⑥ _____ . You know what peyote is, right? It's a hallucinogenic drug used in Huichol rituals. The Huichol thought the peyote was ⑦ _____ . They believed through peyote's hallucinogenic effects, enlightenment and shamanic powers can be achieved. Are you familiar with the word 'hallucinogenic' or 'hallucinate'?

Student   It's... I mean... if you hallucinate, you see ⑧ _____ , either because ⑨ _____ because ⑩ _____ .

Professor   Here you go! Okay, everyone? All right! ... So, it's said peyote gave the Huichol ⑪ _____ . So uh, elements of this world are often ⑫ _____ and bead paintings.

|구문해설| **to the rest of** ~의 나머지 부분에   **that's how ~** (그것이) ~한 방법이다   **be familiar with** ~와 익숙하다, ~와 친밀하다
it's said (that) (사람들이) ~라고 말하다

DICTATION

Exercise 3

🎧 Listen and fill in the blanks.   (S1=M, S2=W)

Student 1	Why do you look so upset?
Student 2	Man! ① _____ , wasn't it?
Student 1	Actually, I didn't think it was so bad. I feel like I did pretty well.
Student 2	Oh... but I think... I failed this exam... ② _____ _____ but the exam was so hard.
Student 1	You know, ③ _____ . Didn't you think you were going to fail the last one, but you still got an A?
Student 2	Well, yeah, I did, but... this time I'm serious... There were ④ _____ _____ and definitely more than five questions I had no idea. I'm too worried... just ⑤ _____ I get the exam back.
Student 1	Well, I ⑥ _____ ... but... well.. I was going to go to see the TA tomorrow... I got some questions to ask on the exam... and if you feel like going together... maybe you can ask about the questions... what do you think?
Student 2	No, what if I hear from her that I failed the exam? ⑦ _____ _____ .
Student 1	No way. ⑧ _____ ! You can just ask about the questions you weren't sure about, and I'm sure she will give you, ⑨ _____ _____ . Then, ⑩ _____ at your answers.
Student 2	Oh-uh, well...

|구문해설| **That was a killer.** 아주 힘들었다 (killer = 아주 힘든 일, 굉장한 것)   **nonstop for** ~을 위해 쉬지 않고, 연속적으로
can't ~ till ~할 때까지 기다릴 수가 없다   **feel like ~ing** ~하고 싶다   **That can't be!** 그럴 리가 없다.

Exercise 4

🎧 **Listen and fill in the blanks.** (S=M, C=W)

Student I want to ① _____ history next year, but I'm not sure what my chances are.

Counselor ② _____ requires the GRE ③ _____ _____ and the possibility of success in graduate school. Thus, the students willing to apply to grad school have to ④ _____. And now, well, looking at your transcript, ⑤ _____ you would have much of a problem with your grades. I mean you have enough to get into some of the nice schools...

Student But do you think I could get into a top school? Is there any other things ⑥ _____?

Counselor It will be better if you have three or four recommendations, and those recommendations ⑦ _____. And I advise you to try to obtain research experience.

Student Oh, I see.

Counselor And, well, is there ⑧ _____ you have been involved in?

Student I've worked on the student newspaper since my freshman year. And I'm the president of the history club. But will that be enough?

Counselor What are you talking about? It's ⑨ _____ that you are very ⑩ _____ doing five or six things that ⑪ _____.

Student Really? Oh, good. That makes me feel a lot better.

|구문해설| **grad school** = graduate school 대학원 **willing to** 기꺼이 ~하려고 하는, 자진하여 ~하는 **give one's full attention to** ~ 에 전적으로 정성을 쏟다, 열중하다

Actual Test 1

TOEFL Listening

Listen to part of a lecture about apitherapy. Then answer the questions.

Note-taking >>>

What Apitherapy is

Target

Beneficial Effect

*apitherapy 봉독(벌독) 요법 anti-inflammatory 항염증의, 항염증약 degenerative 퇴행성의, 퇴화적인

1 What is the lecture mainly about?

Ⓐ Rheumatoid arthritis and its symptoms
Ⓑ The pain of bee sting and rheumatoid arthritis
Ⓒ Components of bee venom and their effects
Ⓓ A bee sting therapy and its effectiveness

2. Which of the following is true about apitherapy?
   Ⓐ It is a recent practice that uses bee venom to help with arthritis.
   Ⓑ It has become one of the most popular arthritis therapies.
   Ⓒ It has been proved to be effective for joint problems.
   Ⓓ It is not approved because of its possible negative effects.

3. Listen to part of the lecture again.
   Why does the professor say this:
   Ⓐ To acknowledge that the therapy sounds unusual
   Ⓑ To summarize people's attitudes about bee stings
   Ⓒ To emphasize that apitherapy using bee sting is really painful
   Ⓓ To give his personal opinion on the therapy of bee sting

4. What does the professor mean when he says this:
   Ⓐ There's no medicine invented using the chemicals that are effective to treat people.
   Ⓑ Bee sting therapy is effective enough to help people with rheumatoid arthritis.
   Ⓒ More studies on the chemicals that work for rheumatoid arthritis have to be done.
   Ⓓ Bee sting therapy must not be used until the chemicals are successfully identified.

Actual Test 2

TOEFL Listening

Listen to part of a conversation in the campus health center. Then answer the questions.

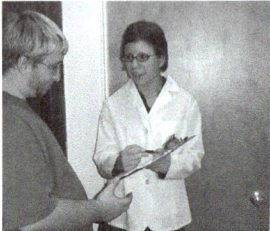

Note-taking >>>

Man's problem

Conditions

1 Why does the nurse ask for the student's ID?
   Ⓐ To verify that he has not been to the clinic
   Ⓑ To ask if he has the ID with him
   Ⓒ To confirm that he is eligible for free health care
   Ⓓ To get his personal information for the record

170

2. What does the nurse say about the campus pharmacy?
   - Ⓐ It offers a discount to students who are getting their prescriptions filled.
   - Ⓑ It is located next to the clinic.
   - Ⓒ Its medications are offered free of charge.
   - Ⓓ It is mandatory that students use it.

3. Listen to part of the conversation again.
   Why does the student say this:
   - Ⓐ To explain why he is not feeling well
   - Ⓑ To imply that he has a minor health problem
   - Ⓒ To confirm if he came to the right place
   - Ⓓ To complain about the long process

4. Listen to part of the conversation again.
   What does the nurse mean when she says this:
   - Ⓐ To express that other IDs will not work
   - Ⓑ To ask the man to say that again
   - Ⓒ To ask the man to specify what he means
   - Ⓓ To show her feeling for him

DICTATION

Actual Test 1

🎧 **Listen and fill in the blanks.** (P=M)

Professor Umm... most of us try to ① _____, right? But believe it or not, many people are currently turning to bee stings... umm... do I intentionally ② _____? Oh... no! But, the fact of the matter is, if you could imagine ③ _____ rheumatoid arthritis... a bee sting barely hurts. Actually people suffering from rheumatoid arthritis ④ _____ by bees or ⑤ _____ _____. Oh, yeah!... ah... it's called uh, apitherapy... Apitherapy is the medical use of honeybee products... it has been practiced since ancient times. In the modern world honeybee venom has found wide uses in treating arthritis and other inflammatory and degenerative disease. Well... the apitherapy most commonly refers to use of bee venom, ⑥ _____ (BVT) to help with rheumatoid arthritis.. you know the problems ⑦ _____ ... ⑧ _____ by the medical community, the studies that have been done on the therapy indicate that it is, uh, in fact, pretty effective. Why is this? Well, we don't... we're not sure, but we do know that among the 18 active substances in bee venom, several are ⑨ _____ _____. The anti-inflammatory substances that are believed to be responsible for the beneficial effects seen ⑩ _____ _____ with severe rheumatoid arthritis and some other neurological syndromes. Uh, we haven't been very successful ⑪ _____, but why bother... ⑫ _____ _____ seems to really work for a lot of people?

|구문해설| **believe it or not** 믿거나 말거나   **suffer from** ~(의 병)으로 고통받다   **be willing to** 기꺼이 ~하려고 하다, 자진해서 ~하다
while + 주어 + 동사 ~하는 반면에, ~하는 동안에   **be successful at** ~에 성공하다

Actual Test 2

🎧 **Listen and fill in the blanks.**

(N=W, S=M)

Nurse	What can I do for you?
Student	① _____ !
Nurse	Oh, okay... you'll just have to wait a bit. Have you visited the student health center before?
Student	Uh-uh. ② _____ .
Nurse	Okay. And ③ _____ . Can I see your ID?
Student	Umm... wait... Oh! Great, well... how about other IDs?
Nurse	I'm sorry?
Student	④ _____ .
Nurse	Well, is there anything else that can verify that you're a student here? Our health services ⑤ _____ .
Student	Oh, I have my license. Will my driver's license work?
Nurse	That will be fine. If the doctor ⑥ _____ , you'll have to pay for it. ⑦ _____ at the campus pharmacy, though.
Student	Okay... is there anything else I need to do?
Nurse	Yes. Just ⑧ _____ asking you about your medical history, any other health concerns, those kinds of things.
Student	Okay. Should I come back after my class, ⑨ _____ thirty minutes?
Nurse	I'll have the doctor see you as soon as possible.

|구문해설| **Social Security Number** 사회 보장 번호　**be free** 무료이다　**get it for a discount** 할인된 가격으로 얻다

Vocabulary Review

A Choose and write the correct word that matches each definition.

| avoid | relax | cancel | depict | sacred |
| therapy | endorse | verify | prescribe | disrupt |

1. _____ becomes less stiff or firm
2. _____ believed to be holy or concerned with religion
3. _____ make certain that you support or approve of
4. _____ check something is true by scientific examination
5. _____ write what medicine or treatment should be taken
6. _____ prevent something from operating or continuing
7. _____ keep away from something or someone
8. _____ postpone or annul something that was scheduled
9. _____ give a description in writings or paintings
10. _____ a particular treatment of someone with mental or physical illness

B Use the phrase below to complete the sentences.

| involve in | familiar with | enough to | instead of | suffer from |

1. Do you know how many cars were _____ the crash?
2. I wonder why Koreans use 'our' _____ 'my' like our family, our brother, etc.
3. It's not cold _____ snow.
4. The reporter says residents in the area are now _____ water famine.
5. I'm sorry that I'm not _____ the company's mailing system.

PROGRESS TEST

Listening Comprehension Section Directions

This section measures your ability to understand conversations and lectures in English. You will hear each conversation or lecture only one time. After each conversation or lecture, you will answer some questions about it. The questions typically ask about the main idea and supporting details. Some questions ask about a speaker's purpose or attitude. Answer the questions based on what is stated or implied by the speakers.

You may take notes while you listen. You may use your notes to help you answer the questions. Your notes will not be scored. If you need to change the **volume** while you listen, click on the Volume icon at the top of the screen. In some questions, you will see this icon: 🎧 This means that you will hear, but not see part of the question.

Some of the questions have special directions. These directions appear in a gray box on the screen. Most questions are worth one point. If a question is worth more than one point, it will have special directions that indicate how many points you can receive. You must answer each question. After you answer, click on **Next**. Then click on **OK** to confirm your answer and go on to the next question. After you click on **OK**, you cannot return to previous questions.

You will have 20 minutes to answer the questions in this section. A clock at the top of the screen will show you how much time is remaining. The clock will not count down while you are listening to test material.

Progress Test 5

TOEFL Listening

Listen to part of a discussion about midwives. Then answer the questions.

TOEFL Listening

1. What is the discussion mainly about?
   - Ⓐ The benefits of using a doctor rather than a midwife
   - Ⓑ A comparison of midwifery practices across the globe
   - Ⓒ Kinds of diseases laboring mothers are prone to get
   - Ⓓ The reasons for the reduced number of midwives in the 19th century

2 Listen to part of the discussion again:
   What does the professor mean when he says this:
   - A He isn't sure what the reasons are.
   - B He wants the students to participate.
   - C He thinks the reasons are obvious.
   - D He doesn't think the students know.

3 Listen to part of the discussion again:
   What can be inferred about the students?
   - A They share the same opinion.
   - B They both disagree with the professor.
   - C Neither is sure what the causes are.
   - D They disagree about the causes.

4 According to the professor, why were doctors hesitant to share information?
   - A They did not want to compete with midwives.
   - B They were not aware of the midwives.
   - C They felt the midwives wouldn't understand.
   - D They believed that the information was well-known.

5 Why does the professor mention sterilized instruments?
   - A To give an example of something midwives used before doctors did
   - B To show that they were uncommon in hospitals until very recently
   - C To give an example of implements which helped to reduce the mortality rate
   - D To suggest that they were a common cause of childbed fever in women

Progress Test 6

TOEFL Listening

Listen to part of a conversation between a professor and student. Then answer the questions.

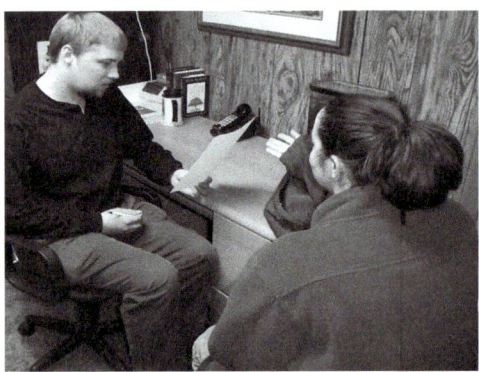

TOEFL Listening

1 Why does the student go to see the professor?

- Ⓐ To ask his advice on an internship
- Ⓑ To ask for a recommendation
- Ⓒ To find out his opinion on Starmark Publishing
- Ⓓ To tell him that she got an internship

2. Why does the professor mention the size of Starmark?
   - Ⓐ To imply it is too small to be taken seriously
   - Ⓑ To suggest that there are too many employees there
   - Ⓒ To indicate that it might be an impersonal place to work
   - Ⓓ To state that it might have a position for her after she graduates

3. How does the professor feel about Starmark?
   - Ⓐ He thinks it's a good company for her to prepare for her career.
   - Ⓑ He doesn't really have much information on the company.
   - Ⓒ He is critical of the company's internship program.
   - Ⓓ He is somewhat worried because it is one of the biggest publishing companies.

4. Listen to part of the conversation again: 🎧
   Why does the professor say this: 🎧
   - Ⓐ To advise that her career is useless without an academic degree
   - Ⓑ To confirm that he well understands what she wants
   - Ⓒ To indicate that he needs some information about her
   - Ⓓ To suggest that it would be beneficial if she has any professional certificate

5. What will the professor likely do when he receives the email?
   - Ⓐ He will write the letter of recommendation.
   - Ⓑ He will forward her résumé to a publishing company.
   - Ⓒ He will wait until she brings him the recommendation form.
   - Ⓓ He will recommend a good career path for her.

DICTATION

Progress Test 5

🎧 Listen and fill in the blanks. (P=M, S1=W, S2=M)

Professor	The role of the midwife ① _____ is an ancient practice seen in almost all cultures. However, by the mid-19th century, more and more women began to use primarily male doctors rather than female midwives ② _____ . There were a number of reasons for this change. Does anyone have any thoughts on what these might be?
Student 1	Well, I know that ③ _____ in the past than it was today, and those days maybe, uh… the belief was spread that ④ _____ to give birth in a hospital with a doctor than at home with a midwife.
Student 2	I'll bet it was more about money. As it became more… uh… more profitable to be a doctor, ⑤ _____ and possessed all the information ⑥ _____ .
Professor	Actually, you're both right. By the mid-19th century, as doctors learned more about ⑦ _____ like childbed fever, which was one of ⑧ _____ childbearing women, and the need to wash their hands and ⑨ _____ , mortality declined. Of course, passing this information ⑩ _____ would have had ⑪ _____ . But doctors, as Mike said, were competitive, and wanted to increase their business, which is basically what happened. Now, let's look at the particular ways ⑫ _____ during this time.

|구문해설| **the role of the midwife in** ~하는 데 있어서 산파의 역할은   **assist with** ~을 돕다

I'll bet 난 ~라고 장담한다, 내가 ~을 보증하겠다   **related to** ~에 관련된

180

Progress Test 6

Listen and fill in the blanks. (S=W, P=M)

Student	Hi, Professor Jackson. ① _____ today.
Professor	Sure, Janie, come on in. What can I do for you?
Student	Well, ② _____ this summer at Starmark Publishing... if I get it, it will be a really good experience.
Professor	Terrific. Starmark is a big company. ③ _____, which can help you get a job when you graduate, but if you enjoy working there, ④ _____ find a position for you.
Student	⑤ _____. But anyway, the reason I wanted to talk to you was ⑥ _____ writing me a recommendation for the internship. I need two references. I thought ⑦ _____ from an English professor.
Professor	Absolutely. ⑧ _____ or something?
Student	No, not really. They just want a letter talking about why I'd be good for the job. ⑨ _____.
Professor	Okay. And you know what else would help me? ⑩ _____, so I can mention some of ⑪ _____, extra-curricular activities, that kind of thing.
Student	Sure, no problem. I can email those to you when I get home.

|구문해설| **have an appointment** 약속이 있다   **apply for an internship** 인턴십에 지원하다   **to see if** ~인지 아닌지 확인하기 위해   **mind ~ing** ~하기 싫어하다, ~하는 것을 원치 않다   **fill out (a form)** (서류, 문서를) 작성하다

Vocabulary Review for Progress Test

A Choose and write the correct word that matches each definition.

| hiring | position | publishing | competitor | midwife |
| sterilize | childbirth | curricular | internship | accomplishment |

1. _____ a woman who is trained in aiding the delivery of babies
2. _____ the act of giving birth to a child
3. _____ make things completely clean and free from bacteria
4. _____ the period of time when someone is an intern
5. _____ your ability acquired by training
6. _____ a job in a company or organization
7. _____ related to an academic course of study
8. _____ printing copies of books, which are sent to shops to be sold
9. _____ employing someone or paying someone to do a particular job for you
10. _____ a person who takes part in a competition so you want to defeat him

B Use the phrase below to complete the sentences.

| a number of | rather than | apply for | fill out | have an appointment |

1. I haven't decided yet which company I'll _____ .
2. You can place an order by _____ this order form.
3. _____ people including me refused to join the conference.
4. Generally speaking, people prefer to follow directions _____ make their own decisions.
5. Did you forget you _____ with a client at 6?

FINAL TEST

Listening Comprehension Section Directions

This section measures your ability to understand conversations and lectures in English. You will hear each conversation or lecture only one time. After each conversation or lecture, you will answer some questions about it. The questions typically ask about the main idea and supporting details. Some questions ask about a speaker's purpose or attitude. Answer the questions based on what is stated or implied by the speakers.

You may take notes while you listen. You may use your notes to help you answer the questions. Your notes will not be scored. If you need to change the **volume** while you listen, click on the Volume icon at the top of the screen. In some questions, you will see this icon: 🎧 This means that you will hear, but not see part of the question.

Some of the questions have special directions. These directions appear in a gray box on the screen. Most questions are worth one point. If a question is worth more than one point, it will have special directions that indicate how many points you can receive. You must answer each question. After you answer, click on **Next**. Then click on **OK** to confirm your answer and go on to the next question. After you click on **OK**, you cannot return to previous questions.

You will have 20 minutes to answer the questions in this section. A clock at the top of the screen will show you how much time is remaining. The clock will not count down while you are listening to test material.

Final Test 1

TOEFL Listening

Listen to part of a lecture in a psychology class. Then answer the questions.

TOEFL Listening

1 What aspect of Piaget's theory does the professor mainly discuss?
- Ⓐ How it has changed since it was created
- Ⓑ How it relates to the process of learning
- Ⓒ How it is compared to teaching theories
- Ⓓ How it is based on Piaget's experiences

2. What does the professor say about the sensorimotor phase?

   Ⓐ It begins at the age of two.
   Ⓑ The senses develop from stimuli.
   Ⓒ Knowledge comes from the senses.
   Ⓓ Toy makers concentrate on this phase.

3. Which of the following is a characteristic of the concrete phase? Choose TWO correct answers.

   Ⓐ Children can develop rational thinking skills.
   Ⓑ Teachers can help children answering a question.
   Ⓒ Children enjoy figuring things out themselves.
   Ⓓ Teachers should encourage children to ask questions.

4. In the lecture, the professor talks about Piaget's cognitive development theory. Indicate whether each phrase is part of that theory. Click on the correct box for each phrase.

	Yes	No
Very sensitive to even small changes		
Consider toys and dolls as their friends		
Learn while asking many questions		
Abstractly answer to rational questions		
Learn and understand the relationship among given facts		

5. Why does the professor say this : 🎧

   Ⓐ To persuade that the term is inappropriate
   Ⓑ To reveal the major topic of study for the day
   Ⓒ To explain the meaning of the phase name
   Ⓓ To highlight a general developmental obstacle

Final Test 2

TOEFL Listening

Listen to part of a conversation between a professor and a student. Then answer the questions.

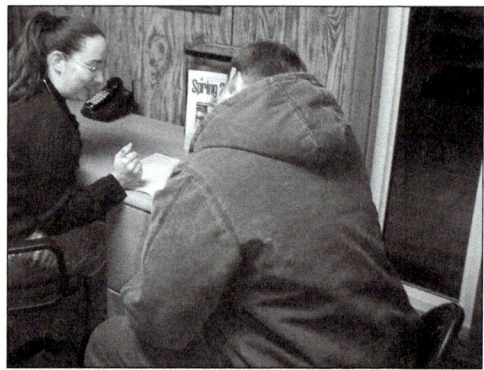

TOEFL Listening

1. Why does the man go to see his professor?

   Ⓐ To get the professor's notes from class
   Ⓑ To inquire about viewing a documentary
   Ⓒ To ask a question about a DVD he saw
   Ⓓ To seek more information about the project

2 Why doesn't the student rely on his classmate for the information?

- Ⓐ He feels the information is incomplete.
- Ⓑ He thinks that the professor's notes are better.
- Ⓒ He hasn't been able to get the student's notebook.
- Ⓓ He knows the information on rituals is erroneous.

3 What does the professor mean when she says this :

- Ⓐ He should pay closer attention to the material that he missed.
- Ⓑ The deadline should be regarded as highly important.
- Ⓒ He still has time to study for the midterm.
- Ⓓ The documentary's contents will be on an upcoming exam.

4 Listen to part of the conversation again :
What can be inferred from the following statement?

- Ⓐ The professor would rather not write the note.
- Ⓑ The professor isn't sure if he can get the note.
- Ⓒ The note may not achieve the professor's intention.
- Ⓓ The note should only be used if absolutely necessary.

5 What will the student most likely do next?

- Ⓐ Go to the library to view a documentary
- Ⓑ Go to the library to meet up with Debbie
- Ⓒ Go to find a book on the Yanomami
- Ⓓ Go to see if the DVD is back from a class

NEXUS makes your next day

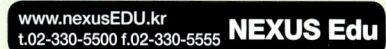
NEXUS Edu

이것이 This is 시리즈다!

THIS IS GRAMMAR 시리즈
▶ 중·고등 내신에 꼭 등장하는 어법 포인트 철저 분석 및 총정리
▶ 다양하고 유용한 연습문제 및 리뷰, 리뷰 플러스 문제 수록

THIS IS READING 시리즈
▶ 실생활부터 전문적인 학술 분야까지 다양한 소재의 지문 수록
▶ 서술형 내신 대비까지 제대로 준비하는 문법 포인트 정리

THIS IS VOCABULARY 시리즈
▶ 교육부 권장 어휘를 빠짐없이 수록하여 초급·중급·고급·어원편으로 어휘 학습 완성
▶ 주제별로 분류한 어휘를 연상학습을 통해 효과적으로 암기

• Reading, Vocabulary – 무료 MP3 파일 다운로드 제공

THIS IS 시리즈

THIS IS GRAMMAR 시리즈
초·중·고급1·2 넥서스영어교육연구소 지음 | 205×265 | 250쪽 내외(정답 및 해설, 워크북 포함) | 각 권 12,000원

THIS IS READING 시리즈
1·2·3·4 넥서스영어교육연구소 지음 | 205×265 | 192쪽 내외(정답 및 해설, 워크북 포함) | 각 권 10,000원

THIS IS VOCABULARY 시리즈
초급 / 중급 권기하 지음 | 152×225 | 350쪽 내외 | 각 권 8,500원 / 9,500원
고급 / 어원편 권기하 지음 | 180×257 | 400쪽 내외 | 각 권 11,000원 / 12,000원

무료 MP3 파일 다운로드 제공
www.nexusEDU.kr

NEXUS makes your next day

www.nexusEDU.kr
t.02-330-5500 f.02-330-5555
NEXUS Edu

문법을 기초로 한 체계적인 영어 글쓰기

초·중급 실력을 가진 학습자들에게 영작의 기초가 된다.

- Grammar-Based Writing | 문법을 기초로 한 체계적인 영어 글쓰기
- Step by Step & Integrated Approach | 단계별 접근 방식을 통한 자연스러운 영어 글쓰기
- Writing on Various Subjects | 다양한 주제의 영어 글쓰기
- Writing with Various Purposes | 다양한 목적의 영어 글쓰기

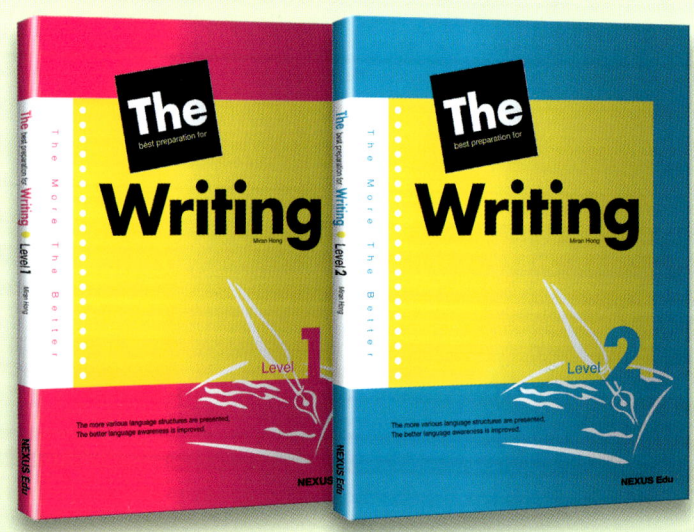

The best preparation for **Writing** 시리즈   Level 1 / Level 2
The Writing Level 1: Miran Hong 지음 | 값 9,500원
The Writing Level 2: Miran Hong 지음 | 값 9,500원

성공적인 학습을 위한 단계별 전략!
Development & Progress for Completion

NEXUS TOEFL® iBT

넥서스영어교육연구소

정답 및 해설

Listening 2

Level

TOEFL® is a registered trademark of Educational Testing Service.
This publication is not endorsed or approved by ETS.

NEXUS Edu

성공적인 학습을 위한 단계별 전략!
Development & Progress for Completion

NEXUS TOEFL® iBT

정답 및 해설

Listening

Level

NEXUS Edu

CHAPTER 01
MAIN IDEA

Sample

교수 좋아요, 여러분. 오늘은 20세기의 괄목할만한 작가 중 한 명인 제임스 조이스에 대해 얘기하려고 합니다. 여러분은 그가 아일랜드 출신의 소설가이자 시인이라는 것, 그리고 대문호로서 널리 알려져 있음을 잘 알고 있으리라 봅니다. '젊은 예술가의 초상'이나 '율리시즈'와 같은 작품은 시대를 초월한 최고의 작품으로 손꼽히지요.
조이스는 대부분의 성인기를 타국에서 보냈지만, 그의 아일랜드에서의 경험, 말하자면... 초년기의 경험은 그의 작품에 본질적인 요소이며, 그리고 에... 그의 소설에 나오는 모든 배경을 제공하고 있습니다. 오늘 우리는 아일랜드에서의 경험이 그의 작품에 어떠한 영향을 미쳤는지에 관해 중점적으로 논의하게 될 것입니다. 알겠죠?

강의는 주로 무엇에 관한 것인가?
(A) 제임스 조이스의 대표 작품들
(B) 제임스 조이스가 초년기에 겪은 아일랜드에서의 경험
(C) 초년기의 경험이 제임스 조이스의 소설에 미친 영향
(D) 작품에 반영된 제임스 조이스의 가족과 친구들

정답 (C)

Vocabulary Preview — for Skill Check-up

다음 정의를 듣고 알맞은 단어를 고르시오.

1 philosopher	2 promotion	3 essential
4 campaign	5 absorb	6 research
7 aptitude	8 agrarian	9 entomology
10 neolithic		

1 a person who studies philosophy and specialized in it
  철학을 연구하거나 철학을 전공한 사람
2 an attempt to make a product popular or sell successfully
  제품의 평판을 좋게 하거나 성공적으로 판매하려는 시도
3 basic, indispensable or absolutely necessary to something
  어떤 것에 대한 기본적이고 없어서는 안 될, 혹은 대단히 필요한
4 run for an office or position
  공직이나 (어떤) 지위를 얻으려고 출마하다
5 take in or soak up something like water
  물처럼 어떤 것을 흡수하거나 빨아들이다
6 study something or attempt to find out about something
  어떤 것을 공부하거나 그것에 관해 알아내려는 시도
7 natural ability to learn quickly or do well
  재빨리 습득하고 또 잘 하는 천성적인 능력
8 relating to the land or its cultivation
  토지나 토지의 경작과 관련된
9 study of insects
  곤충의 연구
10 relating to the most recent period when people used stone for making things
  인간이 물건을 만들 때 돌을 사용하던 가장 최근 시기의

다음 단어를 이용하여 아래 문장을 완성하시오.

1 project	2 campaign	3 absorb
4 aptitude	5 personality	6 brand
7 neolithic	8 reference	9 essential
10 promotion		

1 나는 그 프로젝트가 현실적으로 가능한지 아닌지 의심스럽다.
2 그는 대통령 후보자에게 불법 선거 자금을 제공했다고 고발당했다.
3 그 식물들은 토양으로부터 수분과 미네랄을 흡수한다.
4 우리는 창조적 프로젝트 설계 능력을 보유한 사람을 찾고 있다.
5 이것은 당신이 인격장애가 있는지를 결정하는 테스트이다.
6 어떤 자료에 따르면, 그 제품의 브랜드 가치는 천문학적 숫자로 환산된다.
7 신석기 시대 사람들은 돌을 사용하여 도구를 만들었다.
8 그는 곤충학과 관련된 참고도서 몇 권을 원했다.
9 자신의 일에 흥미를 느끼고 친밀한 동료들과 일하는 것 모두 만족스러운 직장 생활을 하는 데 필수적이다.
10 그는 자신의 최근 영화를 홍보하기 위해 현재 도쿄에 머무르고 있다.

Skill Check-up — Topics of Lectures

1 강의는 주로 무엇에 관한 것인가?
(A) 다음 수업 시간을 위해 읽어 두어야 할 읽기 자료 요약
(B) 시간 단위가 인성을 형성한다는 이론
(C) "나는 누구인가?"에 대한 철학자들의 상이한 대답

정답 (B)

해설 교수는 인성에 관한 이 철학자의 이론을 살펴보겠다고 했다. (C)는 지난 시간에 다룬 내용이다.

 스크립트

P I'd like to <u>start things off with the reading you did for class today</u>, and especially <u>the philosopher's theory of personality</u>, that is, how he thinks we should answer the question "Who am I?", Okay? Previously, <u>we've been checking out</u> different theories over the past few classes, right? Some say '<u>soul</u>,' others say '<u>brain chemistry</u>,' and so on. People have been <u>grappling with this question for ages</u>. This person, however, considers <u>life's stages to be the essential thing</u> that defines us. What am I getting at? I mean during our teenage years and then, say, during our middle-age years <u>our personalities can be remarkably different.

교수 오늘은 여러분들이 예습해 온 읽기 자료를 가지고 얘기를 시작하겠습니다. 특히 인성에 대한 이 철학자의 이론, 그러니까 "나는 누구인가"라는 질문에 대해 그는 우리가 어떻게 대답해야 한다고 생각하는지에 대해 살펴보고자 합니다. 좋죠? 앞서 몇 번의 수업을 통해 우리는 여러 가지 이론을 다루어 보았습니다. 그렇죠? 어떤 사람들은 그것을 '영혼'이라고 하고, 어떤 사람들은 '뇌의 화학작용'이라고 하는 등 여러 가지가 있습니다. 수 세기 동안 사람들은 이 질문에 대해 고심했습니다. 그러나 이 사람은 인생의 각 시기가 우리를 정의하는 본질적인 요소라고 인식합니다. 이것은 무엇일까요? 제 말은 십대 시절과, 그 이후의 중년기에 우리의 인성이 현격히 달라질 수 있다는 것입니다.

2 토론은 주로 무엇에 관한 것인가?
(A) 인류 역사에 미친 기술의 지속적인 영향
(B) 산업혁명과 도구 사용의 급격한 변화
(C) 고대 기술과 현대 기술 간의 연관성

정답 (A)

해설 교수는 technology(기술)를 단일 개체가 아닌 '연속체', 즉 세대를 거치며 변화해 온 ongoing process로서의 기술이라고 정의하고 있다.

🎧 스크립트

P A question. What's technology given us? Yes, Chris?
S Well, that's... computers, cell phones, you name it.
P Right, but it's much more than that. My point this time is that we need to see it as part of a continuum.
S Ah, I see... so that's why we devoted so much class time to studying tool use in early humans, for example? And then we saw how that led to the Industrial Revolution?
P You got it. What we saw through looking at those examples is that technology fundamentally is an ongoing process, making influences on our lives, not just cell phones and computers.

교수 질문 하나 하겠습니다. 우리에게 기술이란 무엇인가요? 네, 크리스?
학생 음, 그러니까... 컴퓨터, 휴대폰, 그 밖에 뭐든지요.
교수 그래요, 그러나 기술이란 그 이상의 무엇입니다. 지금 내가 말하고자 하는 것은, 우리는 기술을 연속체의 일부로 파악할 필요가 있다는 것이에요.
학생 아, 알겠어요. 예를 들자면, 우리가 많은 수업 시간을 할애해서 인간이 초기에 사용했던 도구들에 관해 공부한 것도 그런 이유인거죠? 그리고 그것이 어떻게 산업 혁명으로 이어졌는가를 공부했던 것도요?
교수 그렇지요. 그러한 예를 통해 우리가 알 수 있는 것은 근본적으로 기술이란 단순히 휴대 전화나 컴퓨터 같은 것이 아니라, 우리 삶에 영향을 주면서 계속 발전해가는 일련의 과정이라는 겁니다.

3 토론은 주로 무엇에 관한 것인가?
(A) 성공적인 제품 홍보 요소들
(B) 젊은 층에게 판매하기 적합한 제품 선택하기
(C) 현대 문화에 있어서의 마케팅과 광고

정답 (A)

해설 효과적인 상품 광고를 위해 알아야 할 점을 자동차 판매를 예로 들어 설명하고 있다. 첫째, 해당 소비층을 알아야 하고, 둘째, 그 소비층이 볼 만한 매체를 통해 광고해야 한다고 지적한다.
(B)는 판매 대상을 젊은 층으로만 제한하였고, (C)는 토론의 내용을 벗어나 있다.

🎧 스크립트

P   Okay... So, uh, we talked about most of the things we need to remember to create an effective branding campaign, so what do you think is the most important?
S1 The first thing we need to have is a specific target for the product.
S2 Well, the most important... I mean... we really need to make sure that your advertisements are clearly associated with what you're targeting.
P   You're both right. Let me give an example. If you want your new car to stand for youth, which is pretty specific... then you need to advertise it in young people's magazines and during their TV shows, and show young people driving the cars, and so on.

교수 좋아요. 그러니까, 에, 우리는 효과적인 브랜드 캠페인 창출을 위해 기억해야 할 사항들을 대부분 논의해 보았습니다. 여러분은 무엇이 가장 중요한 요소라고 생각합니까?
학생1 우리에게 필요한 첫 번째 요소는 그 제품의 구체적인 대상입니다.
학생2 음, 가장 중요한 요소는... 그러니까 광고와 목표 대상을 명확하게 연관시키는 것입니다.
교수 두 학생의 의견은 다 옳습니다. 예를 하나 들어보도록 하죠. 만약 여러분이 (자사의) 신(新) 차를 젊음을 상징하는 제품으로 만들고 싶다면... 젊음을 의미한다는 것 자체가 특정한 것이죠, 여러분은 그 차를 젊은이들을 위한 잡지라든가 TV 쇼에 광고를 내보내야 하고, 젊은이들이 그 차를 운전하고 있는 모습을 보여준다든가 하는 등의 일을 해야 합니다.

4 토론은 주로 무엇에 관한 것인가?
(A) 고대인들이 피라미드 건설을 위해 사용한 흡수팽윤 기법
(B) 액체가 흡수될 경우 발생하는 특정 세포의 확장
(C) 물에 의한 바위의 심각한 부식 과정

정답 (B)

해설 강의의 중심 주제는 Imbibition이다. 교수는 세포 팽창을 바위에 나무 못을 박아 깰 때 물이 한 역할을 비교하며 설명하고 있다. (A)와 (C)는 전체의 한 일부분(예)에 지나지 않는다.

🎧 **스크립트**

P OK, so today we're going to <u>look at</u> imbibition. So, uh, imbibition is a fancy word for <u>the swelling caused by</u> fluid absorption. Examples?
S Well, the book said it's like <u>when a seed absorbs water</u> and it <u>cracks open</u>.
P Right. It's clear, then?
S Not exactly. I mean why does <u>the water cause it to crack</u>?
P Hmm… well, the water causes cellular expansion. You know, let's say you <u>drill a hole in a rock</u>. Then you put a wooden stick in the hole tightly, and then you <u>soak the stick in water</u>. Well, the stick expands and the rock breaks. The Great Pyramids' stones <u>were cut that way</u>, you know. That's what I'm talking about.

교수 좋아요, 그럼 오늘은 흡수팽윤에 관해 살펴보겠습니다. 자, 음, 흡수팽윤이란 액체를 흡수함으로써 발생하는 팽창에 해당하는 말로 미사여구 같은 것입니다. 예를 들면 (어떤 것이 있을까요)?
학생 음, 책에서는 씨앗이 물을 흡수할 때 균열이 생겨 터지는 것과 같은 것이라고 하더군요.
교수 맞습니다. 그럼, 의미는 이해가 된 거죠?
학생 그렇지는 않아요. 제 말씀은 그러니까, 물 때문에 왜 씨앗에 균열이 일어나는 건가요?
교수 흠… 에, 물은 세포 팽창을 유발합니다. 그러니까, 바위에 구멍을 뚫는다고 해 봅시다. 그리고 그 구멍에 나무 막대기를 꽉 꽂은 후에, 그 막대기를 물에 담급니다. 그러면, 그 막대기가 팽창하고 바위가 깨지게 됩니다. 저 대(大) 피라미드의 바위도 이러한 방식으로 잘랐습니다. 제가 얘기하려는 것은 이겁니다.

Skill Check-up — Purposes of Conversations

1 여자가 교수에게 의논하고 있는 이유는 무엇인가?
(A) 프로젝트 발표 일정을 취소하기 위해
(B) 과제 제출 기한을 늦추기 위해
(C) 다음 주 교수와의 약속을 잡기 위해

정답 (B)

해설 학생은 교수가 내준 프로젝트 아웃라인을 기한 내에 잡을 수 없을 것 같다고 얘기한다. 학생이 교수에게 원하는 것은 무엇이 될지 짐작해 본다. I'll visit your office next Friday. 라고 했으므로 (A) To cancel ~은 답이 될 수 없다.

🎧 **스크립트**

S Excuse, Professor, I think I'll have some trouble <u>finishing the project outline on time</u>. Actually, <u>I haven't even considered yet</u> what I'm going to do on it. I tried to keep the schedule as best as I can, but… I also have to do <u>some research for other classes</u>.
P Umm… what is the date to <u>hand in the outline</u>? Is it next Tuesday?
S Yeah, right.
P <u>How much time do you need</u>, then?
S Around three days, maybe. <u>I'll visit your office next Friday</u>.
P OK, I wish you luck!

학생 저기요, 교수님, 제가 기한 내에 프로젝트 개요를 완성하는 데 문제가 좀 있을 것 같습니다. 실은 어떤 것을 해야 할지조차 생각을 못한 상태입니다. 일정에 맞추려고 최선을 다했지만, 다른 수업에 쓸 자료 조사도 해야 해서요.
교수 음… 내가 이 클래스에 프로젝트 개요를 언제까지 제출하라고 했나요? 다음 주 화요일까지인가요?
학생 예, 맞습니다.
교수 그러면 시간이 얼마나 더 필요하죠?
학생 3일 정도요. 다음 주 금요일에 교수님 연구실을 방문하겠습니다.
교수 좋아요. 행운을 빌어요.

2 남자는 여자가 무엇을 하기를 원하는가?
(A) 교수님으로부터 받은 편성 자료를 구해 달라.
(B) 꿀벌의 의사소통에 관한 유용한 정보를 제공해 달라.
(C) 곤충들의 의사소통에 관한 참고도서를 찾아 달라.

정답 (B)

해설 남자는 곤충에 남다른 취미를 가진 여자에게 '꿀벌의 의사소통'이라는 과제 주제에 적합한 아이디어를 구하고 있다.

🎧 **스크립트**

S1 I decided to write about <u>how honeybees communicate</u>.
S2 Did you study some <u>entomology books</u> in the library?
S1 Oh, sure. But I was <u>so confused</u> because there's too much information printed there. I want to hear something from an expert. <u>You're into all insects</u>!
S2 Well… about the communication, right. Honeybees are interesting, especially because they dance. It's <u>a sort of body language</u>. They use body language to give <u>the other bees in the hive</u> information about food, shelter, and other things.

S1 But it's not very precise at all, like real language, is it?
S2 Actually, you'd be surprised. Bees can use this dance language to explain — within a few centimeters! — where the best food source is.

학생 1 난 꿀벌들이 어떻게 의사소통하는가에 관한 글을 쓰기로 결정했어.
학생 2 도서관에서 곤충학 관련 서적을 조사해봤니?
학생 1 어, 물론. 그런데 정보가 너무 많아서 더 혼동이 되네. 전문가의 의견을 듣고 싶어. 네가 곤충에 대해 많이 알잖아.
학생 2 글쎄, 의사소통에 관해서라, 이거지. 꿀벌은 참 흥미로워. 특히 그들은 춤을 추거든. 그건 일종의 신체 언어(바디 랭귀지) 같은 건데, 꿀벌 통에 있는 다른 벌들에게 식량이나 은신처 같은 다른 여러 정보를 전달하려고 바디 랭귀지를 사용하지.
학생 1 그렇지만 그건 진짜 언어처럼 그렇게 정확하지는 않을 거 아냐, 그렇지 않아?
학생 2 실은, 너 아마 놀랄걸. 벌들은 춤이라는 언어로 설명을 해. 심지어 몇 센티미터 내 어디에 가장 좋은 먹이가 있는지 까지도 가능하지.

3 여자가 교수를 찾아간 이유는 무엇인가?
(A) 그녀가 해야 할 과제에 쓸 유용한 자료를 얻기 위해
(B) 교수와 함께 그 책에 관해 상세히 논의하기 위해
(C) 그녀가 어디에서(어떤 자료에서) 더 많은 정보를 찾을 수 있는지 묻기 위해

정답 (C)

해설 학생은 강의 내용에 관련된 참조할 만한 책을 추천해달라고 한다. 교수로부터 직접적인 정보를 얻으려는 것이 아니므로 (A)는 답이 될 수 없다.

🎧 스크립트

S Excuse me, professor, I have a question about these books that you mentioned when we talked about the article today.
P OK, which books in particular?
S The one saying that men seem to have a stronger aptitude for things related to space, while... umm... but women are better at communication.
P Oh, yes. The name of the book is... umm "To Communicate." It shows that this may be a result of different brain structures.
S I was thinking maybe I want to do a little more research for my paper. And I was wondering if I could get more suggestions for other reference books.
P Actually, I didn't hand it out in the class, but I have a copy, the list of the books. Here it is.

학생 실례합니다, 교수님 오늘 이 자료에 관해 토의할 때 교수님께서 언급한 책들에 관해 질문이 있어서요.
교수 그래요. 특히 어떤 책을 말하는 건가요?
학생 남성은 공간과 관련된 것에 보다 뛰어난 능력을 드러내는 반면, 음... 여성은 의사소통 능력이 더 뛰어나다고 언급한 책이요.
교수 아, 그래요. 그 책 제목이... 음 "의사소통하기"예요. 이 책에서는 그 원인이 두뇌 구조가 다르기 때문이라고 주장하죠.
학생 제가 과제를 위해서 좀 더 조사를 하면 좋겠는데, 다른 참고 도서로 추천해 주실만한 게 있는지 궁금합니다.
교수 사실은, 수업 시간에 나눠주지는 않았지만, 그 책들의 목록이 한 부 있어요. 여기 있군요.

4 남자가 여자에게 받으려고 하는 것은 무엇인가?
(A) 여자의 수업 필기
(B) 수업 시간에 받은 유인물
(C) 숙제에 관한 유용한 정보

정답 (A)

해설 남자는 시험에 관해 걱정하고 있다. 여자는 수업 시간에 받은 handout을 참고하라고 제안하지만 남자가 원하는 건 여자의 노트필기 복사이다.

🎧 스크립트

S1 I'm still confused about the Neolithic Agrarian Revolution. I'm worried about the test.
S2 Hmm... the big thing is that metal tools really brought about a major change in human existence. This was around 8,000 B.C. You should read the handouts from the class.
S1 Actually, I have them. I mean... it would be better if I could get what the professor said in the class.
S2 Well... I guess you'll have to see my notes then.
S1 Why don't I make a quick copy of that part and return it right after?
S2 Sure, no problem. And actually I won't be using it until tomorrow anyway.

학생 1 난 아직도 신석기 시대의 농업혁명에 대해 잘 모르겠어. 시험이 걱정 돼.
학생 2 음... 중요한 건 금속 도구가 인류의 생존에 아주 중요한 변화를 초래했다는 거야. (금속 도구의 사용은) 기원전 8,000년 경이었어. 수업 시간에 나눠 준 유인물을 읽어 봐.
학생 1 사실, 그거 갖고 있기는 한데, 그래도 교수님께서 수업 시간에 강의하신 내용을 알면 더 좋을 것 같아서.
학생 2 그럼... 내가 필기한 것을 봐야겠구나.
학생 1 내가 그 부분을 빨리 복사하고 곧바로 돌려주면 안 될까?
학생 2 그래, 그렇게 해. 사실 난 내일까지는 그거 필요 없어.

Exercise

1 A - (A) B - (C)
2 A - (B) B - (B)
3 A - (C) B - (B)(D)
4 A - (D) B - (B)

Exercise 1
커뮤니케이션 수업에서의 강의 일부를 듣고 물음에 답하시오.

🎧 스크립트

P We've been looking at the different ways to promote positive messages about your company. The things we've discussed were mostly about what kind of things companies create in order to make their image better or more appealing to customers... but, uh, what I want to focus on now is... what we're going to do when something undeniably... just negative happens. This is an area that we call umm... "crisis communications". Now, say, uh, say that your product has been accused of causing people to get sick and the customers are demanding compensation because you hurt them. Let's say you're given the task of dealing with the crisis. Then, how do you deal with it as the spokesperson? What would you say in public? Okay... there could be a couple of things you can do when you deal with these situations... and I will be mentioning those as we look at several cases... but before we get into any of those... the first thing you need to keep in mind is that basically uh, you, you want to take control of the situation as soon as possible, showing that you, uh, your company is considering the situation seriously and you're really worried about it. Denying makes you look, well, suspect. Expressing concern and assuring the public that you are taking, uh, care of the situation — no matter if the crisis is your fault or not — ultimately makes you look much better. And image is what this is all about.

교수 우리는 지금껏 회사의 긍정적 메시지를 증진시키기 위한 여러 가지 방안을 살펴보았습니다. 그동안 우리가 얘기한 것은 주로, 기업이 더 좋은 이미지를 구축하거나 고객의 관심을 더 끌어내기 위해 어떤 일을 하는지에 관한 것이었습니다. 그러나 에, 지금 제가 주목하고자 하는 것은... 불가피하게 부정적 사건이 발생한 경우 어떻게 행동해야 하느냐에 관한 것입니다. 이것이 우리가 말하는, 음 '위기 상황 커뮤니케이션' 이라는 분야입니다. 자, 말하자면, 에, 귀사 제품으로 인해 고객에게 질병이 발생하였고, 피해를 입은 고객들은 보상을 요구하고 있습니다. 여러분에게 이 위기 상황을 극복해야 한다는 과제가 주어졌다고 가정해 봅시다. 그러면, 대변인으로서 여러분은 어떻게 대처할 것입니까? 대중 앞에서 뭐라고 말하겠습니까? 좋아요... 이러한 상황을 헤쳐나가기 위해 여러분이 취할 수 있는 몇 가지 방안이 있을 수 있겠습니다. 앞으로 몇 가지 경우를 살펴보면서 그 방안들을 언급하도록 하겠습니다. 그렇지만 그것들을 살펴보기 전에... 여러분이 제일 먼저 명심해야 할 것은 기본적으로, 음, 여러분은 가능한 한 빨리 그 상황을 통제하고자 한다는 것입니다. 여러분이, 에, 여러분의 기업이 이 상황을 심각하게 생각하고 있으며, 이 상황을 진심으로 염려하고 있음을 보여주면서 말이죠. (상황을) 부정하게 되면 여러분은, 그러니까, 의혹의 눈길을 받게 됩니다. (여러분이) 근심하고 있음을 나타내고, 대중에게 귀사가 이 상황에 대해 책임질 것이라는 확신을 심어주는 것이, 여러분(회사)의 잘못이든 아니든 상관없이 말이죠, 궁극적으로 여러분을 훨씬 더 훌륭하게 보이도록 할 것입니다. 그리고 이미지란 바로 이런 것입니다.

어휘 appealing 마음을 끄는, 매력적인 undeniably 부정하기 어렵게, 명백히 compensation 보상 spokesperson 대변인, 대표자 concern 걱정, 근심; 관심 assure 확신시키다, 보증하다 the public 대중, 민중 ultimately 궁극적으로, 결국, 마지막으로 be accused of ~로 고소(고발)당하다 deflect 비끼다, 빗나가다 implement ~을 실행하다

A 강의는 주로 무엇에 관한 것인가?
(A) 이미지 문제를 해결하는 방법
(B) 이미지 문제를 가능한 빨리 처리하는 것이 얼마나 중요한가
(C) 회사에 대한 긍정적인 메시지 증진시키기
(D) 회사의 문제점에 대한 책임을 회피하는 방법

해설 교수는 부정적인 이미지가 만들어 질 수 있는 예를 들며, 회사 입장에서는 우선 우려를 먼저 표명하는 일을 제일 먼저 해야 한다고 한다. 이어지는 강의는, 이런 우려를 표명한 다음 무슨 일을 해야 할지가 등장할 것이다.

B 교수가 이전에는 무엇에 관해 얘기했는가?
(A) 까다로운 시장에서 상품을 판매하는 방안
(B) 비인기 상품 광고에 대한 접근법
(C) 긍정적인 기업 이미지를 창출하는 방법
(D) 피해 대책을 수행하는 기술

해설 강의의 시작 부분 We've been talking about~에서 알 수 있듯 지난 강의에서 다룬 내용은 '어떻게 긍정적인 이미지를 홍보하느냐' 였다.

Exercise 2
역사 수업에서의 토론의 일부를 듣고 물음에 답하시오.

🎧 스크립트

P The movable type printing press was a machine which made it possible to produce many books at that time. I think you've already read also about the background and the effect of Gutenberg's invention. In today's class, we'll have the opportunity to look over how the invention of the printing press profoundly influenced the culture and religion of the time. Let me ask you guys a question first. Where do you suppose the printing press affected culture?

S1 I read in the textbook that it seriously impacted religion.

P You're on a roll. Keep going.

S1 Let's see… It was closely related to the Protestant Reformation. The religious reformation was not sudden, I mean, the printing press laid the groundwork for it. The great invention allowed a much broader audience to read Martin Luther's German translation of the Bible and it spread Luther's other writings.

S2 I guess it also caused a change in the power of priests. As the translation of more Bibles were printed, people had their own book and they didn't need priests reading to them — they could read their own Bibles. So the clergy lost some power.

P Right. And this led to what?

S2 Umm… you got me.

P It led to a transformation of education. Before, the clergy held power through their knowledge. They were the teachers of the day. But now the poor and the middle class, not just the rich, could learn to read more easily. And as we mentioned, now that books were machine-printed, spelling and grammar became standardized.

교수 이동형 인쇄기는 당시 많은 양의 책을 생산할 수 있게끔 한 기계였습니다. 여러분도 구텐베르크의 발명품이 만들어진 배경과 영향에 대해 이미 많은 자료를 읽었으리라 생각됩니다. 오늘 수업 시간에는 인쇄기의 발명이 당시 문화와 종교에 어떻게 커다란 영향을 미쳤는지 살펴볼 기회를 갖고자 합니다. 우선 여러분께 질문을 하나 하도록 하지요. 여러분은 인쇄기가 문화의 어떤 부분에 영향을 미쳤다고 생각합니까?

학생 1 종교에 엄청난 영향을 미쳤다고 교재에서 읽었습니다.

교수 네, 좋습니다, 계속해 보세요.

학생 1 음… 청교도 혁명과 밀접한 관련이 있습니다. 종교 개혁은 갑작스럽게 일어난 것이 아닙니다. 그러니까, 인쇄기가 그 초석을 마련했다는 것입니다. (인쇄기의) 대(大) 발명으로 훨씬 더 많은 수의 독자들이 마틴 루터가 독일어로 해석한 성경을 읽을 수 있었고, 이런 현상은 루터의 다른 글들에까지 확산되었습니다.

학생 2 제 생각에는 그것이 성직자들의 권력에도 변화를 초래했던 것 같습니다. 성경을 번역한 책들이 더 많이 출판되면서 사람들은 자신만의 성경을 갖게 되었고, 성경을 읽어주던 성직자들이 더 이상 필요하지 않게 되었습니다. 그들 스스로 성경을 읽을 수 있게 되었으니까요. 그래서 성직자들은 어느 정도의 권력을 상실하게 되었습니다.

교수 맞습니다. 그래서 어떠한 결과를 낳았나요?

학생 2 음… 그건 잘 모르겠습니다.

교수 교육의 변화를 낳았습니다. 그 이전까지 성직자는 자신들의 지식을 이용해 권력을 장악했습니다. 그들은 당대의 교사였습니다. 그러나 이후로는 부유층 뿐 아니라, 빈민층과 중산층도 더욱 쉽게 읽는 방법을 배울 수 있었지요. 그리고 이미 언급했다시피 그 이후 책들은 기계로 인쇄되었고, 철자법이나 문법이 표준화되었습니다.

> **어휘** movable 움직일 수 있는, 이동하는 printing press 인쇄기
> profoundly 깊이있게; 심오하게 the clergy 성직자들
> transformation 변형, 변모 standardized 표준화된, 규격화된
> lay the groundwork for ~의 토대가 되다

A 토론은 주로 무엇에 관한 것인가?
(A) 이동형 인쇄기로 인쇄된 다양한 형태의 서적들
(B) 인쇄기가 당시 문화와 종교에 미친 영향
(C) 중산층의 교육과 관련된 인쇄 서적의 활용
(D) 성직자의 일상에 미친 종교적, 비종교적 그리고 언어학적 영향

해설 인쇄기의 발명이 당시 문화, 종교 등 생활상에 미친 영향에 대하여 이야기하고 있다.

B 이동형 인쇄기의 발명이 미친 영향으로 언급되지 <u>않은</u> 것은 무엇인가?
(A) 중산층의 교육 개선
(B) 서적 출판에서의 성직자의 역할 약화
(C) 언어 사용을 지배하는 규칙의 표준화
(D) 교육 과정의 변화

해설 성직자들이 서적 출판에 직접 관여하지는 않았으므로 그 범주가 잘못되었다.

Exercise 3
사회학 수업에서의 강의의 일부를 듣고 물음에 답하시오.

🎧 스크립트

P Now remember that we left off talking about a few factors that made industrialization happen? But today, I'd like to talk about women of the industrialization period. In particular, I want to talk about the ways in which industrialization not only changed the perception of women's roles — in the home and in society — but it also changed the daily experiences of women, Okay? Basically, what we're gonna look at is how new technologies changed the country's job market and pushed women out of the home and into the job market. And then how that change... created an incredible amount of tension in our culture.... in terms of what was expected of women. For your understanding, I'll use some visual aids during the lecture. Okay... first let's look into how industrialization brought change to the job market. As new technologies accelerated, it was possible to do most work without much time or effort. As a result, factory owners employed women, and sometimes children instead of experienced men because women worked for low wages. A number of male laborers lost their jobs. In other words, women's social activities were triggered by male unemployment. Now, let's glance over what was expected of women at that time. Traditionally women were occupied with housework and caring for their children at home. Keeping house was their duty. From the old point of view, getting out of the home to work was quite a shock.

교수 지난 시간에 산업화를 가져온 몇 가지 요인에 관해서 논의하다 그만둔 것을 기억하나요? 오늘은 산업화 시기의 여성에 관해 논의해 보고자 합니다. 그런데 특히, 산업화가 가정에서나 사회에서의 여성의 역할에 대한 인식을 변화시킨 것 외에, 여성의 일상 체험을 변화시킨 방법들에 대해 논의하고자 합니다. 알겠죠? 기본적으로 우리가 살펴볼 점은, 새로운 기술이 어떻게 국가의 노동력 시장을 변화시켰으며, 어떻게 여성을 가정에서 노동력 시장으로 내보냈는가 하는 점입니다. 그리고 여성에 대한 기대라는 관점에서, 어떻게 그 같은 변화가... 우리 문화에 엄청난 긴장 상태를 초래했는지 보겠습니다. 여러분의 이해를 돕기 위해, 이번 강의 시간에는 시각자료를 활용하도록 하겠습니다. 좋아요... 먼저 산업화가 어떠한 방식으로 노동력 시장에 변화를 가져왔는지 살펴봅시다. 새로운 기술이 가속화됨에 따라 대부분의 작업이 많은 시간과 노력 없이도 가능하게 되었습니다. 그 결과, 공장주들은 숙련된 성인남성 대신에 값싼 임금으로도 노동을 한다는 이유로 여성을, 때로는 아동들까지 고용하였죠. 그리고 많은 남성 노동자들이 실직하게 되었습니다. 다시 말해, 여성의 사회 활동은 남성의 실업으로 인해 촉발되었습니다. 이제, 당시의 여성에 대한 기대가 어떤 것이었는지 살펴보도록 합시다. 전통적으로 여성은 가사를 전담했으며, 가정에서 육아를 담당했습니다. 가사는 그들의 의무였습니다. 전통적인 관점으로 보면 (여성이) 일을 하기 위해 집밖으로 나오는 것은 꽤 충격적인 것이었습니다.

어휘 industrialization 산업화 perception 인식, 인지, 지각 incredible 놀라운, 훌륭한, 굉장한 tension 긴장, 긴박 상태 accelerate 가속화하다 trigger 유발하다 unemployment 실직 an amount of 상당한 양의 in terms of ~에 관하여, ~의 점에서 (보면) be occupied with ~에 종사하다 keep house 가사일하다

A 강의의 주제는 무엇이 될 것인가?
(A) 여러 종류의 긴장(상태)과 신(新) 기술
(B) 경제 전환점을 이룬 20세기
(C) 산업화로 인한 여성 생활 방식의 변화
(D) 19세기와 20세기의 여성 역할의 비교

해설 교수는 산업화로 인해 야기된 여성의 역할 변화에 대해 강의하겠다고 밝혔다. 그 중에서도 신기술의 발전이 여성들을 취업 시장으로 내몰게 된 배경에 대해 다룰 것임을 명시하고 있다.

B 여성이 밖에서 일하게 된 이유는 무엇인가? 정답 두 개를 고르시오.
(A) 수공업 제품 생산에 재능이 있었다.
(B) 고용주들이 여성을 고용함으로써 돈(인건비)을 절감하고자 했다.
(C) 공장주들이 남성들을 통제하지 못했다.
(D) 덜 숙련된 노동자들로도 생산이 가능했다.

해설 여성들이 가사 노동 대신 밖에서 일을 하게 된 계기는 1) 적은 시간과 노력으로 생산이 가능해졌다는 점, 2) 숙련된 노동자였던 남성보다 적은 임금으로 고용이 가능했다는 점 때문이었다. (C)는 언급된 바 없다.

Exercise 4
두 학생의 대화의 일부를 듣고 물음에 답하시오.

🎧 스크립트

S1 Do you have a second? I need to talk to you about something for my class.
S2 Well, I have a class in 15 minutes. Make it short.
S1 Yeah... remember the class that we had last week about therapy... considering time into medical treatments or something?
S2 Right... yeah... What about it?
S1 For some reason, I don't have the article the professor handed out.
S2 Which article are you talking about? I remember there... um... two or three articles he gave us.
S1 That's... uh... The article talks about the correlation between time, blood pressure and heart attacks. It says our bodies' blood pressure spikes when we wake up in the morning... and uh... heart attacks are um... more common at those times, or

something. That's what I'm looking for.
S2 I know what you mean.
S1 Do you have it now?
S2 Actually, I left my stuff in my dorm, though. Have you tried the library?
S1 I'm on my way back from the library now.
S2 All right... You want me to get them for you later?
S1 You think you could do that for me?
S2 I'll give you a copy of them after class.
S1 Oh, thanks.

학생 1 잠시 시간 있어? 수업과 관련해서 의논할 일이 있어.
학생 2 글쎄, 15분 뒤에 수업이 있는데. 간단히 말해 봐.
학생 1 그래, 지난 주 수업 기억나? 치료법에 관한 것인데... 시간을 의학 치료법이나 뭐 그런 것에도 고려한다는 것 말이야.
학생 2 맞아, 그랬지. 그게 뭐?
학생 1 사정이 좀 생겨서, 교수님께서 나눠주신 자료가 나한테 없어.
학생 2 어떤 자료 말하는 거야? 내가 기억하기로는... 음... 교수님께서 나눠주신 자료가 두세 개 였던 것 같은데.
학생 1 그게.. 음... 시간과 혈압, 그리고 심장마비 사이의 연관성에 관한 자료야. 그 자료에는 우리가 아침에 일어날 때 혈압이 급격히 상승한다고 되어 있어. 그래서, 음... 그 시기 즈음에 심장 마비가 더 많다는 거야. 내가 찾는 건 그 자료야.
학생 2 네가 뭘 찾는지 알겠다.
학생 1 지금 그거 갖고 있어?
학생 2 실은 그 자료들을 기숙사에 뒀어. 너 도서관은 찾아봤어?
학생 1 지금 도서관에서 돌아오는 길이야.
학생 2 알았어. 나중에 내가 갖다 줄까?
학생 1 그렇게 해줄 수 있겠어?
학생 2 수업 끝나고 한 부 복사해 줄게.
학생 1 그래, 고마워.

어휘 treatment 치료(법), 치료제　blood pressure 혈압　correlation 상호 관계, 상관성　heart attack 심장 발작, 심장 마비

A 여자가 남자와 대화하고 싶어 하는 이유는 무엇인가?
(A) 논문 주제인 시치료(時治療)에 관한 정보를 얻기 위해
(B) 남자가 필기한 내용의 복사본을 얻기 위해
(C) 도서관 어디에서 자료를 찾을 수 있는지 묻기 위해
(D) 지난 수업 시간에 다뤘던 읽기 자료를 빌리기 위해

해설 여자는 교수가 내준 읽기 자료를 분실하여서 남자에게서 그것을 빌리려고 한다.

B 남자는 이후에 무엇을 할 것인가?
(A) 자료를 찾기 위해 도서관에 갈 것이다.
(B) 수업에 참석할 것이다.
(C) 여자와 자료에 대해 토론할 것이다.
(D) 자료를 가지러 기숙사에 갈 것이다.

해설 다음 행동을 예측하는 문제는 마지막 대사에 주목한다.

Dictation　Exercise

Exercise 1

① We've been looking at
② to promote positive messages
③ more appealing to customers
④ when something undeniably
⑤ This is an area that
⑥ crisis communications
⑦ has been accused of causing people to get sick
⑧ how do you deal with it as the spokesperson
⑨ before we get into any of those
⑩ is considering the situation seriously
⑪ Denying makes
⑫ no matter if the crisis is your fault or not
⑬ image is what this is all about

Exercise 2

① movable type printing press
② we'll have the opportunity to look over
③ profoundly influenced
④ the printing press affected culture
⑤ You're on a roll
⑥ was closely related to
⑦ laid the groundwork for it
⑧ allowed a much broader audience to read
⑨ caused a change in the power of priests
⑩ didn't need priests reading to them
⑪ It led to a transformation of education
⑫ through their knowledge
⑬ the poor and the middle class
⑭ became standardized

Exercise 3

① we left off talking about a few factors
② women of the industrialization period
③ the perception of women's roles
④ daily experiences of women
⑤ out of the home and into the job market
⑥ created an incredible amount of
⑦ in terms of what was expected of women
⑧ As new technologies accelerated
⑨ instead of experienced men
⑩ worked for low wages
⑪ were triggered by

⑫ were occupied with housework
⑬ was quite a shock

Exercise 4

① something for my class
② the class that we had last week
③ considering time into medical treatments
④ I don't have the article
⑤ Which article are you talking about
⑥ the correlation between
⑦ our bodies' blood pressure spikes
⑧ more common at those times
⑨ Do you have it now
⑩ I left my stuff in my dorm, though
⑪ I'm on my way back from
⑫ I'll give you a copy of them

Actual Test

1 1 - (B) 2 - (D) 3 - (C) 4 - (A)
2 1 - (C) 2 - (C) 3 - (D) 4 - (B)

Actual Test 1

도서관학 수업에서의 대화의 일부를 듣고 물음에 답하시오.

🎧 스크립트

P In the early 1800s, the paper industry was still using rags as its basic source of fiber as it had for many centuries. However, the rag supply couldn't keep up with the growing demand for paper. The United States alone was using 250 thousand tons of rags each year. And a quarter of that had to be imported. It was clear that a new source of fiber was needed to keep up with the demand for paper. The answer to this problem turned out to be paper made from wood pulp, something that was abundantly available in North America. In Canada, the first wood pulp mill was set up in 1866 and it was immediately successful. But while wood pulp solved the problem of quantity, it created a problem of quality. Wood contains a substance called lignin. The simplest way to make large quantities of cheap paper involved leaving the lignin in the wood pulp. But lignin is acidic and its presence in paper has shortened the life expectancy of paper from several centuries for rag paper to less than a century for paper made from wood pulp. This means that books printed less than a hundred years ago are already turning yellow and beginning to disintegrate, even though books printed much earlier are in perfect condition. This is bad enough for the older books on your bookshelf but it poses a huge problem for libraries and the collections of government documents.

교수 1800년대 초기 제지 산업 분야에서는 지난 수세기 동안 그래 왔던 것처럼 섬유의 기본 재질로 (제지용) 넝마를 사용하고 있었습니다. 그러나 넝마 공급이 늘어나는 종이의 수요를 따라잡지 못하게 되었죠. 미국에서만 해마다 25만 톤의 넝마를 사용했으니까요. 게다가 그 중 4분의 1은 수입까지 해야 했습니다. 종이 수요를 충족시키려면 새로운 형태의 섬유가 필요한 것이 분명했습니다. 이 문제에 대한 해답은 북미 지역에서 풍부한 목재 펄프를 사용해 종이를 만드는 것으로 결론이 났습니다. 1866년 캐나다에 최초의 목재 펄프 제조 공장이 건설되었고, 즉각적인 성공을 이루었습니다. 그러나 목재 펄프를 사용함으로써 양의 문제는 해결되었지만 품질 측면에서 문제를 야기시켰습니다. 목재에는 리그닌이라 불리는 물질이 포함되어 있는데, 값싼 종이를 대량 생산하는 가장 간단한 방법을 사용하면서 목재 펄프에 이 리그닌이 남게 되었습니다. 하지만 리그닌은 산성이라 종이에 이 리그닌이 남아있는 경우 종이의 수명이 단축되지요. 넝마를 사용한 종이는 수 세기 동안 보존이 가능했던 반면 목재 펄프를 사용한 종이는 한 세기를 채 버티지 못했습니다. 이 말은 백년도 안 된 책들이 벌써 노랗게 변색되고 부식되기 시작했다는 얘기가 됩니다. 그 보다 훨씬 전에 인쇄된 책들도 아직 완벽한 상태로 남아 있는데 말입니다. 즉 여러분 책장에 있는 오래된 책들도 꽤 문제지만, 도서관이나 정부 문서 보관에도 상당한 문제가 되고 있습니다.

1 강의는 주로 무엇에 관한 것인가?
(A) 출판 산업계의 성장
(B) 제지(製紙)의 역사
(C) 19세기 종이의 사용
(D) 목재 섬유의 구성 성분

해설 제지 원료가 바뀌게 된 계기와, 제지의 원재료가 바뀜으로써 생겨난 장단점을 언급하고 있다.

2 1800년대 초기 제지 산업에서 새로운 종류의 섬유 재질이 필요했던 이유는 무엇인가?
(A) 출판업자들이 고품질의 종이를 원했다.
(B) 넝마로 만든 종이가 너무 빨리 부식되었다.
(C) 목재 펄프가 너무 비쌌다.
(D) 넝마의 공급량이 부족했다.

해설 공급이 수요를 따라가지 못했다.

3 교수의 말에 따르면, 리그닌의 문제점은 무엇인가?
  (A) (리그닌을) 얻기가 어렵다.
  (B) 리그닌이 없이는 종이를 만들 수 없다.
  (C) 종이를 부식시킨다.
  (D) 목재를 펄프로 만들 수 없게 한다.

해설 리그닌은 산성이라 종이를 쉽게 부식시킨다.

4 교수의 말에 따르면, 도서관이 직면한 문제는 무엇인가?
  (A) 책의 상태가 좋지 않은 것들이 많다.
  (B) 1800년대 초기의 책들을 너무 많이 소장하고 있다.
  (C) 정부 문서를 보관할 장소가 충분하지 않다.
  (D) 이들이 사용하는 종이의 대부분을 수입해야 한다.

해설 도서가 쉽게 부식되기 때문에 상태가 좋지 않다. 보존 및 관리에 문제가 있을 것이다.

Actual Test 2

교수 연구실에서 이루어진 대화의 일부분을 듣고 물음에 답하시오.

🎧 스크립트

S Professor... Can I come in for a minute?
P Sure. Have a seat.
S Well... I've done a lot of research for my genetics paper, but... it's just that I can't decide what to write about... so I sent you an email to get some help.
P Yeah... I got your email... and... well, I was thinking it might be good if you write on the Amish and their genetics... what do you think?
S The Amish? I think I've read about them and seen a television documentary program about their community. They live without any modern conveniences, right? No cars or electric lights... But what does that have to do with genetics?
P Actually, you should focus on the high rate of rare diseases in Amish communities. It occurs because, in such a closed community, there is a low rate of genetic diversity.
S What do you mean by genetic diversity?
P Well, it's really a matter of odds. What happens is that there is a limited pool of partners for marriage, and so people who marry in these societies are mostly distant relatives. There aren't a lot of different genes being passed on, as in an open society. And then, if there is a gene for a rare disease in a family, if both people are members of that, this can significantly increase their children's chances of getting the gene for the disease.
S Oh, I see. This topic sounds quite interesting. I'd like to work on it as you recommended.

학생 교수님, 잠시 들어가도 될까요?
교수 그래요. 앉아요.
학생 저... 유전학 과제를 위해 조사를 많이 해봤지만 무엇에 관해 쓸지를 아직 결정하지 못했습니다. 그래서 도움을 구하려고 교수님께 이메일을 보냈었어요.
교수 네, 학생의 이메일은 받았어요. 글쎄요, 내가 생각하기에는 학생이 아미시 사람들과 그들의 유전적 특질에 관해 글을 써 보면 좋을 것 같은데, 어떻게 생각해요?
학생 아미시 사람들이요? 그들 공동체에 관한 글을 읽어본 것 같아요. TV 다큐멘터리로도 접해봤고요. 현대의 이기(利器)의 혜택을 거부한 채 살아가는 사람들이죠, 맞나요? 자동차나 전기도 없이 말이에요. 그런데 그 사람들이 유전학과 어떤 관계가 있나요?
교수 실은, 아미시 집단에서 희귀 질병의 발병률이 높다는 데 초점을 맞추어야 합니다. 이런 현상은 아미시 집단처럼 폐쇄된 사회에서는 유전적인 다양성의 비율이 낮기 때문에 일어나는 것이니까요.
학생 유전적인 다양성이 무슨 뜻인가요?
교수 음, 그건 정말 확률 상의 문제예요. 그게 무엇인가 하면, (폐쇄된 사회에서는) 결혼 상대의 범주가 한정되어 있기 때문에 이런 사회에서 결혼하는 구성원들은 대개 서로가 먼 친척뻘이 됩니다. 개방적인 사회에서처럼 (다음 세대로) 전달되는 유전자가 그다지 다양하지 않아요. 그래서 한 가계에 희귀 질병에 대한 유전자가 있고 배우자 둘 다 그 가계의 일원일 경우, 자식이 그 질병에 대한 유전자를 보유할 확률이 상당히 높아지지요.
학생 아, 그렇군요. 이 주제가 아주 흥미롭겠네요. 추천해 주신대로 이 주제로 과제를 작성해 보겠습니다.

1 남자가 교수를 찾아간 이유는 무엇인가?
  (A) (자신이 정한 과제의) 주제에 대해 교수의 의견을 듣기 위해
  (B) 아미시 사람들을 만날 수 있는 방법을 찾기 위해
  (C) 과제에 대해 교수와 상의하기 위해
  (D) 아미시 사람들과 유전학과의 상관 관계를 확인하기 위해

해설 남학생은 교수를 찾아와 유전학 과제 주제로 무엇을 정할지에 관해 상의하고 있다. 교수는 학생에게 Amish 사람들의 생활 습관을 얘기하면서 이들 생활상과 유전적 결과를 연구해 보라고 조언한다.
  (A) - 아직 Topic을 정하지 못했다고 했다.
  (B)(D) - Amish에 관한 얘기는 교수와 만난 이후에 들은 것이다.

2 먼 친척끼리 결혼하면 어떤 일이 발생하는가?
  (A) 자손들에게 여러 다양한 유전자들이 전달된다.
  (B) 출생률이 현저히 감소한다.
  (C) 물려줄 수 있는 유전자 수가 한정된다.
  (D) 아이들은 부모의 유전자를 물려받을 가능성이 더 적다.

해설 같은 종족끼리 결혼을 하면 다른 종족에게서나 볼 수 있는 유전자를 새로 받아들이지 못하기 때문에 물려주는 유전자가 한정될 수밖에 없다.

3 교수의 말에 따르면, 유전학적 다양성이란 무엇인가?
(A) 근친혼의 경향
(B) 폐쇄 사회에서 발생하는 문제점
(C) 진보적인 기술 사용의 거부
(D) 여러 다양한 (유전) 형질의 존재

해설 Amish 사람들의 결혼 관례로 볼 때 확률적으로 '다양한 유전자가 공존할 가능성'이 낮다.

4 유전적 특질과 아미시 사람들의 관계에 관해 옳은 것은 무엇인가?
(A) 희귀 질병이 드물기 때문에 더욱 건강하게 살아왔다.
(B) 그들의 사회적 생활양식은 희귀 질병의 발병률이 높아지는 결과를 초래했다.
(C) 그들의 결혼 양상을 통해 새로운 유전자가 발생했다.
(D) 그들은 폐쇄 공동체를 형성하는 능력이 유전되는 것 같다.

해설 아미시 사람들은 외부 세계와 단절된 형태로 생활하기 때문에 같은 종족끼리 결혼을 한다. 이로 인해, 그 종족이 가진 유전적 질병이 다음 세대(결국, 같은 종족)에게 전이되는 확률이 높으나 새로운 유전자가 생길 가능성(C)은 낮다.

Dictation — Actual Test

Actual Test 1

① rags as its basic source of fiber
② couldn't keep up with the growing demand
③ a quarter of that
④ a new source of fiber was needed
⑤ that was abundantly available in
⑥ was set up in
⑦ solved the problem of quantity
⑧ The simplest way to make large quantities
⑨ its presence in paper has shortened
⑩ to less than a century
⑪ are already turning yellow and beginning to disintegrate
⑫ but it poses a huge problem

Actual Test 2

① I've done a lot of research
② it's just that I can't decide what to write about
③ if you write on
④ seen a television documentary program

⑤ without any modern conveniences
⑥ focus on the high rate of rare diseases
⑦ in such a closed community
⑧ a low rate of genetic diversity
⑨ a matter of odds
⑩ a limited pool of partners
⑪ There aren't a lot of different genes
⑫ as in an open society
⑬ their children's chances of
⑭ sounds quite interesting

Vocabulary Review

다음 각 정의와 일치하는 단어를 골라 써 넣으시오.

1 distant   2 rare   3 genetics
4 incredible   5 diversity   6 clergy
7 spokesperson   8 relative   9 tension
10 unemployment

1 가까이 연관되지 않은; 아주 먼
2 흔하지 않은; 자주 일어나지 않는
3 유전자로 한 세대에서 다음 세대로 전달되는 특질
4 아주 특이하고 놀라워서 사실이라고 믿지 못하는
5 서로 아주 다른 일련의 것들
6 종교적인 일의 공식적인 지도자
7 단체나 기구를 변호하는 대변인
8 혈연이나 혼인을 통해 가족 관계로 맺어지는 사람
9 정신적·감성적 불안이나 긴장의 상태
10 일을 원하는데도 불구하고 갖지 못하는 것

다음 구문을 사용하여 문장을 완성하시오.

1 participate in   2 bring about   3 in detail
4 was accused of   5 dealt with

1 모든 학생들은 학교 동아리 활동 중 적어도 하나는 참여해야 한다.
2 우리는 이 계획으로 몇 가지 긍정적인 결과가 창출되리라 생각한다.
3 다음 회의 시간에 그 문제를 자세히 논의할 것이다.
4 나의 동료 중 한 명이 절도 혐의로 구속되었다.
5 우리는 그의 문제가 정치적으로 다뤄져야 한다고 믿는다.

CHAPTER 02
SUPPORTING DETAILS

Sample

교수 네, 그래서, 일단 여러분이 자신이 쓸 글에 대해 간단한 아웃라인을 잡았다고 한다면, 실제로 글을 써 내려가기 전에 '자유로운 글쓰기'를 하기 위해 얼마간의 시간을 내야 합니다. 그렇게 하면... 새로운 아이디어를 생각해 내는 데 도움이 됩니다. '자유로운 글쓰기'가 성공적이려면, 음, 시간 제한을 두는 것입니다. 우선, 이를테면 10분 정도라든가, 이렇게 글을 쓰는 데 시간을 정해 두는 겁니다. 그런 다음 (그 시간 내에) 쓸 수 있는 만큼 글을 써 보세요. 머리에 떠오르는 그 어떤 것도 좋습니다.

학생 저, 그렇지만 머리에 떠오르는 모든 것을 다 쓰는 것은 아니겠지요. 제 말은 그런 글은 (어떤 주제로) 초점이 맞춰지지 못할 테니까요.

교수 음, 이렇게 생각해 보죠. 우선 너무 많은 생각을 하지 않는 거예요. 그러면 여러분의 정신이 맑아져서 새롭고 흥미로운 것들을 떠올릴 수 있습니다. 다시 말하면, 여러분은 보다 창의적이 될 수 있습니다.

교수는 자유로운 글쓰기에 대해 어떤 이야기를 하고 있는가?
(A) 어떤 아이디어는 가치 없는 것이기 때문에 무시해야 한다.
(B) 머리에 떠오르는 모든 것을 활용해서는 안 된다.
(C) (글쓰기에) 10분 이상을 소비해야 한다.
(D) 머리에 떠오르는 내용은 무엇이든 유용할 수 있다.

정답 (D)

Vocabulary Preview for Skill Check-up

다음 정의를 듣고 알맞은 단어를 고르시오.

1 extinct   2 inhabitant   3 sensory
4 guarantee   5 incentive   6 register
7 geography   8 myth   9 invade
10 dialect

1 no longer existing
   더 이상 존재하지 않는
2 a person who lives in a particular place
   특정 지역에서 사는 사람
3 relating to the physical senses
   신체 감각에 관련이 된
4 ensure that something will definitely happen
   어떤 일이 틀림없이 일어날 거라고 확신하다
5 something that causes a person to act positively
   사람이 적극(긍정)적으로 행동하게끔 하는 어떤 것
6 enroll one's name on an official list
   공식적인 목록에 자신의 이름을 올리다
7 study of the earth's surface, seas, climates, towns
   지구의 표면, 해양, 기후, 도시의 연구
8 a traditional well-known story about social customs or religious beliefs
   사회적 관습이나 종교적 신념에 관해 전통적으로 잘 알려진 이야기
9 enter another country by military force, especially for conquest
   군사력으로, 특히 정복을 목적으로 다른 나라에 들어가다
10 a regional variety of language spoken by the members of a particular group
    특정 그룹의 구성원들이 사용하는 언어의 지역적 다양성

다음 단어를 이용하여 아래 문장을 완성하시오.

1 sensory   2 invade   3 registered 4 guarantee
5 extinct   6 translate 7 dialect   8 inhabitant
9 solar   10 recall

1 나이를 먹어갈수록 우리의 육체적·감각적 능력이 쇠퇴한다고 한다.
2 조지 부시 미 대통령은 신이 그에게 아프가니스탄과 이라크 침공을 명령했다고 말했다.
3 너무 많은 학생들이 그 수업에 수강 신청을 하자 학교는 정원수를 늘렸다.
4 정부는 식품안전 보장을 위한 기준안을 마련하기로 약속했다.
5 공룡이 멸종한 원인에 대한 몇 가지 가설이 있다.
6 여러 국가의 출판업자들이 해리 포터를 (그들의 언어로) 출판 번역하려고 애썼다.
7 화자의 사투리 사용과 다양한 목소리 톤으로 청자는 화자들을 구별할 수 있었다.
8 이들 산악 지역의 전형적인 거주자는 야채만을 먹는다.
9 그는 집을 개조하여 태양 에너지로 난방을 할 수 있도록 했다.
10 그 회사는 2005년 9월 이후 생산된 모든 불량 자동차를 리콜하겠다는 정책을 마련했다.

Skill Check-up Important Information

1 교수의 말에 따르면, Champ란 무엇인가?
  (A) 탐험가들이 발견한 선사 시대 어류
  (B) Champlain 호수에 사는 것으로 알려진 크고 흔한 어류
  (C) 이 호수에 서식하는 것으로 알려졌으나 존재 여부가 입증되지 않은 생물

정답 (C)

해설 중심 소재는 전설 속의 생명체 Champ이다. Champ에 대한 여러 의견이 있으나 명백한 실존 근거가 나오지 않는한 그저 전설일 뿐이라는 게 교수의 결론이다.
(B) – 흔한 종류의 어류라는 것은 일부의 주장일 뿐 증거 자료는 없다.

 스크립트

P For some reason, the world's large lakes are <u>common sources of myth</u>. Any of you heard of the uh, Creature of Lake Champlain? Its name is Champ and <u>it's been supposedly sighted</u> hundreds of times, even by explorer Samuel de Champlain in 1609.

S So, what is it, then? I mean it's something, right?
P It's uh... well... some say Champ is a plesiosaur, a large extinct fish. Others claim that it's simply a large lake sturgeon, a common fish found in Lake Champlain. But let's put it this way: until there is undeniable documentation of this mysterious creature existing, he'll just be a mystery.

교수 여러 이유로 세계의 큰 호수들은 흔히 전설의 소재가 됩니다. 여러분 가운데 누구, 에, Champlain 호수 생물에 관해 들어본 적이 있나요? 그 생물의 이름은 Champ이고, 1609년에 탐험가 Samuel de Champlain이 발견하기까지 수백 차례 발견된 것으로 추정됩니다.
학생 그럼, 그것이 뭔가요? 그러니까 뭔가 특별한 것이군요?
교수 그것은, 에, 어떤 사람들은 Champ를 장경룡이라고 하는데, 이미 멸종된 커다란 물고기입니다. 또 어떤 사람들은 그냥 단순히 Champlain 호수에서 발견되는 흔한 물고기인 대형 호수 철갑상어라고 주장합니다. 그런데 이렇게 생각해 봅시다. 이 미지의 생명체에 대한 명백한 증거 자료가 존재하지 않는 한, 이 생명체는 단지 신비의 존재일 뿐이겠지요.

2 남자의 문제는 무엇인가?
(A) 그는 어떤 책이 과제에 적합할지 결정하지 못했다.
(B) 사서가 그 책을 회수할 수 없다고 말한다.
(C) (과제를 위해 필요한) 책이 이미 다른 학생에게 대출되었다.
정답 (C)

해설 남학생이 원하는 것은 과제에 필요한 책을 구하는 것이다. 현재 이 책은 대출되어 있는 상태지만 도서관 사서가 그 책을 회수하여 남학생이 이용할 수 있도록 할 것이다.

🎧 스크립트

S I desperately need this book for my paper, but it's not due back for a month.
L How soon is your paper due?
S Not for another two weeks.
L Perfect. I can recall the book for you. The person who has it now will get a notice to return the book this Friday.
S But what if he doesn't return it?
L Umm, there's no guarantee he will, but we charge a big fine for not returning recalled books. It's a very good incentive!

학생 제가 과제를 작성하려면 이 책이 꼭 필요한데 한 달 동안 책이 회수되지 않네요.
사서 과제 제출 기한이 언제인가요?
학생 2주도 안 남았어요.
사서 좋아요. 학생을 위해 그 책을 회수하도록 하죠. 그 책을 대출한 학생에게 금요일까지 반납하라는 통보를 할게요.

학생 하지만 그가 만약 반납하지 않으면 어떡하죠?
사서 음, 그가 반납할 거라고 장담은 못하지만, 책을 반납하지 않으면 많은 벌금을 물도록 조치한답니다. 반납을 유도할 수 있는 좋은 제도지요.

3 사람들이 같은 식품의 맛을 다르게 느끼는 이유는 무엇인가?
(A) 미뢰의 개수가 다르기 때문에
(B) 미각 기관의 크기가 다르기 때문에
(C) 혀의 모양이 다르기 때문에
정답 (B)

해설 사람마다 미각 기관의 크기가 다르며, 맛을 느끼는 기관이 클수록 맛을 더 강하게 느낀다.

🎧 스크립트

P As I mentioned earlier, we all don't taste things in the... in the same way. Some people, for example, love the taste of broccoli; I know a lot of you eat it very often, am I right? Meanwhile other people like me might think it's the worst taste in the world. Why is that? Well, there's a physiological explanation for this. Some people just have bigger taste buds than others! Taste buds are those sensory receptors on your tongue that let you know what you're eating. And so the bigger taste buds you have, the more you taste. It seems too simple, but what I can say is... it's true...

교수 일전에 말했듯이, 우리 모두가 똑같은 방식으로 맛을 느끼는 것은 아닙니다. 예컨대 어떤 사람들은 브로콜리의 맛을 아주 좋아하죠. 제가 알기로는 많은 사람들이 꽤 자주 브로콜리를 먹는다고 하는데, 맞나요? 반면에 또 어떤 사람들은, 저처럼 브로콜리를 세상에서 가장 맛이 없는 음식이라고 생각하기도 할 겁니다. 왜 그럴까요? 음, 이에 대해 생리학적인 설명이 있습니다. 어떤 사람들은 다른 사람보다 큰 미뢰를 갖고 있다는 겁니다. 미뢰는 혀에 존재하는 감각 기관으로 여러분이 섭취하는 음식이 무엇인지 식별하도록 하죠. 그래서 (다른 사람들) 보다 큰 미뢰를 가지고 있는 경우 맛을 더 강하게 인식하게 되는 겁니다. 아주 단순한 것 같아도, 제가 말씀드릴 수 있는 건, 이것이 사실이란 겁니다.

4 남자의 수강 신청 문제에 대해 여자가 제시한 해결 방안은 무엇인가?
(A) 담당 교수에게 (추가로) 수강을 할 수 있도록 해달라고 요청하라.
(B) 그다지 많지 않은 사람들이 등록하는 중급반에 수강 신청하라.
(C) 가능하다면 다음 학기 지리학 수업에 등록하라.
정답 (A)

해설 남자가 지리학 수강 신청을 하지 못해서 실망스러워하자 여자는 해당 과목 교사에게 부탁해 보라고 한다. 일반적으로 교사가 학생을 받아들이겠다는 양식에 서명을 하면 강의를 들을 수 있다.

🎧 스크립트

S1 Arg! I'm so frustrated! I keep trying to register for this geography class, but I can't get in! If I don't get in this semester, I'll be really behind.

S2 That's the problem with intro classes. They fill up so fast. The other thing is that there are too many first year students this semester.

S1 Maybe. Anyway, is there any way I can get in?

S2 Maybe you could ask the professor to let you in. You can usually get in when a professor signs a form to allow a student to join a class that's already full.

S1 Yeah, that might work.

학생 1 아, 정말 지치겠어. 이 지리학 수업을 신청하려고 계속 시도하고 있는데, 신청이 안 돼. 이번 학기에 수강하지 못하면 난 정말 뒤처질 거야.

학생 2 그게 바로 기초 과목이 갖는 문제라니까. 기초 과목은 정원이 너무 빨리 차거든. 게다가 이번 학기에는 신입생들도 너무 많잖아.

학생 1 그런가 봐. 어쨌든, 내가 수강할 수 있는 방법이 없을까?

학생 2 교수님께 수강하게 해 달라고 부탁드려 봐. 수강 인원이 이미 차 버린 수업이라도 대개 교수가 수강을 허가하는 양식에 서명을 하면 수강할 수 있거든.

학생 1 그래, 그 방법이 통하겠군.

Skill Check-up True or False

1 교수가 비디오에 관해 말한 것은 무엇인가?
(A) (영상이) 매끄럽게 제작되지 않았다.
(B) 할리우드 영화적 특성을 지녔다.
(C) 성인들 사이에서 전쟁을 옹호하는 분위기가 생겨났다.

정답 (A) T (B) F (C) F

해설 교수는 리얼리티를 살린 영상을 전달함으로써 사람들에게 전쟁의 참혹성을 알리고 더불어 반전 감정을 불러일으켰다고 얘기하고 있다. 영상 매체가 어떻게 사실성을 전달했는지를 주목해서 들어본다.

🎧 스크립트

P OK, so we've been talking about the Viet-Nam War's effect on American youth. But today I want to expand that to a discussion of something that affected Americans in general – I mean all Americans – and made us leave that war-torn country. You see, video news stories seen nightly led to an early end of the war. Sounds crazy, huh? Well, it's not when you consider that night after night, Americans watched those horribly graphic, jerky, roughly prepared images on their TVs. The images often had the quality of home movies... I mean they weren't your typical well-done Hollywood production. This made it seem to the viewers as if they were really there.

교수 자, 그러니까 우리는 지금까지 베트남 전쟁이 미국 젊은이들에게 미친 영향에 대해 이야기해 보았습니다. 오늘은 이것이 일반적인 미국인들, 그러니까 모든 미국인들에게 영향을 미친, 그리고 우리로 하여금 전쟁으로 피폐해진 그 나라를 떠나게 만들었던 무언가에 대한 논의로 확대해 보겠습니다. 여러분도 알다시피, 밤새 영상으로 보도되는 뉴스 때문에 이 전쟁은 조기 종식되었습니다. 믿겨지지 않나요? 글쎄요, 밤이면 밤마다, 미국인들이 자신들의 TV를 통해 아주 투박하고 끔찍할 정도로 생생하게 처리된 영상들을 봐왔다고 생각하면 그렇지 않을 겁니다. 흔히 그런 영상들은 가정에서 찍은 비디오 정도의 완성도에 불과합니다. 말하자면, 세련되게 제작된 전형적인 할리우드 영화가 아니었단 말입니다. 하지만 이는 (오히려) 시청자들이 마치 실제로 현장에 있는 것처럼 느끼게 하였습니다.

2 교수가 고대 영어에 대해 말한 것은 무엇인가?
(A) 게르만 어는 기원전 3세기에 두 개의 분파로 분리되었다.
(B) 영국 제도 침략이 영어의 변화 속도를 늦추었다.
(C) 고대 영어는 서 게르만 언어와 앵글로 언어가 조합된 것이다.

정답 (A) F (B) F (C) T

해설 현재의 영어는 초기 여러 번의 변화 과정을 거쳐 생성된 것이다.
(A) - BC 2세기경 세 개 분파로 나뉘었다.
(B) - 변화가 늦춰진 것이 아니라 새로운 언어로 탄생되었다.

🎧 스크립트

P The English we speak today is the result of a long process of change. Well, even the early history of English is pretty eventful. It began as a Germanic branch of the Indo-European language. In about 2 BC, this Germanic language split up into three different dialects, one of which was called West Germanic. People who spoke this language invaded the British Isles, and then the language mixed with the native language of the Angles, the inhabitants there. This became Anglo-Saxon, or what we know today as Old English. Now... mmm... why don't we take a look at table 4 on page 65... to see the process?

교수 오늘날 우리가 사용하는 영어는 오랜 기간의 변천 결과입니다.

음, 영어는 그 초기 역사조차 상당히 파란만장합니다. 영어는 인도-유럽 언어의 한 게르만계 분파로 시작되었습니다. 기원전 2세기에 이 게르만 어는 세 개의 방언으로 분리되었고, 그 중 하나가 서 게르만 어라고 불렸죠. 이 언어를 사용하는 사람들이 영국 제도를 침략했고, 이후에 그곳의 주민인 앵글로 족의 토착 언어와 혼합됩니다. 이것이 앵글로 색슨, 즉 오늘날 우리가 알고 있는 고대 영어입니다. 이제, 음... 65쪽의 표 4를 보면서 그 과정을 살펴보도록 할까요?

3 화자들이 파도에 의해 생성된 에너지에 관해 말한 것은 무엇인가?
(A) 파도에 의해 생성된 에너지는 그다지 성공적이지 않았다.
(B) 파도는 인류에게 많은 에너지를 공급할 수 있다.
(C) 조수 전력 발전기는 강을 이용해 에너지를 만든다.

정답 (A) T (B) F (C) F

해설 토론의 주제는 해양을 이용해 전력을 얻을 수 있는 방법들이다. 파도를 이용한 전력 생산은 규모나 전력량 면에서 부족하지만 최근 조수간만의 차를 이용한 새로운 방법이 등장하여 그 가능성과 생산성에 기대가 높다.

🎧 스크립트

P The ocean seems to <u>offer an unlimited source of power</u>. Yet... well... it's difficult to harness its energy.
S1 Didn't you say that we could <u>capture the energy generated by waves</u>, or something?
S2 Yeah... but wave-generated energy is small-scale and <u>largely unsuccessful</u>.
P Well, don't discount it just yet, OK? Lately, more success has come from using the power of tides to create energy. <u>Shore-based dams</u> use the rise and fall of water that occurs <u>as tides go in and out</u>. They generate electricity much as hydroelectric dams do on rivers. <u>Tidal power is a renewable energy source</u> because tides are caused by <u>the orbital mechanics</u> of the solar system. So tidal power is considered endless, well, as far as humans are concerned.

교수 바다는 전력을 제공하는 무한한 원천인 듯합니다. 그렇지만, 글쎄요, 그 에너지를 동력화하는 것은 어렵습니다.
학생 1 파도나 그와 비슷한 것을 이용해 발생되는 에너지를 획득할 수 있다고 말씀하셨잖습니까?
학생 2 음... 그렇지만 파도로 생성된 에너지는 공급량도 적고, 그다지 성공적이지 않잖아요.
교수 글쎄, 아직은 섣불리 과소평가하지 말도록 하세요. 최근, 조수의 동력을 이용한 에너지 생산 결과는 보다 성공적이었습니다. 해변에 위치한 댐들은 밀물과 썰물로 인해 발생하는 물의 낙폭을 이용하는데, 이들은 강에 위치한 수력발전 댐만큼이나 많은 에너지를 만들어내지요. 조수간만의 차로 생겨나는 전력은 재생 가능한 에너지 원천입니다. 왜냐하면 조수는 태양계 궤도에서의 운동으로 생성되는 것이니까요. 그래서 인간이 관심을 기울이는 한 조수 전력은 무한합니다.

4 여자가 로제타스톤에 대해 말한 것은 무엇인가?
(A) 로제타스톤 자체에 당시 알려진 모든 상형문자의 형태가 나타나 있었다.
(B) 연구원들은 (기존의) 알려진 언어를 이용하여 미지의 언어를 번역할 수 있었다.
(C) 로제타스톤이 발견되기 전에 사람들은 상형문자의 존재조차 알지 못했다.

정답 (A) F (B) T (C) F

해설 Rosetta Stone에는 상형문자를 고대 그리스어로 번역해놓은 것이 있어서, 이를 통해 상형문자를 최초로 해독할 수 있게 되었다.

🎧 스크립트

S1 When the professor said she'll talk about the Rosetta Stone next class, did she mention anything else? Like, why it is important, <u>its historical value</u> or anything like that?
S2 Uh, yeah, she <u>made a short comment</u> on its importance. That's all. Nothing special.
S1 The importance?
S2 That's, umm, <u>it enabled researchers</u> to finally understand hieroglyphs. They hadn't been able to <u>translate it until the stone was discovered</u>.
S1 How did this stone help them do that?
S2 Luckily, on the stone, there was a translation of the hieroglyphs <u>into ancient Greek</u>. Because they understood ancient Greek, they were able to understand the hieroglyphs.

학생 1 교수님께서 다음 시간에 로제타스톤에 대해 다루겠다고 말씀하셨을 때 그 외에 다른 언급도 하셨니? 이를테면, 로제타스톤이 중요한 이유라든지, 역사적 가치나 그런 것들 말이야.
학생 2 어, 그래, 그 중요성을 간단히 언급하긴 하셨어. 그게 다야. 특별한 건 아니었어.
학생 1 중요성?
학생 2 그게, 그러니까... 로제타스톤으로 인해 연구자들이 마침내 상형문자를 이해할 수 있게 됐대. 로제타스톤이 발견되기 전에는 상형문자를 해석하지 못했었다는군.
학생 1 그 돌이 (상형문자를 해석하는 데) 어떤 역할을 한 거야?
학생 2 운좋게도 그 돌 표면에 상형문자를 고대 그리스어로 해석해놓은 게 있었던 거야. 그 사람들이 고대 그리스 어는 이해했기 때문에, 그 상형문자도 해석할 수 있게 된 거지.

Exercise

1 A - (C) B - (C)
2 A - (B) B - (A)(D)
3 A - (B) B - (C)
4 A - (C) B - (A)(C)

Exercise 1

환경 수업에서의 강의의 일부를 듣고 물음에 답하시오.

🎧 스크립트

P A dam is basically an obstruction intentionally built in a river for a couple of different reasons. OK, sometimes umm… they're constructed to control flooding, sometimes to divert water to irrigate fields on farms… and uh, at other times they're built to produce hydroelectric power — that is, electricity that is generated by water power. Now, these have been around for a long time, but it wasn't until the 1930s that they really began being built on the massive scale that say, the Hoover or Aswan Dams were built on. Until this time, dams had little effect on the rivers. But once huge dams began being built, we've seen a lot of problems that occur alongside the benefits that dams give human societies. One problem is the flooding of large areas of land. For example, in the West African country of Ghana, the Upper Volta River was dammed in the late 1970s in order to generate electricity for the people of the country, as well as to sell to other countries. However, in blocking the river with the dam, a huge lake of water was created. This completely flooded out land that people in the Upper Volta Region had been living and farming on for hundreds, thousands, of years. So, money was brought in by electricity, but the farmers had to move into another place for resettlement. At that time, around 78,000 people emptied their towns and villages.

교수 기본적으로 댐이란 몇 가지 이유 때문에 강에 계획적으로 건설된 장애물입니다. 자, 때때로 음… 댐은 강의 범람을 방지하기 위해, 또 때로는 물길을 돌려 논밭에 물을 대기 위해서도 건설됩니다. 그리고 에, 어떤 경우에는 수력전력 즉, 수력을 이용해 발생시킨 전기를 생산하기 위해서도 세워집니다. 자, 오랜 동안 댐은 이런 식이었습니다. 그러나 1930년대가 되자 Hoover 댐이나 Aswan 댐과 같이 대규모 댐이 축조되기 시작했지요. 이때까지만 해도 댐은 강에 거의 영향을 주지 않았습니다. 그러나 일단 대규모의 댐이 건설되기 시작하면서 인간 사회에 혜택을 줌과 동시에 많은 문제점도 야기한다는 것을 알게 되었습니다. 한 가지 문제점은 대규모 토지의 범람입니다. 예컨대 1970년대 후반 가나의 서아프리카 지역인 Upper Volta River에, 내수용 전력 생산은 물론 국외 전기수출을 위해서 댐이 건설되었습니다. 그런데, 댐으로 강을 막아버리자 거대한 호수가 만들어졌습니다. 이로 인해 Upper Volta River 주민들이 수백, 수천 년 동안 경작을 하면서 살아온 땅이 완전히 침수되었습니다. 전력 생산으로 많은 수익을 창출했지만, 농민들은 새로이 정착할 땅을 찾아 이주해야 했습니다. 당시 78,000여명의 주민이 그들의 마을과 촌락을 떠났습니다.

어휘 obstruction 장애물 intentionally 계획적으로 flooding 범람 divert 전환하다 irrigate (토지에) 물을 대다 hydroelectric 수력 발전의 generate (열, 전기를) 발생시키다 block ~을 막다 resettlement 재정착 flood out ~에 홍수가 나다

A 다음 중 댐 건설의 이점으로 언급되지 <u>않은</u> 것은 무엇인가?
(A) 물을 사용하여 농사에 도움이 될 수 있다.
(B) 전력 판매로 인해 수익이 창출된다.
(C) 댐으로 생성된 호수를 관광산업으로 개발할 수 있다.
(D) 물의 흐름을 통제하여 홍수를 방지한다.

해설 댐을 짓는 목적은, 1)홍수 통제 2)토지 관개용 물 공급 3) 수력 발전이다. (B)는 강의 마지막 부분에 언급(money was brought in by the electricity)되어 있다.

B 대규모 댐 건설로 야기된 문제점은 무엇인가?
(A) 댐 운용에 막대한 자금이 든다.
(B) 대규모 댐 건설로 인해 농부들이 궁핍해졌다.
(C) 어떤 사람들은 (다른 곳을 찾아) 재정착해야 했다.
(D) 대규모 댐을 운용하려면 엄청난 노력과 시간이 요구된다.

해설 대규모 댐이 건설된 후의 문제점은 바로 댐 건설지의 수몰(flooding)이다. 이로 인해, 강의 맨 마지막에 언급했듯이, 해당 지역에 거주하는 주민들은 다시 정착할 곳을 찾아 이사를 가야 했다.

Exercise 2

영어 수업에서의 대화의 일부를 듣고 물음에 답하시오.

🎧 스크립트

P I guess you've had an experience like this… someone is speaking your language, but the words they use and the way they pronounce those words, make it seem like they are speaking another language.

S1 Oh, yes, it doesn't happen often, but sometimes when I talk with one of my club members, who is from another state, I feel that way.

S2 Even in my family gatherings, I notice it frequently. My mother has been living here in New York since her twenties and she's from a small village in a western state. She sounds like a New Yorker, but whenever she talks with her parents, she speaks the way my grandparents do.

P That's a typical case! Then why does this happen? I could say that's, it's because a few words might be peculiar to some region. Yet, uh, for the most part, the structures and the vocabulary are identical to the so-called standard language. We call this variation a dialect.

S How's it different from a separate language? A separate language refers to a branch of the same language, too.

P Good question. To be a separate language, the majority of the words should be different from the standard version. Also, the grammar should be significantly different, such as verb usage, or the syntax—that is the order the words come in a sentence. If these conditions are fulfilled, we truly have a separate language.

교수 아마 여러분은 이런 비슷한 경험을 해 보았을 겁니다. 어떤 사람이 여러분의 모국어로 말하고 있는데 그들이 사용하는 단어들이나 그 단어들을 발음하는 방식이 마치 다른 언어를 구사하고 있다는 느낌을 주는 경우 말입니다.

학생 1 아, 그래요. 자주는 아니지만, 가끔 저희 동아리 회원 한 명과 이야기를 하고 있을 때, 음, 그 사람은 다른 주에서 왔거든요. 그 때 그런 걸 느꼈어요.

학생 2 심지어 저희 가족 모임에서도 자주 그런 느낌이 들어요. 저의 어머니께서는 20대 이후로 뉴욕에서 살고 계시지만, 서부 어느 한 주(州)의 작은 마을 출신이세요. 어머니는 (평상시에는) 뉴욕 사람처럼 말씀하시는데 외할머니 외할아버지와 말씀을 나누실 때면 그 분들과 같은 억양으로 말씀하세요.

교수 그게 바로 전형적인 경우에 해당합니다. 그렇다면, 왜 이런 일이 발생할까요? 아마 그건, 몇몇 단어들이 어떤 특정 지역에서만 사용되는 특이한 것이기 때문이라고 할 수 있어요. 그러나, 에, 대부분의 경우 언어 구조나 어휘는 소위 말하는 표준어와 동일하죠. 우리는 이러한 변이를 방언이라고 합니다.

학생 1 그건 분리 언어(separate language)와 어떤 점에서 다른 가요? 분리 언어(separate language)도 같은 언어 내에 속하는 한 어파(語派)를 의미하잖습니까?

교수 좋은 지적입니다. 분리 언어가 되기 위해서는 어휘의 대부분이 표준어의 어휘와 달라야 합니다. 또한 문법, 다시 말해 동사 용법이나, 문장 내에서 단어가 위치하는 순서를 의미하는 통사 같은 것들이 현격히 달라야 하죠. 이러한 조건이 충족될 때라야, 진정한 분리 언어라고 할 수 있습니다.

어휘 pronounce 발음하다 New Yorker 뉴욕 주(미 북동부) 사람 region 지역, 범위 identical 동일한, 똑같은 so-called 이른바, 소위 variation 변화, 변동 usage 언어 용법, 어법; 사용법 syntax 구문론, 문장론 fulfill 충족시키다 peculiar to (~에게) 독특한, 고유한

A 교수가 방언의 어휘에 관해 말한 것은 무엇인가?
(A) 표준어와 완전히 다르다.
(B) 지역마다 조금씩 다르다.
(C) 방언으로 말한 것은 언제나 이해하기 쉽다.
(D) 표준어의 어휘와 동일하게 발음된다.

해설 몇몇 단어는 특정 지역에서만 사용하는 것이라 낯설게 들리나 대부분의 경우 표준어와 동일할 때, 그런 말을 방언이라고 한다. (A)는 전혀 별개의 언어를 일컫는다.

B 분리 언어를 구성하는 요소로 언급된 것은 무엇인가? 정답 두 개를 고르시오.
(A) 전혀 다른 어휘
(B) 친숙한 발음
(C) 복잡한 통사
(D) 상이한 동사 구조

해설 교수는 마지막에 "To be a separate language ~"라며 이 문제에 대한 해답을 제시하고 있다. 발음이나 구문론의 복잡함은 문제가 되지 않는다.

Exercise 3

두 학생의 대화의 일부를 듣고 물음에 답하시오.

 스크립트

S1 Hello Ted, you skipped class the other day. I was wondering if there was something wrong with you.

S2 I really wanted to get some sleep that morning 'cause I stayed overnight two days in a row at the lab. I had to wrap up the project with some graduate students. Anyway, what did I miss in the last class?

S1 We talked a lot about the role of the mind in affecting the body.

S2 Like sound mind leads to a sound body?

S1 Well... not in that way. One thing we looked at was the placebo effect.

S2 What is that?

S1 You know, a placebo is a sugar pill or something without medicine in it.

S2 A sugar pill?

S1 Well, um... actually there's more than that. The other important thing about placebos is how they work in the pill-taker's mind. You see, they think that placebos really contain medication, not just sugar.

S2 So, what's the role of the mind's relation to the pill? And what's the placebo effect exactly?

S1 What they found out after all, through a

series of experiments, is many people's bodies respond to the placebo, as though it really does contain medicine. If they think that they are getting medicine, they even get better.

S2 That's amazing! It's just another example of the mind having powers we barely understand, I think.

학생 1 안녕 Ted. 너 저번에 수업 빠졌었지. 너한테 나쁜 일이 생긴 게 아닐까 걱정했어.
학생 2 실험실에서 연이어 이틀 동안이나 밤을 샜더니 그날 아침에는 정말 잠을 더 자고 싶더라고. 대학원생들 몇 명과 마무리해야 할 프로젝트가 있었거든. 어쨌든 지난번 수업에서 내가 못 듣고 놓친 게 뭐지?
학생 1 신체에 영향을 미치는 정신의 역할에 대해 많이 얘기했어.
학생 2 건강한 정신이 건강한 육체를 만든다는 그런 것?
학생 1 음... 그건 아니고. 우리가 살펴본 건 플라시보 효과였어.
학생 2 그게 뭔데?
학생 1 알다시피 플라시보는 의약 성분이 첨가되지 않은 알약 형태의 설탕 같은 거잖아.
학생 2 알약 형태의 설탕?
학생 1 그러니까, 음... 실제로는 그 이상이지. 플라시보에 대해 또 한 가지 중요한 점은 그것이 복용한 사람의 마음에 어떤 식으로 영향을 미치는가 하는 점이야. 알다시피 이 설탕 알약을 복용한 사람들은 플라시보가 단순한 설탕이 아니라 실제로 의약 성분을 함유하고 있다고 믿거든.
학생 2 그래서 그 약에 대한 마음의 역할이 뭐야? 그리고 플라시보 효과라는 게 정확히 뭐야?
학생 1 일련의 실험을 통해 최종적으로 알아낸 바는, 플라시보가 마치 실제로 의약 성분을 함유한 것처럼 많은 사람들이 반응을 한다는 거야. 자신들이 약을 복용하고 있다고 믿으면 실제로 효과를 본다는 거지.
학생 2 그저 정말 놀라운데. 우리는 좀처럼 이해하기 어렵지만 마음이 힘을 갖고 있다는 걸 보여 주는 또 하나의 실례인 것 같아.

어휘 medication 투약, 약물 치료 barely 간신히, 겨우, 가까스로 stay overnight 밤을 새다 in a row 연속적으로 wrap up (숙제 등을) 다하다 respond to ~에 반응하다, 응하다

A 대화에 따르면, 플라시보가 의미하는 것은 무엇인가?
 (A) 정신적으로 익숙하지 않은 약의 한 종류
 (B) 실제 의약 성분을 포함하지 않은 알약
 (C) 정신 치료를 유발하는 사고 방식
 (D) 정신이 육체를 치유한다는 주장을 담은 이론

해설 약을 복용하는 사람들은 그 약에 치료에 도움이 될 만한 성분이 들어있을 거라고 믿지만 실제로는 그저 '약인 것처럼' 보이는 물질이다.

B 플라시보 효과를 초래하는 것은 무엇인가?
 (A) 의사가 비밀리에 환자에게 약을 처방한다.
 (B) 환자들이 실제로는 아프지 않다는 사실을 깨닫는다.
 (C) (환자들이) 속아서 그 알약을 진짜 약이라고 믿게 된다.
 (D) 의사가 환자의 증상을 오진한다.

해설 Placebo Effect의 가장 큰 특징은 사람들로 하여금 스스로 좋다고 믿게끔 하는 데 있다.

Exercise 4
두 학생의 대화의 일부를 듣고 물음에 답하시오.

 스크립트

S1 What's your paper about, Allie?
S2 I'm writing about the transformation of European painting in the early Renaissance, from really flat figures to more realistic ones.
S1 Are you going to talk about Hockney's theory?
S2 Actually, I don't know about that. What is it?
S1 Hockney says that the great masters of those days actually used a camera obscura to help them create more realistic figures.
S2 I think I can add his theory in my paper. Please tell me more about it.
S1 Well, Hockney, who's a painter himself, claims that there's all kinds of evidence to show that these painters used a camera obscura.
S2 A camera obscura? How does it work?
S1 Simple. It's like this. Cover the windows of your bedroom so it's totally dark. Then make a small hole in the cover. A ray of light through the hole makes an image on the opposite wall, that is to say, you'll see a full-color image of what's outside, except the image is upside-down and opposite like a mirror image.
S2 That's cool! How did he figure out that painters used the camera obscura?
S1 Because so many of the subjects in the paintings were left-handed, the change was sudden, and not everything was in focus. Hockney felt like he had good reason to think a projection device was used.

학생 1 Allie, 너의 과제 주제는 뭐니?
학생 2 초기 르네상스 시대의 유럽 회화의 변천에 대해 쓰고 있어. 아주 단순한 인물상에서 좀 더 사실적인 인물상으로 변화한 것에 대해서 말이야.
학생 1 Hockney의 이론에 대해 다루려는 거니?
학생 2 사실, 그에 대해서는 잘 몰라. 그게 뭔데?
학생 1 Hockney는 당대의 위대한 예술가들이 보다 사실적인 인물

을 창조해내기 위해 사실은 카메라 옵스큐라를 이용했다고 주장하고 있어.

학생 2 내 과제에 그의 이론을 덧붙일 수 있을 것 같다. 좀 더 자세히 설명해 봐.

학생 1 음, Hockney 자신도 화가인데, 그는 그 당시 예술가들이 카메라 옵스큐라를 이용했음을 입증하는 증거가 다수 존재한다고 주장해.

학생 2 카메라 옵스큐라? 어떻게 작동하는 건데?

학생 1 간단해. 이런 거지. 방이 완전히 어둠에 잠기도록 침실의 창문을 모두 가리는 거야. 그런 다음에 그 가리개에 작은 구멍을 내. 그러면 구멍을 통해 광선이 들어오면서 반대편 벽에 이미지를 만들게 되지. 즉 너는 외부에 있는 천연색 이미지를 (그 벽에 비친 빛을 통해) 볼 수 있게 되는 거야. 단, 그 이미지들은 거울에 생긴 상처럼 상하가 뒤집혀 있고, 좌우도 바뀌어 있지. 그것만 제외한다면 밖의 실제 이미지와 동일해.

학생 2 멋진걸. 그는 화가들이 카메라 옵스큐라를 이용했다는 걸 어떻게 알아낸 거야?

학생 1 그림의 많은 제재들이 좌우가 바뀌어 있는데다 그러한 변화도 급격하고 작품에 쓰인 소재가 모두 초점이 맞춰져 있지도 않았거든. 그래서 Hockney는 프로젝션 장치가 사용되었다고 추론하게 된 거지.

어휘 transformation 변형, 변모 Renaissance 르네상스 flat (색조·명암이) 단조로운 realistic 실제적인, 현실적인 opposite 반대편의, 맞은 편의 projection 영상, 영사 device 장치, 고안품 figure out ~을 알아내다

A 남자가 카메라 옵스큐라에 관해 말한 것은 무엇인가?
(A) 예술가로서 Hockney의 야망이 카메라 옵스큐라의 개발로 이어졌다.
(B) 주류 예술가들은 Hockney가 카메라 옵스큐라를 사용했음을 입증했다.
(C) 카메라 옵스큐라는 보다 사실적인 회화 작품을 그리는 데 기여했다.
(D) 몇몇 사진작가들이 새로운 예술 양식을 시도하기 위해 카메라 옵스큐라를 사용했다.

해설 화가 Hockeny는 르네상스 시기의 대가들이 보다 사실적인 그림을 그리기 위해 카메라 옵스큐라를 사용했다는 이론을 펼쳤다.

B 화가들이 카메라 옵스큐라를 사용했다는 증거로 언급된 것은 무엇인가? 정답 두 개를 고르시오.
(A) (그림속) 인물들이 왼손잡이다.
(B) 그림의 변형이 미세했다.
(C) 몇몇 소재는 초점이 맞지 않았다.
(D) 문서로 된 증거자료가 존재했다.

해설 left-handed와 not everything was in focus가 해답이 된다.

Dictation — Exercise

Exercise 1

① an obstruction intentionally built in
② control flooding
③ divert water to irrigate fields on farms
④ generated by water power
⑤ it wasn't until the 1930s
⑥ on the massive scale
⑦ once huge dams began being built
⑧ alongside the benefits
⑨ the flooding of large areas of land
⑩ as well as to sell to
⑪ in blocking the river with the dam
⑫ had been living and farming on
⑬ money was brought in
⑭ had to move into another place
⑮ emptied their towns and villages

Exercise 2

① the way they pronounce those words
② it doesn't happen often
③ has been living here in
④ She sounds like a New Yorker
⑤ speaks the way my grandparents do
⑥ a few words might be peculiar to some region
⑦ are identical to
⑧ this variation a dialect
⑨ refers to a branch of the same language
⑩ the majority of the words
⑪ verb usage
⑫ the syntax
⑬ the order the words come in a sentence

Exercise 3

① skipped class
② I stayed overnight
③ in a row at the lab
④ wrap up the project
⑤ the role of the mind
⑥ sound mind leads to a sound body
⑦ without medicine in it
⑧ how they work in the pill-taker's mind

⑨ the role of the mind's relation to the pill
⑩ through a series of experiments
⑪ it really does contain medicine
⑫ they even get better
⑬ the mind having powers

Exercise 4

① really flat figures
② more realistic ones
③ create more realistic figures
④ add his theory
⑤ these painters used a camera obscura
⑥ so it's totally dark
⑦ A ray of light through the hole
⑧ on the opposite wall
⑨ a full-color image of what's outside
⑩ upside-down
⑪ opposite like a mirror image
⑫ were left handed
⑬ not everything was in focus
⑭ a projection device was used

Actual Test

1 1 - (B) 2 - (A) 3 - (A) 4 - (D)
2 1 - (C) 2 - (B) 3 - (D) 4 - (B)

Actual Test 1
공생에 관한 생물학 수업에서의 토론의 일부를 듣고 물음에 답하시오.

 스크립트

P There's a variety of ways for organisms to interact in an environment. One common way is called symbiosis. This means that one organism interacts with another organism and that they live together for survival. The question I'd like to discuss now is whether symbiotic relationships are beneficial or harmful for participants.

S1 Symbiotic relationships can be harmful rather than beneficial. I'm talking about parasites. For instance, a tapeworm lives inside the intestines of another animal, uh, to survive, and it eats all of the food that the other animal takes in. So what happens to the other animal? It's likely to die of malnutrition.

S2 Not all symbiotic relationships are harmful. Some are neutral; they neither hurt nor harm the organism. And some are beneficial.

P Yeah, right. Can you give me an example of beneficial symbiosis?

S2 Umm... we can look at the example of the cattle egret and the cow. Cows are covered with small insects, downright annoying. If they transmit disease, potentially, the cow could die, or at least get really sick. The egret, a uh... small bird, living on the back of the cow, eats the insects and well, this keeps the cow healthy. The egret needs the cow to survive, but both organisms benefit from the relationship.

P Another example is the goby fish and the shrimp. The goby fish sometimes lives together with a shrimp. The shrimp, almost blind, is vulnerable to predators when above the ground, digs a burrow in which it lives with the goby fish. In case of danger, the goby fish touches the shrimp with its tail to warn it of danger. When that happens, they both quickly retreat into the burrow. That's what we call mutualism, a form of symbiosis.

교수 유기체는 환경 내에서 다양한 방식으로 상호작용을 합니다. 흔한 방식 중 하나는 공생이라 일컬어지는데, 이것은 하나의 유기체가 다른 유기체와 상호작용하면서 생존을 위해 함께 살아가는 것을 의미합니다. 이제 토의하려는 문제는 이런 공생 관계가 이로운 것인지, 아니면 관련 생물에게 해로운 것인지에 관한 겁니다.

학생 1 공생 관계는 이로운 것이기 보다는 해로울 수 있습니다. 기생 생물을 얘기해 보겠습니다. 예를 들어 촌충은 어, 생존을 위해 다른 동물의 장 속에 기생하면서 그 동물이 섭취하는 모든 양분을 먹습니다. 그러면 그 동물에게는 어떤 일이 벌어질까요? 영양실조로 죽게 될 겁니다.

학생 2 모든 공생 관계가 해로운 성질을 띠지는 않아요. 어떤 것은 중립적이고요. 그러니까 그들은 유기체를 해하거나 피해를 끼치지 않습니다. 또 어떤 것들은 이롭기도 하죠.

교수 네, 맞아요. 유익한 관계를 맺는 공생의 예를 들어보겠어요?

학생 2 음... 황로와 젖소의 예를 들 수 있겠습니다. 작은 곤충들이 젖소를 에워싸고 있는데, 아주 성가신 일이지요. 만약 이 곤충들이 질병을 옮긴다면, 어쩌면 젖소는 죽을 수도 있습니다. 아니면 적어도 심각한 병에 걸릴 수가 있습니다. 황로는, 음, 작은 새인데요, 젖소의 등에 살면서 그 곤충들을 먹습니다. 그래서 젖소가 건강을 유지할 수 있습니다. 황로는 생존하기 위해 젖소를 필요로 하지만, 두 유기체 모두 이 관계를 통해 이득을 보게 되는 거죠.

교수 또 하나의 예로 망둥이와 새우를 들어보죠. 망둥이는 종종 새우와 살아갑니다. 시력이 상당히 약한 새우는 물이 얕은 곳으로 올라오면 침입자에게 쉽게 공격을 받기 때문에 굴을 파고 거기서 망둥이와 함께 살지요. 위험이 닥칠 경우 망둥이가 새우의 꼬리를 건드려 위험을 알립니다. 그래서 위험이 발생하면 둘은 신속히 땅굴 속으로 함께 피신합니다. 이런 것이 공생의 한 형태인 상리공생입니다.

1 토론에 따르면, 공생이란 무엇인가?
(A) 자연 환경에서 발생하는 위험한 상황
(B) 두 유기체 사이의 상호 의존 관계
(C) 기생으로 인한 결과의 한 예
(D) 동물과 환경의 상호 관계

해설 Symbiosis(공생)란 하나의 유기체가 다른 유기체에 기대어 생존하는 것을 가리킨다.

2 화자의 한 사람이 기생 생물에 대해 말한 것은 무엇인가?
(A) 공생의 부정적인 형태의 실례이다.
(B) 숙주 생물에 거의 영향을 미치지 않는다.
(C) 기생 생물이 숙주 생물로부터 어떻게 이익을 취하는지 불분명하다.
(D) 숙주 생물의 생존에 필요한 영양분을 제공한다.

해설 Parasites의 한 예로 든 tapeworm은 다른 동물의 창자에 기생하며 그 영양분을 빼앗아 먹는다. 때문에 정작 그 동물은 영양 결핍에 시달린다. 한 쪽이 이득을 얻음으로써 다른 한 쪽이 손해를 보는 관계이다.

3 황로와 젖소의 관계는 어떠한 특징을 갖는가?
(A) 양쪽 유기체 모두에게 이로움
(B) 양쪽 유기체 모두에게 이롭지도 해롭지도 않음
(C) 한 유기체는 이익을 얻고, 다른 유기체는 피해를 입음
(D) 한 유기체는 이익을 얻고, 다른 유기체에게는 영향을 주지 않음

해설 황로는 젖소의 몸에 붙어있는 곤충을 잡아먹음으로써 영양을 섭취하고 젖소를 질병이나 죽음으로부터 구한다.

4 망둥이는 새우의 생존에 어떻게 도움을 주는가?
(A) 새우를 위해 굴을 깊게 판다.
(B) 건강을 유지할 수 있도록 새우에게 먹이를 제공한다.
(C) 새우를 대신하여 포식자와 싸운다.
(D) 새우가 포식자로부터 피신할 수 있도록 경고 신호를 보낸다.

해설 망둥이는 거의 앞이 안 보이는 새우가 파 놓은 굴에 함께 살면서, 침입자가 있을 때에는 새우의 꼬리를 만져 위험을 알린 다음, 함께 굴로 피신한다. (B)와 (C)는 언급된 바가 없다.

Actual Test 2

교수와 학생의 대화의 일부를 듣고 물음에 답하시오.

🎧 스크립트

S Professor, I have a question.
P Sure. Go on.
S Well, I think electroshock treatment is really barbaric and ineffective, but it is still being used in psychiatry, right?
P Yes, that's true. Though at first it seemed to do a good job at curing people of mental disorders like severe depression and schizophrenia, there were many, many complaints about it as well. Especially when it was first used, treatment was performed without the use of anesthesia or muscle relaxants. It was painful and scary for people. Later, when effective medication for major mental disorders was developed a half-century ago, the need for the electroshock treatment lessened.
S So why would psychiatrists start using it again?
P Well, one of the things that we've found is that the medications that replaced shock treatment didn't work for everybody. In some cases, shock treatment really was much more effective for a serious problem like schizophrenia.
S Even though it is a horrible experience?
P Well, these days, it isn't nearly so bad. The patients are medicated before treatment and treated much better than they were in the early days of this treatment. But still, as you mentioned, electroshock treatment generates debate in both psychology and among the general public.

학생 교수님, 질문이 하나 있습니다.
교수 그래요. 해 보세요.
학생 저, 제가 생각하기에 전기충격 요법은 정말 야만적이고 비효과적인 것 같은데 정신병리학에서는 여전히 사용되고 있지 않습니까?
교수 네, 사실입니다. 초기에는 심각한 우울증이나 정신분열증과 같은 정신장애 환자들을 치료하는 데 효과가 있는 것 같았지만, 그에 대한 불만도 상당했습니다. 특히 처음 이 치료법이 사용되었을 때는 마취제나 근육 이완제 없이 시술되었는데, 이는 사람들에게 아주 고통스럽고 두려운 일이었지요. 이후, 그러니까 50년 전에 대표적인 정신장애 치료에 효과적인 약품이 개발되자 전기충격 요법에 대한 필요가 줄어들었습니다.
학생 그러면 왜 정신과 의사들이 다시 이 치료법을 사용하기 시작한 건가요?
교수 음, 그 한 가지 이유는 이 전기충격 요법을 대체했던 의학 치료법이 모든 사람들에게 효능을 보이는 게 아님을 알게 되었기 때문이죠. 어떤 경우에는, 정신분열증 같은 심각한 문제일 때 충격 요법이 훨씬 더 효과적이었으니까요.

학생 끔찍한 경험인데도 말입니까?
교수 음, 요즘은 그다지 심하지가 않습니다. 환자는 시술 전에 약물 치료를 받는데다 초기의 시술에 비해 훨씬 더 나아진 치료법이 사용되니까요. 그러나 학생이 말했다시피 전기충격요법은 정신과 의료진과 일반 대중 사이에 여전히 논란을 불러일으키고 있습니다.

1 학생이 알고 싶어 하는 것은 무엇인가?
(A) 어제 교수가 강의에서 다뤘던 것
(B) 전기충격 요법의 정의
(C) (전기) 충격 요법 사용이 다시 활성화된 이유
(D) (전기) 충격 요법에 대한 교수의 견해

해설 학생은 전기 충격 요법을 야만적이고 비효율적인 치료법이라고 생각한다. 폐지되었다가 다시 부활된 이유를 묻고 있다.

2 전기 충격 요법의 시술이 중단된 이유가 <u>아닌</u> 것은 무엇인가?
(A) 환자들에게 부정적 경험이었다.
(B) 모든 환자에게 효과는 있었지만 너무 비쌌다.
(C) 약이 더 효과가 있는 것으로 보였다.
(D) 야만적인데다 비효과적으로 보였다.

해설 전기 충격 요법에 대한 몇 가지 불만이 있었고, 당시 새로운 약물 치료법이 개발되었다.

3 전기충격 요법이 다시 활성화된 이유는 무엇인가?
(A) 정신장애 치료약품에 독성물질이 함유되어 있었다.
(B) 정신장애 환자들이 (전기충격 요법을) 다시 활성화할 것을 요구했다.
(C) 의사들이 생각할 수 있는 유일한 방안이었다.
(D) 의약품이 효과가 나타나지 않을 때 전기 충격 요법은 효과가 있었다.

해설 정신분열증에는 전기충격이 더 효과적이었다.

4 교수의 말에 따르면, 현대의 전기충격요법이 과거의 전기충격 요법과 다른 점은 무엇인가?
(A) 환자가 받는 고통은 더 심하지만 효과는 더 크다
(B) 보다 인도적인 방식으로 시술된다.
(C) 현대의 전기치료법에 사용되는 전력이 적다.
(D) 정신과 의사들은 일부 환자들에게 있어 신(新) 기술이 과거의 치료법만큼 효과적이지 않음을 밝혔다.

해설 교수는 "these days, it isn't nearly so bad."라며 예전만큼 고통스럽거나 야만적이지 않다고 말한다. 또한 치료가 시작되기 전에 약물을 투여함으로써 고통을 덜 느낀다는 것을 암시한다.

Dictation — Actual Test

Actual Test 1

① for organisms to interact
② live together for survival
③ are beneficial
④ can be harmful
⑤ it eats all of the food
⑥ It's likely to die of
⑦ Some are neutral
⑧ neither hurt nor harm
⑨ some are beneficial
⑩ downright annoying
⑪ living on the back of the cow
⑫ is vulnerable to predators
⑬ digs a burrow
⑭ with its tail to warn it of danger
⑮ both quickly retreat into the burrow

Actual Test 2

① electroshock treatment
② barbaric and ineffective
③ curing people of mental disorders
④ severe depression
⑤ many complaints about it as well
⑥ painful and scary for
⑦ for major mental disorders
⑧ the need for
⑨ lessened
⑩ the medications that replaced shock treatment
⑪ for a serious problem
⑫ The patients are medicated
⑬ they were in the early days of this treatment
⑭ generates debate

Vocabulary Review

다음 각 정의와 일치하는 단어를 골라 써 넣으시오.

1 experiment   2 theory   3 divert
4 interact   5 generate   6 medication
7 pill   8 transformation 9 organism
10 hydroelectric

1 어떤 것에 대한 과학적 실험
2 어떤 것을 설명하는 개념
3 처음 의도했던 것과는 다른 길로 가게 하다
4 서로의 행동 또는 상태에 영향을 미치는 다른 두 가지
5 에너지나 전력을 생산하다
6 질병의 증상을 치료하거나 질병을 예방하는 데 사용되는 약
7 씹지 않고 삼키는 약
8 어떤 것이 다른 것으로 변화하거나 바뀌게 하는 것

9 독립적으로 기능할 수 있는 능력을 가진 생물
10 흐르는 물의 에너지를 사용하여 전력을 생산하는 것과 관련한, 혹은 전력 생산에 사용된

다음 구문을 사용하여 문장을 완성하시오.

1 In general   2 responded to   3 identical to
4 peculiar to   5 effect on

1 일반적으로 심장마비로 고통을 받는 사람들은 과체중이다.
2 예상 외로 그녀는 그의 말에 민감하게 대꾸했다.
3 한국 브랜드와 거의 유사하게 만들어진 일부 중국 제품들이 대중의 비난을 받고 있다.
4 한복은 한국 고유의 문화이다.
5 사람들은 영화가 아이들에게 긍정적으로나 부정적으로 영향을 미친다고 믿는다.

Progress Test

1 1-(A) 2-(B) 3-(C) 4-(B)(D) 5-(C)
2 1-(B) 2-(C) 3-(C) 4-(B)   5-(A)

Progress Test 1
의학 수업 강의의 일부를 듣고 물음에 답하시오.

🎧 스크립트

P Over the last few classes, we've discussed how western medicine has attempted to bring eastern medicine teachings into its practice. Western practitioners have made efforts to incorporate two of the world's major medical schools of thought. What I'd like to look at today is a recent study of eastern medicine that uh, basically... shows that acupressure and exercise can help old people remain healthy. Now, acupressure, a therapy, claims that various, distant, and seemingly unrelated parts of the body are connected. It involves placing physical pressure on different pressure points on the surface of the body, by hand, with the elbow, or with the aid of various devices. Thus, acupressurists will stimulate part of the foot in order to treat a headache and so on. Now, interestingly, a study looked at the Chinese practice of older people walking on cobblestone streets for exercise. Cobblestones are those rounded rocks and used for paving streets, right? Not only does the practice exercise the body, but the pressure of the cobblestones on the feet seems to benefit overall health. The effect of walking on cobblestones was verified by the study. It monitored a group of 60 older people who just walked for an hour a day three days a week, while another group walked just half an hour three days a week but on cobblestones. The results were pretty fantastic. In the cobblestone walking group, people's blood pressure dropped significantly and their balance improved markedly. However, the regular walking group didn't see these benefits at all.

교수 지난 몇 차례의 수업을 통해 우리는 서양 의학계가 어떤 방식으로 동양 의학 교수법을 접목시키려 했는지에 대해 논의했습니다. 서양의 의학자들은 이 세계 주요 두 의학계의 사상을 통합하고자 노력했습니다. 오늘 살펴보고자 하는 것은 최근에 이뤄진 동양 의학에 관한 연구입니다. 에, 기본적으로, 이 연구에서는 지압과 운동이 노인들의 건강 유지에 도움이 된다는 것을 보여주고 있습니다. 자, 지압이란 하나의 치료법으로서 멀리 떨어져서 서로 관계가 없어 보이는 인체의 각 부분들이 사실은 서로 연결되어 있다고 주장하는 이론입니다. 지압이란 손이나 팔꿈치, 또는 그 밖의 여러 보조 기구들을 이용해 신체 표면의 특정 지압 지점에 물리적 압력을 가하는 것입니다. 그래서 침술사들은 두통 같은 질병을 치료하기 위해 발의 특정 부위를 자극하지요. 자, 흥미롭게도 운동 삼아 자갈길을 걸어 다니는 노인들을 상대로 한 중국의 의술에 관한 연구가 있었습니다. 자갈은 표면이 둥근 돌로써 포장도로를 만드는 데 사용하는 겁니다, 그렇죠? 그런데 이것이 신체 운동이 될 뿐 아니라 발에 가해지는 자갈의 압력이 건강 전반에 이득이 되는 것 같습니다. 자갈길 걷기의 효과는 연구를 통해 확실하게 입증되었습니다. 일주일에 삼 일, 하루 한 시간 동안 걷기 운동을 했던 60세 이상의 노인 그룹과, 일주일에 삼 일, 하루 30분씩 자갈길 걷기 운동을 실행했던 노인 그룹을 대조하여 실험하였는데, 그 결과는 상당히 놀라웠습니다. 자갈길을 걸었던 그룹에 속한 노인들의 혈압이 현격히 떨어졌고, 그들의 균형감 또한 뚜렷하게 향상되었습니다. 그러나 일반적인 걷기 운동을 했던 그룹은 이런 효과를 전혀 보이지 않았습니다.

1 이 강의의 주제는 무엇인가?
(A) 자갈길 걷기의 장점을 입증하는 최근 연구
(B) 운동과 지압술을 접목하려는 서양 의학의 시도
(C) 중국 노인과 서양 노인의 건강 상태 비교
(D) 고혈압을 운동으로 낮출 수 있는 방법

해설 중국 의술의 하나인 지압이 운동과 접목될 때 구체적으로 어떤 효과가 나타났는지에 대한 연구 결과를 보여 주고 있다.

2 교수의 말에 따르면, 지압이란 무엇인가?
(A) 중국에서 흔히 사용되는 약의 한 종류
(B) 별개의 신체 부분들이 서로 연결되어 있다는 가설에 기초한 치료법

(C) 노인들의 건강 불균형을 초래하는 원인
(D) 심장 마비 증세로 고통 받는 사람들에게 추천하는 운동의 한 유형

해설 지압사들은 두통 같은 증세를 치료하기 위해 (머리에 직접적인 치료를 하는 게 아니라) 발의 특정 부위를 지압했다. 이는 우리 몸의 각 부분들이 발과 연결되어 있다는 가정 하에서 행해지는 일이다.

3 교수의 말에 따르면, 자갈은 무엇인가?
(A) 지압에 사용된 약의 한 종류
(B) 연구에 등장하는 그룹을 일컫는 의학 용어
(C) 도로 포장에 사용되는 일종의 둥근 돌
(D) 고혈압 치료를 위해 사용되는 방법

해설 지압의 효과를 높이기 위해 사용된 도구의 일종이지 약물은 아니다.

4 다음 중 이 연구에 등장하는 두 그룹에 관해 교수가 언급하지 않은 것은 무엇인가? 정답 두 개를 고르시오.
(A) 거의 같은 연령대이다.
(B) 동일한 표면의 길을 걸었다.
(C) 주당 삼 회 운동을 했다.
(D) 건강상의 균형이 향상되었다.

해설 60대의 노인들로 구성되었으며, 일주일에 세 번, 특정 시간만큼(각 30분, 1시간) 걷도록 했다.

5 자갈길을 걸었던 그룹에 대한 연구 결과는 무엇인가?
(A) 보행자의 체중 감량을 유발했다.
(B) 보행자의 정서 안정을 향상시켰다.
(C) 혈압을 낮추는 데 도움이 되었다.
(D) 건강 전반에 대한 의식을 형성했다.

해설 운동 시간은 적으나(30분) 자갈 위에서 걷기를 한 노인들만 혈압이 떨어지는 효과를 보았다.

Progress Test 2

두 학생의 대화의 일부를 듣고 물음에 답하시오.

 스크립트

S1 I can't believe they're raising tuition again. I don't know how I'm going to afford it.
S2 Well, I got a job through campus employment services. It's only part-time, but it'll cover the cost of textbooks and even offset the cost of tuition a bit. It's actually not a bad job, either.
S1 So, it's like an on-campus job or something? Like working in the library? Those jobs are so boring.
S2 No, actually, private employers in town list their job openings with campus employment services. So, there are a lot of different choices. I'm running errands for a group of lawyers downtown.
S1 Cool. That'll come in handy when you apply to law school. I wonder if there are any finance-related jobs... that'd be really good for my résumé... I'm graduating soon.
S2 Well, you should just go to the office and check it out. It's open during normal business hours... all you have to do is go in and ask for the off-campus jobs binder. They list the openings by field.
S1 It's that simple, huh? Well, in addition to providing some extra cash, it'd make my parents happy. They've been bugging me to get a part-time job for months.
S2 It really does help you out when you graduate to have some experience.

학생 1 수업료를 또 올린다니 말도 안 돼. 수업료를 어떻게 마련해야 할지 모르겠네.
학생 2 글쎄, 난 교내 취업알선 서비스를 통해 일자리를 얻었어. 시간제 일이긴 하지만 교재 구입비와 약간의 수업료를 충당할 수 있을 정도는 돼. 사실 업무도 그리 나쁘지는 않고.
학생 1 그러면, 교내 아르바이트 같은 거야? 도서관에서 일하는 것처럼 말이야? 그런 일은 너무 지루해.
학생 2 아냐. 실제 시내의 개인 고용주가 교내 취업알선 서비스를 통해 공석인 일자리를 올려놓거든. 그렇기 때문에 선택할 수 있는 일자리가 많아. 난 시내 (법률회사에서) 변호사들의 업무 보조 일을 하고 있어.
학생 1 괜찮네. 네가 로스쿨에 지원할 때 그 경험이 아주 유용하겠는걸. 거기 뭐 재무 관련 일자리도 있을까? 내 이력에도 꽤 도움이 될 텐데. 나 곧 졸업하잖아.
학생 2 글쎄, 우선 사무실로 가서 확인해 봐. 통상적인 업무 시간대에 열려있거든. 그냥 들어가서 캠퍼스 밖에서 할 수 있는 일자리가 있는지 문의하면 돼. 분야별로 일자리 목록이 있어.
학생 1 아주 간단하네. 음, 돈도 좀 벌 수 있는데다 우리 부모님께서도 좋아하시겠다. 지난 몇 달 동안 우리 부모님은 나더러 아르바이트를 구하라고 타박하셨거든.
학생 2 그런 경험이 졸업할 때 정말 큰 도움이 될 거야.

1 여자가 한 말에 따르면 다음 중 시간제 일자리를 얻는 것에 대해 사실이 <u>아닌</u> 것은 무엇인가?
(A) (남자가) 학비의 일부를 충당할 수 있을 것이다.
(B) 등록금을 벌 수 있을 것이다.
(C) 업무 경험이 (나중에) 일자리를 얻는 데 도움이 될 것이다.
(D) 그가 선택할 수 있는 다양한 일자리가 있다.

해설 등록금의 일부를 충당할 수 있다고 했다.

2 교내 일자리에 대해 남자는 뭐라고 얘기하는가?
(A) 그는 도서관에서 일할 자격이 없다고 생각한다.
(B) 그는 교내에서 제공되는 일자리에 대해 알지 못한다.
(C) 그는 교내 일자리가 흥미롭지 않다고 생각한다.

(D) 그는 교내 일자리가 경력에 도움이 되지 않을 것이라고 생각한다.

해설 도서관 일자리 같은 on-campus job 은 boring 하다고 했다.

3 대화에 따르면, 현재 여자가 일하고 있는 곳은 어디인가?
(A) 교내 도서관
(B) 은행
(C) 법률 회사
(D) 컴퓨터 실습실

해설 여자는 현재 시내에 있는 법률회사에서 변호사들의 업무를 돕고 있다. (B)는 남자가 원하는 일이다.

4 여자의 일자리에 대해 남자는 뭐라고 얘기하는가?
(A) 여자에게는 틀림없이 지루한 일일 거라고 생각한다.
(B) 여자에게 좋은 경험이 될 거라고 생각한다.
(C) 그녀의 직업 목표와 어떻게 관련이 되는지 확신하지 못한다.
(D) 자신이 원하는 일자리를 그녀가 갖게 되어 화가 난다.

해설 여자가 장차 로스쿨에 들어갈 때 유리하게 작용할 것이라고 말했다.

5 다음 중 남자가 재무 분야의 일자리를 찾고 있는 이유로 언급된 것은 무엇인가?
(A) 그는 장래의 구직 활동에 도움이 되리라 믿는다.
(B) 그는 재무를 전공해야 할지 아닐지를 알아보려고 한다.
(C) 그는 대학원 진학을 고려하고 있다.
(D) 그는 그 일자리가 도움이 된다고 생각하지 않는다.

해설 졸업을 하고 직장을 구할 때 도움이 될 것이라고 생각한다.

Dictation — Progress Test

Progress Test 1

① bring eastern medicine teachings into its practice
② a recent study of eastern medicine
③ acupressure and exercise
④ seemingly unrelated parts
⑤ pressure points on the surface of the body
⑥ the aid of various devices
⑦ stimulate part of the foot
⑧ walking on cobblestone streets
⑨ used for paving streets
⑩ the pressure of the cobblestones on the feet
⑪ was verified by the study
⑫ monitored a group of 60 older people
⑬ just half an hour
⑭ cobblestone walking group
⑮ their balance improved markedly

Progress Test 2

① they're raising tuition again
② afford it
③ got a job through
④ it'll cover the cost of
⑤ offset the cost of tuition
⑥ it's like an on-campus job or something
⑦ list their job openings
⑧ I'm running errands for
⑨ any finance-related jobs
⑩ It's open during normal business hours
⑪ ask for the off-campus jobs binder
⑫ They've been bugging me

Vocabulary Review — Progress Test

다음 각 정의와 일치하는 단어를 골라 써 넣으시오.

1 résumé	2 tuition	3 afford
4 incorporate	5 pressure	6 acupressure
7 stimulate	8 offset	9 opening
10 verify		

1 학력 사항이나 경력 사항에 관한 간단한 소개
2 대학이나 전문대학의 수업료로 지불하는 금액
3 어떤 것의 대가로 지불하기에 충분한 돈을 소유하다
4 전체로 만들다
5 어떤 대상을 세게 누를 때 발생하는 힘
6 신체의 특정한 부위를 누름으로써 병을 치료하는 요법
7 반응을 더 이끌어내도록 고무시키다
8 다른 것으로 보상하다
9 취업할 수 있는 좋은 기회
10 어떤 것이 사실임을 확정하다

다음 구문을 사용하여 문장을 완성하시오.

| 1 in order to | 2 into practice | 3 In addition to |
| 4 come in handy | 5 run errands | |

1 내 주치의는 내게 체중을 감량하려면 규칙적으로 조깅을 해야 한다고 권했다.
2 Jim이 그의 아이디어를 실행하자마자 회사가 조금씩 발전하기 시작했다.
3 운동 이외 여러 방식의 식이요법으로도 체중감량이 가능하다.
4 나는 국제적인 근무 환경에서 일을 하고 있어서 여러 언어를 구사할 수 있는 능력이 쓸모가 있다.
5 그녀는 동생에게 간식거리를 사오라고 하든지 이런저런 것들을 가져오라는 심부름을 종종 시킨다.

CHAPTER 03
PROCESS / CLASSIFICATION

Sample

교수 자, 일전에 말했듯이 셀 애니메이션에서의 중요한 포인트는 애니메이팅 작업을 좀 더, 에 효율적으로 진행하는 것이라 볼 수 있습니다. 그러면 애니메이터(만화제작자)들이 이러한 방식을 어떻게 실행할까요? 그들은 셀 애니메이션 작업을 할 때, 별개의 다른 투명 종이 위에 각 캐릭터를 그립니다. 캐릭터마다 별개의 종이를 사용한다는 걸 명심하세요, 알겠지요? 배경도 각각 독립적으로 불투명한 종이 위에 그립니다. 그런 다음, 애니메이션 촬영을 할 때 이 캐릭터를 각 프레임 내에 있는 배경의 표면에 겹치게 놓아둡니다. 이렇게 되면 애니메이터의 작업이 훨씬 수월해집니다.

다음 중 셀 애니메이션의 단계에 속하는 것은 무엇인가? 옳은 것에 체크하시오.

	Yes	No
수석 화가가 프레임(틀)을 그린다.		✓
캐릭터를 투명 종이에 그린다.	✓	
스케치를 컴퓨터로 스캔한다.		✓
배경을 불투명 종이에 그린다.	✓	
캐릭터들을 배경의 가장 윗부분에 놓는다.	✓	

Vocabulary Preview — for Skill Check-up

다음 정의를 듣고 알맞은 단어를 고르시오.

1 scholarship 2 introvert 3 bourgeoisie
4 converge 5 volcano 6 fresco
7 chamber 8 career 9 application
10 doom

1 financial aid provided to students by a college or foundation
   학교나 단체가 학생들에게 제공하는 학자금 보조
2 a quiet, shy person who finds it difficult to talk to people
   사람들과 대화하는 것을 어려워하는 조용하고 부끄러움을 타는 사람
3 the middle-class people who own most of the wealth in a capitalist system
   자본주의 시스템에서 부의 대부분을 차지하는 중산층 사람들
4 come together at a particular place
   특정 장소로 함께 모이다
5 a mountain that emits hot melted rock, gas, steam, and ash from inside
   내부에서 녹은 뜨거운 바위, 가스, 증기 그리고 재를 내뿜는 산
6 a picture that is painted on a plastered wall
   회반죽 벽에 그려진 그림
7 an enclosed space or room for a particular purpose
   특별한 목적을 위해 마련된 닫힌 공간이나 방
8 a particular occupation that you are trained for
   당신이 훈련되어 있는 특정 업무
9 a formal written request for admission or employment
   입회 또는 고용을 요구하는 공식 요청서
10 an unpleasant or disastrous destiny
   불쾌한, 혹은 비참한 운명

다음 단어를 이용하여 아래 문장을 완성하시오.

1 scholarship 2 introvert 3 converge
4 career 5 application 6 authorized
7 transcript 8 challenging 9 commitment
10 ecosystem

1 그의 반 친구 중 한 명이 뛰어난 학업 성적으로 장학금을 받았다.
2 사람들은 보통 내성적인 사람이 수줍음을 많이 탈 것이라 여기지만, 수줍음을 많이 타는 사람들이 모두 다 내성적인 것은 아니다.
3 토론이 진행될수록, 맨 처음에는 회의 참석자 모두의 의견이 불일치하는 것 같았으나, 그들의 의견이 수렴되기 시작했다.
4 그는 성공적인 영화 인생을 마감하며 영화제에서 공로상을 수상하기를 기대했다.
5 나는 신용카드 발급 신청서를 작성했다.
6 미 대통령은 자국 방위를 위해 군을 대동할 수 있는 권한이 있다.
7 학업성적표란 개인의 학업 성과에 대한 전반적인 기록이다.
8 그 영화감독은 또 한 번 자신의 영화에 출연하여 영화 속에서 계속 매력적인 역할을 맡아보고 싶다고 말한다.
9 그 회사는 자사의 혁신, 고품질 제품 생산, 서비스 기준 표준화에 전력을 다했다.
10 이 실험은 지역 해양 생태계에 환경 파괴를 가져왔다.

Skill Check-up — Identifying Process

1 다음 각 구절이 성공적인 사진 찍기 단계로 언급되었으면 Yes, 아니면 No를 쓰시오.

카메라가 본체 내부에 빛을 모은다.	Yes
필름의 결정들이 빛에 반응한다.	Yes
빛의 양을 조절하기 위해 조리개가 열린다.	No

해설 사진을 찍는다는 것은 1) 빛의 양을 조절하여, 2) 렌즈가 일부 빛을 필름에 수렴하면, 3) 필름의 작은 알갱이들이 빛과 화학 반응을 일으켜 렌즈 앞의 상을 기록하는 과정이다.
조리개(Aperture)에 대한 언급은 없다.

🎧 스크립트

P To successfully <u>record a photographic image</u>, first... light has to be <u>blocked in all but one place</u> by the camera body. This is called the trapping stage. Then, in convergence, <u>the lens causes these light rays</u> to slow and bend, then <u>converge on the film</u>.

Finally, in registration, tiny, light-sensitive grains on the film <u>react chemically to the light</u> and record the image in front of the camera lens.

교수 사진의 상을 성공적으로 기록하기 위해서는 우선, 카메라 본체의 한 부분을 제외한 모든 부분에 빛을 차단시켜야 합니다. 이것을 트래핑 단계라고 합니다. 다음 작업은 빛을 수렴하는 일인데, 렌즈가 광선의 속도를 늦춰서 굴절시킨 후, 필름 위 한 점에 광선이 모아지도록 합니다. 마지막 단계는 기록하는(찍는) 것입니다. 필름의 작고도 빛에 민감한 알갱이들이 빛에 화학 반응을 일으키면서 카메라 렌즈의 정면에 비치는 상을 기록합니다(찍습니다).

2 다음 각 단계가 화산 폭발 과정과 일치하는 것에 체크하시오.

	Yes	No
마그마의 형성	✓	
마그마의 냉각		✓
화구구의 출현	✓	
마그마가 산을 생성함		✓

해설 화산 폭발은 다음의 단계를 거친다. 1) 마그마가 형성되고, 2) 마그마가 지각을 향해 상승하여 3) 마그마 체임버(magma chamber)에 집적되면 4) Volcanic cone(화구구)이 형성되어 5) 결국 폭발을 일으킨다.

🎧 스크립트

P Volcanoes begin underground, then <u>rise up through the crust</u>, finally bursting through the crust. The first stage is birth. <u>Rock from the Earth's interior</u> is made <u>molten or liquid</u> by high temperature. It's called magma. It rises and <u>leaks into the crust</u>. Because it is so hot, it rises easily. Then, comes collection. The magma <u>collects in a magma chamber</u> near the surface of the earth. Often, <u>a volcanic cone</u> will appear on the surface, signaling an imminent eruption. Last, the magma <u>bursts through</u> the surface or the cone, <u>spewing into the air</u>. This is the explosion.

교수 화산은 지구 내부에서 시작하여 지각을 향해 치솟는 다음 마지막으로, 지각을 뚫고 외부로 폭발합니다. 첫 번째 단계는 형성입니다. 지구 내부에 있는 바위가 높은 열로 인해 융해되거나 액체화되는데, 이것을 마그마라고 하죠. 이 마그마가 솟아올라 지각을 통해 지표면으로 새어나옵니다. 온도가 아주 높기 때문에 쉽게 (지각을 향해) 치솟습니다. 그 다음 단계는 집적(Collection)입니다. 마그마는 지표면 가까운 곳에 있는 마그마 체임버에 집적됩니다. 종종 지표면에 화구구가 출현하여 조만간 분출이 일어날 것이라는 신호를 보내기도 하지요. 마지막으로 이 마그마가 지표면 또는 화구구를 통해 공기 중으로 분출되는데, 이것을 폭발이라고 합니다.

3 다음 중 프레스코 화법의 단계에 속하지 <u>않</u>는 것은 무엇인가? 정답 두 개를 고르시오.

벽에 회반죽을 칠한다.	☐
건조된 석고에 그림의 상들을 새긴다.	✓
안료를 물과 혼합한다.	☐
안료를 건조된 회반죽벽에 바른다.	✓

해설 프레스코란 회반죽을 칠한 벽이 채 마르기 전에 안료를 덧붙이는 작업이다.

🎧 스크립트

P Frescoes are, uh, paintings <u>made in wet plaster</u>. How is it done? The painter would <u>mix up his pigments</u>, or colors, with water. And then he'd, he'd <u>apply a coat of plaster on the wall</u>. Then, he would put the pigment on his brush, and, uh, paint it directly on the wet plaster. <u>When the plaster dried</u>, the color would, uh, <u>be locked in there</u>. This is why these paintings have lasted so long.

교수 프레스코 화법이란, 에, 젖은 회반죽에 그려진 그림을 말합니다. 어떻게 그리느냐 하면, 화가가 안료, 그러니까 그림물감을 물과 혼합합니다. 그러고 나면 화가는 벽 표면에 한 층의 회반죽을 칠합니다. 그런 다음 붓에 물감을 묻혀서 젖은 회반죽 위에 바로 그립니다. 이 회반죽이 건조되면, 그림물감이, 그러니까 에, 회반죽에 그대로 보존되는 겁니다. 프레스코 기법으로 그려진 그림들이 오래도록 보존되는 이유도 여기에 있습니다.

4 다음 중 장학금을 타는 단계로 언급된 것은 Yes, 그렇지 않은 것은 No라고 쓰시오.

부모가 지출한 돈의 양을 입증하라.	No
장학재단 직원과 인터뷰하라.	Yes
회계 사무실에서 장학금을 수령하라.	Yes
장학재단에 성적증명서를 보내라.	No

해설 Needs-based scholarship 을 수령하려면 1) 신청서를 작성하여 2) 부모님의 2년간 세금 증명서를 수령한 후 3) 인터뷰를 거쳐 4) (자격 요건이 증명되면) 장학금을 받는다.
부모의 소비에 관한 언급은 없으며, 성적 증명은 Academic scholarship 을 원할 때 필요한 서류이다.

🎧 스크립트

S1 John, did you have to <u>send in</u> your high school transcripts <u>to get the financial aid</u>?
S2 <u>That's only if</u> you're applying for an academic scholarship. What I have, a <u>needs-based</u> scholarship is more, uh, well... <u>it's like a grant</u>.
S1 Yeah? How do you apply?
S2 Well, first drop by Financial Aid and <u>pick up an application</u>.

S1 I can do that online, right?
S2 For the initial application, no — it's hard copy only. So you fill that in. Oh, and ask your parents for their tax forms for the last two years. The school needs to know how much money they made. Then send it all in. About two weeks later, you'll be called in for an interview with the financial aid officer. If you qualify, she'll authorize the aid and you can head over to the cashier and pick up your check.

학생 1 John, 너 학자금 보조를 받을 때 고등학교 성적증명서를 보내야 했니?
학생 2 성적 장학금 수혜 신청을 할 때만 그래. 내가 받는 건 생활보조 장학금(Needs-based Scholarship)인데, 어, 그건 일종의 보조금 같은 것이거든.
학생 1 그래? 어떻게 지원하는 건데?
학생 2 음, 우선 장학재단에 들러서 지원서를 받아 와.
학생 1 온라인 지원도 가능하겠지?
학생 2 처음 지원할 때는 안 돼. 직접 문서로만 작성해야 해. 그러니까 지원서에 기재를 하고, 아, 그리고 부모님께 지난 2년간의 세금 증명서를 준비해 달라고 부탁해. 학교에서 부모님의 수입 정도를 확인할 필요가 있거든. 이렇게 준비된 서류 모두를 보내. 약 2주 후에 장학 재단 직원이 너에게 전화를 해서 인터뷰를 요청할 거야. 자격 요건이 충족되면 보조를 승인할 것이고, 그러면 출납원에게 가서 수표를 수령할 수 있어.

Skill Check-up — Classifying Information

1 교수는 일(Job)과 전문 직업(Career)의 어떤 점을 비교하는가?
(A) 얼마나 많은 열정을 바칠 자세가 되어 있는가
(B) 얼마나 많은 기술이 요구되는가
(C) 얼마나 많은 시간이 작업에 소요되는가

정답 (A)

해설 Job은 구직자의 교육이나 관심사와 무관하며, 도전적인 것과 거리가 있고(not challenging), 돈을 버는 수단에 지나지 않음에 비해 Career는 교육이나 관심사, 경험을 확대시키고, 책임감과 의무를 필요로 하는 일이다.

🎧 스크립트

P Okay. When we talk about employment opportunities, there are two types; jobs and careers. A job doesn't engage your education or interests. This is negative if you want something challenging. However, if you just want a way to make money, a job can be a good thing. On the other hand, a career is something you build on your education, interests, and experience. It's positive if you can focus and spend a lot of time on your work. However, if you are not prepared to... uh, to make a commitment to your work, a career will not be your best choice.

교수 좋아요. 우리가 취업 기회를 논의하고자 할 때, 거기에는 일(Job)과 전문 직업(Career)이라는 두 가지 종류가 있습니다. 일은 여러분의 교육 정도나 관심사를 반영하지 않습니다. 따라서 여러분이 무언가 도전적인 일을 하고 싶은 거라면 일은 부적합합니다. 그러나 단지 돈을 벌 생각이라면 일이 알맞아요. 반면, 전문 직업은 여러분의 교육 정도나 관심사를 반영하여 경험을 쌓아가는 것입니다. 여러분이 자신의 일에 집중하고 거기에 많은 시간을 소비할 자세가 되어 있을 때 바람직합니다. 그러나 여러분이, 그러니까, 자신의 일에 열정을 바칠 준비가 되어있지 않다면, 전문 직업을 갖는 것은 최상의 선택이 될 수 없습니다.

2 다음 중 Doom Model의 예로 알맞은 것은 무엇인가?
(A) 우리 생애 동안 세계 석유 공급량이 고갈될 것이다.
(B) 광물질이나 광석은 이미 바닥나기 시작했다.
(C) 인구 성장률이 감소하기 시작했다.

정답 (A)

해설 Doom model은 지속적인 인구 성장과 지구 자원의 고갈로 생태계가 붕괴될 것임을 예측한 것이고 Uneven Growth Model은 개발도상국에서는 인구 증가가 감소되고, 전세계적인 추세로 볼 때 인구 증가가 불규칙적일 거라고 내다보는 이론이다.

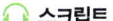 스크립트

S1 The doom model of population growth really didn't pan out, did it?
S2 No. I guess in the 70s researchers predicted that the earth would run out of natural resources within the next few decades because the population would increase so much. As a result, the entire ecosystem would collapse.
P Yeah. The uneven growth model seems more realistic. It takes into consideration the fact that in the most developed countries the population rate is actually declining. The growth rate isn't steady all over the world.

학생 1 인구 증가에 관한 Doom(파멸) 모델은 그다지 성공적이지는 않았습니다. 그렇지요?
학생 2 그렇죠. 제 생각에 70년대에 연구자들은 지구의 천연 자원이 수십 년 내로 고갈될 것이고 인구도 급격히 증가할 거라고 예측했었습니다. 그 결과로 생태계 전반이 붕괴될 거라고 말이지요.
교수 네. 불균형 성장(Uneven growth) 모델이 더 현실적인 것 같아요. 이 모델은 대부분의 개발 도상국가들의 경우 인구율이 사실상 감소하고 있다는 사실을 고려했습니다. (인구) 증가율은 전 세계적으로 볼 때 불규칙적이거든요.

3 다음 각 구절은 누구에 관해 설명하는가?

〈부르주아〉〈프롤레타리아〉
돈을 얼마나 지불해야 하는지를 결정한다. ✓ ☐
공장에서 기계를 사용한다. ☐ ✓
제품 생산을 통해 수익을 창출한다. ✓ ☐

해설 마르크스의 이론에 따르면, 부르주아 계급은 공장과 기계를 소유하고 공장 근로자들에게 임금을 지불하는 반면, 프롤레타리아 계급은 부르주아 계급이 소유한 공장에서 근로자로 일하며 제품을 생산하고 임금을 지급받는다.

🎧 스크립트

P   Okay, so as we look at Marx, we'll hear different terms. One is bourgeoisie. Anyone know what it means?
S1 It's French for "someone who came from the city", or the "burg."
S2 Yeah, but for Marx, the bourgeoisie own the means of production.
P   Right. They own the factories, the machines etc. They determine the wages. And then there is the proletariat. They work in the factories, use the machines to produce the goods. They accept the wages paid by the bourgeoisie.

교수 좋아요. 자, 마르크스에 관해 살펴볼 때면 우리는 여러 가지 용어들을 접하게 될 것입니다. 그 중 하나는 부르주아입니다. 그 의미를 아는 학생 있나요?
학생 1 프랑스 어로 '도시 출신의 사람' 또는 '읍(burg)'이라는 의미예요.
학생 2 네, 하지만 마르크스가 말하는 부르주아는 생산 수단을 소유하고 있죠.
교수 맞습니다. (마르크스의) 부르주아는 공장이나 기계 같은 것들을 소유한 사람들입니다. 그들은 임금을 결정하죠. 그리고 프롤레타리아가 있습니다. 이들은 공장에서 노동을 하고, 기계를 사용하여 상품을 생산합니다. 그리고 부르주아로부터 임금을 받습니다.

4 다음 각 구절이 설명하는 것은 무엇인가?

〈외향적인 사람〉〈내향적인 사람〉
기획 능력이 보다 출중하다. ☐ ✓
사업을 시작하는 일에 덜 열정적이다. ✓ ☐
일반적으로 회사의 지도자이다. ☐ ✓
영업 부서의 상급 간부 지위에 오른다. ✓ ☐

해설 일반적인 기대와 달리 CEO들의 성향을 조사한 한 연구 결과에 따르면 판매 마케팅 분야를 제외한 대부분의 분야에서 이들은 대부분 내향적 성격이었다. 조용하고 절제된 성향의 사람들이 업무 기획이나 운용 부분에 더 적합하기 때문이다.

🎧 스크립트

S1 I learned something interesting in my business management class today about introverts and extroverts. Well, get this. There was a major university study done on CEOs of top corporations. And which personality type would you guess most business leaders have?
S2 Extroverted, for sure. Right?
S1 Actually, the opposite's true. Most of the, uh, the top brass, you know the leaders in a company are not extroverts. They're usually quiet, reserved types who can plan well.
S2 Oh, come on — to lead, say, a sales department, you have to be outgoing.
S1 Oh, right, right. That's true. The only area within a company where extroverts generally rose to the top was in the areas of sales and marketing. Interesting, huh? Oh, and by the way, they're also less likely to start their own companies, too.

학생 1 오늘 경영학 시간에 내향적인 사람들과 외향적인 사람들에 대해 정말 흥미로운 걸 배웠어. 음, 한 번 들어 봐. 대학에서 실시한 주요 연구인데 일류 기업의 CEO들에 관한 것이야. 네 생각에 기업가들은 주로 어떤 성격일 것 같니?
학생 2 그야 물론, 외향적인 성격이겠지. 맞지?
학생 1 사실, 그 반대야. 음, 대부분의 최고 지도자들, 그러니까 기업의 리더들은 외향적이지 않아. 그들은 대개 기획을 잘 하는 조용하고 내성적인 유형에 속해.
학생 2 아니, 그럴리가. 어, 그러니까 영업 부서를 이끌려면 외향적이야 해.
학생 1 아, 그래 맞아. 그건 사실이야. 기업 내에서 일반적으로 외향적 성향의 사람이 책임자 직책까지 올라가는 유일한 영역이 영업과 마케팅이었어. 흥미롭지 않니? 아, 반면에 그들은 자기 회사를 창업할 가능성 또한 적은 사람들이야.

Exercise

1 A - 번역참조 B - (B)(D)   2 A - (D) B - (C)
3 A - 번역참조 B - (B)   4 A - 번역참조 B - (A)

Exercise 1

환경 수업에서의 대화의 일부를 듣고 물음에 답하시오.

🎧 스크립트

P So researchers have been puzzled by the fact that really heavy-duty pollutants have been showing up in the otherwise pristine Arctic. Now, the Arctic Circle is really isolated from the rest of the world, so how these industrial and agricultural pollutants appeared there was at first a bit of a mystery. Anyone have any ideas?

S It's got to be migrating animals, right? Birds, for instance. Anything that spends time in the industrialized regions, but then later spends time in the Arctic.

P You've done your homework. First we've got the birds — many species of land birds migrate very long distances. The most common pattern being for birds is to breed in the temperate or arctic northern zone and winter in warmer regions. All right, in this case, let's take a look at the northern fulmar. Northern fulmar, almost looks gull-like, fly low over the sea. These birds winter in the southern parts of Canada and the northern U.S. They're eating plankton, fish waste and things from polluted waters. Then, they're summering in the Arctic, and their waste and their young contain this pollution which gets into the ecosystem.

교수 그래서 연구자들은 자연 그대로이어야 할 북극지방에 예상과 달리 아주 내구성 강한 오염물질이 나타난 사실에 놀라움을 나타냈습니다. 현재 북극권은 외부 세계로부터 철저히 고립되어 있기 때문에 어떻게 이런 산업이나 농업 오염물질이 이곳에 나타날 수 있었는지 초기에는 다소 수수께끼였지요. 이에 대한 의견이 있는 학생 있습니까?

학생 이동 동물들과 관련이 있지 않습니까? 예를 들어, 새들이 그렇죠. 산업화된 지역에서 시간을 보내다가 나중에 북극 지방에서 머물게 되는 것들이요.

교수 과제를 잘 했군요. 먼저, 새들이 있습니다. 특히 장거리를 이동하는 다양한 종류의 육지 조류들이요. 이 새들에게 가장 일반적으로 나타나는 형태는 온난한 지역이나 북극 지역에서 번식하고 그보다 더 따뜻한 지역에서 겨울을 나는 것입니다. 자, 이런 경우에 해당하는 북부 풀마갈매기를 살펴 보죠. 갈매기와 거의 유사한 생김새를 지닌 북부 지방의 풀마갈매기는 바다 위를 낮게 날아다닙니다. 이들은 캐나다 남쪽 지역이나 북미 지역에서 겨울을 납니다. 그리고 오염된 바다에서 나는 플랑크톤이나, 물고기 배설물 그리고 여러 가지를 먹지요. 그리고 그들은 북극에서 여름을 보내는 겁니다. 그들의 배설물과 새끼들이 오염물질을 포함하게 되고 이 오염물질이 생태계로 편입되는 것이죠.

어휘 puzzle 곤혹하게 하다, 어쩔 줄 모르게 하다 heavy-duty 강력한, 내구성이 강한 pollutant 오염 물질, 오염원 show up 나타나다 pristine 자연 그대로의; 본래의, 초기의 Arctic Circle 북극권 migrating 이주하는, 이동하는 plankton 플랑크톤, 부유 생물

A 다음 각 구절이 북극 지방의 오염의 단계에 속하면 Yes, 그렇지 않으면 No에 체크하시오.

	Yes	No
바다 생물들이 공해로 오염된다.	✓	
캐나다에서 온 배가 북극해를 오염시킨다.		✓
산업으로 인해 수질이 오염된다.	✓	
새들이 자신들의 몸에 오염물질을 묻혀 북극으로 옮긴다.	✓	

해설 오염된 지역(미국, 캐나다 등)의 해양 생물을 먹고 사는 철새들이 계절을 나기 위해 북극권 지방으로 이동하면서 이들 오염 물질도 함께 이동된 것이다.

B 다음 중 사실인 것은 무엇인가? 정답 두 개를 고르시오.
(A) 과학자들은 즉시 북부 지방의 풀마 갈매기를 의심했다.
(B) 플랑크톤은 산업 오염물질에 의해 오염되었다.
(C) 새들이 어떻게 북극지방으로 오염물질을 옮기는지는 명확하지 않다.
(D) 새들의 이동 형태로 오염을 설명할 수 있다.

해설 (A) - 오염 원인을 즉각 알아차렸다면 puzzled by라는 표현을 쓰지 못한다. (C) - 오염된 해양의 플랑크톤을 먹은 새들이 북극권으로 이동한 것이 원인이라고 했다.

Exercise 2

다음 동물학 수업에서의 강의의 일부를 듣고 물음에 답하시오.

🎧 스크립트

P Attempting to distinguish any of the three western accipiters, or hawks from one another can be somewhat difficult. They are easily recognizable as a group, but tend to look a lot like one another. Accipiters or true hawks have short, broad wings and long tails to produce quick flight. These hawks have long shins and long, slender toes. And in size, the female accipier is often much larger than the male. The cooper's hawk is about the size of a crow. Of its relatives, the sharp-shinned hawk is smaller and the northern goshawk is larger. What about the plumage? The plumage of an accipiter isn't really useful in identification, the way it can be with other birds. Only the mature northern goshawk has distinct plumage. Thus, the best thing to look at to make a positive identification is the wing beat of the individual bird. The Cooper's hawk has stiff wing beats as it is flying. The Cooper's hawk flies with several quick wing beats and a glide. The sharp-shinned hawk, however, flies with rapid, snappy wing beats. It appears less stable in flight than other accipiters. Their wing beat is quick, deep strokes and a flapping motion at the "wrist." And the northern goshawk has long, slow wing beats as it flies overhead. It flies with several flaps and a short glide. By noting these details you are more likely to make a correct identification.

교수 세 종류의 서양 맹금류 즉, 매들을 각기 구별하려는 시도는 다소 힘겨운 일입니다. 이들은 분명 개체 그룹으로 인식되지만, 서로의 생김새는 상당히 유사하기 때문입니다. 맹금류 즉, 참매는 날개가 짧지만 넓적하고, 꼬리가 길기 때문에 나는 것이 민첩합니다. 이들 매는 경골 부분이 길며, 발도 길고 날씬합니다. 크기로 보자면 보통은 암 맹금류가 수컷보다 훨씬 큽니다. 쿠퍼매(북미산 매의 한 종류)의 크기는 까마귀 정도 됩니다. 이것과 비슷한 종류인 Sharp-Shinned hawk(줄무늬새매)는 그보다 좀 작고 북부 참매는 그보다 좀 더 크지요. 깃털은 어떨까요? 맹금류의 깃털은 다른 새들과 구별하여 그 동족임을 증명하는 데 그다지 유용하지 못합니다. 단지 완전히 성장을 마친 북부 참매만이 독특한 깃털을 갖고 있습니다. 그러므로 각 새들을 구별할 수 있는 가장 좋은 방법은 그들의 날갯짓입니다. 쿠퍼매는 비행할 때 거세게 날갯짓을 합니다. 이 새는 서너 번 재빠르게 날개를 파닥거리다가 미끄러지듯이 비행하기 시작합니다. 그렇지만 줄무늬새매는 빠르게 파닥거리는듯한 날갯짓을 해서 비행을 할 때는 다른 맹금류보다 덜 안정적인 느낌을 주지요. 이 새의 날갯짓은 재빠른데다 반경이 크고 날갯죽지 부분을 접었다 폈다하는 동작을 동반합니다. 그리고 북부 참매는 공중으로 날아오를 때 천천히 길게 날갯짓을 합니다. 몇 번 날개를 접었다 폈다 하면서 짧게 미끄러져 비행을 시작합니다. 이러한 세부 사항을 이해하게 되면 여러분은 정확하게 이들을 구별할 수 있습니다.

어휘 distinguish 구별하다, 식별하다 recognizable 알아볼 수 있는 plumage (조류의) 깃털, 깃 identification (생물) 동정(=같은 속·종) mature 성숙한, 숙성한 beat (새의) 날개침, 비트 snappy 기운찬, 팔팔한 tend to ~하는 경향이 있다, ~하기 쉽다

A 교수는 서양 맹금류의 어떤 점을 비교하고 있는가?
(A) 새의 깃털
(B) 새들이 교미할 때 보내는 신호
(C) 새들의 날개 크기와 형태
(D) 새들의 날갯짓

해설 새의 생김새나 깃털이 아닌 날갯짓을 보고 각 새를 구별할 수 있다고 했다.

B 쿠퍼매와 참매를 구별할 때 염두에 두어야 할 점은 무엇인가?
(A) 쿠퍼매는 크기 면에서 북부 참매보다 크다.

(B) 참매의 날갯짓은 거세고 빠르다.
(C) 성장이 끝난 북부 참매는 깃털로 다른 새들과 구별할 수 있는 유일한 매이다.
(D) 쿠퍼매의 날개는 길고 좁다.

Exercise 3

사회학 강의에서의 토론의 일부를 듣고 물음에 답하시오.

🎧 스크립트

P Two ways employers judge potential employees is the interview or the psychological test. The interview is the most common. An interview is a conversation between two or more people where questions are asked to obtain information from the interviewee. The hiring person meets with the prospective candidate and asks him or her a series of questions. And the employer tries to see if the candidate has the social skills and intelligence suitable for the workplace. The answers the candidate gives really allow the employers to decide. The psychological test is becoming more common. Psychological testing is used to infer larger generalizations about the individual being tested. Candidates are given a multiple-choice test devised by psychologists. They answer the questions and then the results are interpreted by the test company. By those answers of the individual, the evaluator can compare the behavior of the person to the responses of a normal group.

S1 But an interview just relies on first impressions. Within the first few seconds, he passes judgment on people, which are often wrong... and once the first impression is made, it is actually irreversible. It seems like the psychological test is a much better indicator.

S2 How can a multiple-choice test really say what kind of person you are, though?

P Well, exactly. Both of your points really highlight problems in these processes.

교수 고용주들이 장차 직원이 될 지원자들을 판별하는 두 가지 방법은 인터뷰와 심리 테스트입니다. 인터뷰가 가장 일반적이죠. 인터뷰란 두 사람 또는 그 이상의 사람들 사이의 대화로 인터뷰 대상자로부터 정보를 획득하기 위한 질문을 하는 것

입니다. 고용주가 잠재적인 지원자들을 만나 몇 가지 질문을 하게 되지요. 그리고 이들 지원자들이 사회적 소양이나 근무 환경에 적합한 재능을 가지고 있는지를 살펴봅니다. 지원자의 응답에 따라 고용주는 (누구를 뽑을지) 결정할 수 있습니다. 심리테스트는 (요즘) 더욱 일반화되는 추세를 띠고 있어요. 심리 테스트는 평가받는 개개인에 대한 좀 더 보편적인 사항들을 알아내기 위해 활용됩니다. 지원자들에게는 심리학자들이 고안한 객관식 문항이 주어지는데, 지원자들이 이에 답하면 시험을 주관하는 업체가 그 답안들을 해석합니다. 개인의 응답을 기준으로 평가자는 응답자의 태도와 일반인 그룹의 반응을 비교(분석)하는 것이지요.

학생 1 하지만 인터뷰는 단순히 첫인상에 의존하는 것이잖아요. 고용주는 불과 처음 몇 초 만으로 사람을 판단하게 되니까 종종 이 판단이 잘못된 것일 수도 있습니다. 게다가 일단 첫인상이 형성되면 그 인상을 바꾸기란 사실 어렵습니다. 심리 테스트가 훨씬 더 객관적인 지표인 것 같아요.

학생 2 그렇지만 어떻게 객관식 문제로 개인의 성품을 판단할 수 있겠습니까?

교수 음, 그렇지요. 두 사람 모두 문제점을 제대로 지적했습니다.

어휘 potential 잠재하는, 가능한　hire 고용하다　prospective 기대되는, 장차의, 예상된　candidate 후보자, 희망자　multiple 다수의, 복합적인　devise 궁리하다, 고안하다　interpret 해석하다, 설명하다　impression 인상, 느낌　indicator 지표, 표준, 척도

A 다음 각 문장이 심리 테스트의 단계에 속하면 Yes, 그렇지 않으면 No에 체크하시오.

	Yes	No
지원자들이 일련의 객관식 문항에 응답한다.	✓	
테스트를 주관하는 업체가 응답을 검토한다.	✓	
지원자들은 신체검사를 통과해야 한다.		✓
고용주들이 지원자들의 얼굴 표정을 자세히 살펴본다.		✓

해설 Psychological Test는 선택지가 여러 개인 질문을 주고 개개인이 자신에게 맞는 답을 고름으로써, 그 답으로 지원자의 심리를 파악하는 테스트이다. 테스트 평가는 이 검사를 주관한 회사에서 관할한다.

B 다음 중 인터뷰의 예가 <u>아닌</u> 것은 무엇인가?
(A) 지원자들은 얼굴을 마주 보고 질문에 대답해야 한다.
(B) 심리학자들이 지원자가 한 응답들을 분석한다.
(C) 인터뷰를 하는 사람들은 지원자들이 질문에 대해 응답할 때 신중히 경청한다.
(D) 고용주는 지원자의 응답이 적절한 지를 판별한다.

Exercise 4
두 학생의 대화의 일부를 듣고 물음에 답하시오.

🎧 스크립트

S1 Did you hear about the student presidential election?
S2 Well, not yet. What is the qualification to run for student president?
S1 Well, it's very simple. Candidates for the president must have a 2.5 grade point average and maintain a 2.4 GPA during their terms. I'm going to run for student president.
S2 Oh, really? But you know, uh, to represent students' views within the university will be somewhat tough. You must be responsible for providing a variety of services to students.
S1 I know, but I'd like to try.
S2 Oh, you are serious.
S1 See, you never take me seriously. But it's true. I'm really going for it now.
S2 I see. Well, no wonder you look so busy these days! So what do you have to do, anyway?
S1 Lots! I must have 100 students sign a petition saying I'm fit for the position. Next, I hand in the petition, along with a statement of my platform to the Student Government Office. After that, I'm free to start campaigning.
S2 So what will you change if you're elected, anyway?
S1 If I win, you can bet I'll ask for tennis court rehab funding!
S2 That sounds great! These tennis courts are falling apart. I'll definitely sign the petition.
S1 Hey, thanks. And guess what? I just happen to have the petition right here in my backpack. I'll get it now!

학생 1 너 학생회장 선거에 대해 들었니?
학생 2 음, 아직. 학생 회장에 출마하는 지원 자격이 뭔데?
학생 1 음, 아주 간단해. 후보자들은 평균 평점이 2.5이상이어야 하고, 임기 동안 평점을 2.4 점으로 유지하면 돼. 그래서 난 지원해 보려고 해.
학생 2 정말? 하지만, 너도 알다시피 교내에서 학생들의 의견을 대변하기란 만만치가 않아. 학생들에게 다양한 서비스를 제공해야 할 의무도 지게 될 거야.
학생 1 알아. 그래도 해 보고 싶어.
학생 2 그래. 너 진심이구나.
학생 1 이봐, 넌 내가 하는 말을 진심으로 받아들이는 법이 없구나. 하지만 진심이라고. 이번엔 정말 해 볼 거야.
학생 2 알겠어. 음, 요즘 네가 바빠 보였던 것도 당연하네. 그나저나, 넌 뭘 해야 하는 거니?
학생 1 할 일이 많아. 내가 회장 자리에 적임자라는 것을 증명하는 청원서에 학생 100명의 서명을 받아야 해. 그리고 학생회에 그 청원서와 함께 내 선거유세문도 제출해야 해. 그러고 나면 선

거 운동을 시작할 수 있어.
학생 2 그나저나, 네가 당선되면 뭘 바꿀 거야?
학생 1 내가 당선되면, 반드시 테니스 코트 증축 기금을 요청할 거야.
학생 2 멋진걸. 우리 테니스 코트는 무너질 것 같아. 그 청원서에 꼭 서명할게.
학생 1 야, 정말 고마워. 있잖아, 그런데 마침 내 가방 안에 청원서가 있어. 네 서명 지금 받을게.

어휘 petition 청원서 statement 성명서, 진술 platform 연설, 강연 rehab 부흥, 재건(= rehabilitation) funding 자금 제공, 융자 fit for (~에) 알맞다, 적합하다

A 다음 중 학생회장 선거에 출마하는 단계에 해당하지 <u>않는</u> 것은 무엇인가? 참, 거짓을 체크하시오.

	True	False
동료 학생들의 승인을 얻어낸다.	✓	
학생회에 지원비를 지불한다.		✓
연설문을 제출한다.	✓	
허가받은 기관으로부터 기금을 모금한다.		✓
교내에서 선거 운동을 한다.	✓	

해설 먼저 100명의 학생들로부터 학생 회장직에 적합하다는 서명을 받아서 입후보 연설문과 함께 제출한 후, 본격적으로 캠페인 활동에 나선다.

B 남자가 당선될 경우 선거 공약으로 내건 것은 무엇인가?
(A) 테니스 코트 개조를 위한 기금 획득
(B) 학생의 요구에 귀 기울이기
(C) 테니스 대회를 위한 기금 모금
(D) 승자에게 상금 수여

해설 "If I win, you can bet I'll ask for tennis court rehab funding." 테니스 코트 재건축 비용을 모금하겠다고 했다.

Dictation Exercise

Exercise 1

① have been puzzled by the fact
② showing up
③ these industrial and agricultural pollutants
④ a bit of a mystery
⑤ It's got to be migrating animals
⑥ many species of land birds
⑦ to breed in
⑧ in warmer regions
⑨ fly low over the sea
⑩ fish waste and things from polluted waters
⑪ gets into the ecosystem

Exercise 2

① Attempting to distinguish
② easily recognizable as a group
③ broad wings and long tails
④ slender toes
⑤ about the size of a crow
⑥ isn't really useful in identification
⑦ the wing beat of the individual bird
⑧ as it is flying
⑨ It appears less stable in flight
⑩ it files overhead
⑪ you are more likely to

Exercise 3

① judge potential employees
② to obtain information from the interviewee
③ the prospective candidate
④ suitable for the workplace
⑤ The psychological test
⑥ is used to infer
⑦ devised by
⑧ the results are interpreted
⑨ the evaluater can compare
⑩ relies on first impressions
⑪ passes judgement on
⑫ it is actually irreversible
⑬ highlight problems in these processes

Exercise 4

① the qualification to run for
② grade point average
③ run for student president
④ responsible for providing a variety of services
⑤ I'm really going for it now
⑥ sign a petition saying I'm fit for the position
⑦ along with a statement of my platform
⑧ I'm free to start campaigning
⑨ I'll ask for tennis court rehab funding
⑩ I'll definitely sign the petition
⑪ I just happen to have the petition

Actual Test

1 1 - 번역참조 2 - 번역참조 3 - (B) 4 - (D)
2 1 - (B) 2 - 번역참조 3 (B) (D) 4 (C)

Actual Test 1

교육학 수업에서의 대화의 일부를 듣고 물음에 답하시오.

🎧 스크립트

P Between about 13 and 21, young people undergo a lot of intellectual changes. During this time, humans are in what is known as the variable category of ethical behavior.
S What's the name again?
P Variable. In other words, things aren't set in stone yet. There are a lot of changes taking place. This contrasts with the post-21 year period, which is known as static. What's involved with the variable category? It starts off with a stage we call dualism. In general, the idea is that there are two fundamental kinds of principles. In theology, for example a 'dualist' is someone who believes in Good and Evil. That is to say, the perception of the world is that there is always a right and a wrong. Then this gets a bit more complicated in the gray stage, where young people begin to realize it's not so simple. Near the 17th year, we... the relativistic stage... where we question all judgments and think what we believe now can change later according to time and place. That is to say, uh, we think the truth is not always the same but varies according to circumstance, so one can be right on one hand, and wrong on the other hand. But by 21 we begin to move back to a place where we have a stable set of values. That is, we enter the static category of ethical behavior.

교수 13세에서 21세 사이의 청소년은 많은 지적 변화를 경험하게 됩니다. 이 기간에 인간은 윤리적 태도에 대한 Variable Category로 알려진 시기에 놓이게 됩니다.
학생 어떤 시기라고요?
교수 Variable요. 다시 말해, 사물이 아직 돌처럼 형태가 굳어지지 않은 것을 말하죠. 많은 변화가 일어납니다. 이것은 안정기(Static)라고 알려진 21세 이후의 기간과 대조됩니다. 가변기에 속한 것은 무엇일까요? 이는 Dualism이라고 일컬어지는 단계로 시작됩니다. 일반적으로 이 Dualism은 두 가지 근본 원리가 있다는 것입니다. 예를 들어, 신학에서는 Dualist는 선과 악을 믿는 사람을 뜻합니다. 즉, 언제나 옳은 것과 그렇지 않은 것으로 세계를 인식합니다. 그 다음에 거치는 단계는 좀 더 복잡한 Gray stage로, 이 단계에서 청소년들은 세상이 그리 단순하지 않다는 걸 깨닫게 됩니다. 17세가 될 무렵에는, Relativistic stage에 이르게 됩니다. 이 시기에는 모든 판단에 대해 회의를 품게 되고, 우리가 믿고 있는 모든 것이 시간과 장소에 따라 변할 수도 있다고 생각하게 되죠. 그 말은 그러니까, 에, 진실이 항상 같을 수는 없고 상황에 따라서 변할 수 있다고 생각하는 겁니다. 그래서 한편으로는 옳지만 다른 한편으로는 틀릴 수도 있다고 생각하지요. 그러나 21세에 이르면, 우리는 안정적인 가치관을 갖는 상태로 돌아갑니다. 즉 윤리적 태도에 있어서 안정기에 진입하게 되는 겁니다.

1 다음 각 단계에 따라 아래 진술을 분류하여 체크하시오.

	Dualism	Gray Stage	Relativism
흑백논리의 관점	✓		
누가 옳은 것인지 결정하기 쉽지 않다.		✓	
양측 모두 다 옳을 수 있다.			✓
문제가 복잡하다.		✓	
단 한 사람만이 옳다.	✓		

해설 Dualism - 흑백논리가 적용되어 옳고 그른 것이 명백히 구분되는 단계
Gray Stage - 사물을 바라보는 시각이 복잡해져서 무엇이 옳고 그른지를 명확히 판단하지 못하는 단계
Relativistic Stage - 어떤 일에 대한 판단 자체에 의구심을 품으며 모든 판단에 대해 확신을 갖지 못하는 단계

2 다음 중 가변기에 해당하는 것은 무엇인가? 두 개의 선택지를 고르시오.

정해진 가치관에 근거하여 선택한다.	
오래된 관습과 편견에 따라 결정한다.	
세상(일)은 명쾌하게 선택할 수 있는 사안들로 구성되어 있다고 간주한다.	✓
누군가가 절대적으로 옳다는 것에 대해 회의를 품기 시작한다.	✓
사회적 기대에 근거하여 자신의 입장을 바꾼다.	

해설 Variable category of ethical behavior은 크게 3 단계(Dualism, Gray stage, relativistic stage)로 구분된다고 했다. 각 3단계에 해당되는 특성을 고르면 된다.

3 다음 중 Dualistic 단계의 예에 해당하는 것은 무엇인가?
(A) 자신의 주변 사람 누구도 진실을 말하고 있지 않을 거라고 의심한다.
(B) 모든 이야기는 양면성을 띠고 있음을 인식하지 못한다.
(C) 논쟁적인 사안에 대해 확신하지 못한다.
(D) 자신의 도덕적 가치관에 근거하여 선택한다.

해설 Dualism 은 모든 것을 흑백논리로만 구분하는 단계이므로, 모든 사물에는 여러 가지 측면이 존재함을 인식하지 못한다.

4 다음 중 가변기에 해당하는 태도로 알맞지 <u>않은</u> 것은 무엇인가?
(A) 양측 모두가 옳기 때문에 어떠한 결정도 내릴 수 없다.

(B) 복잡한 세상사를 옳고 그른 것으로 단순화시킨다.
(C) 양측 모두 이점이 있기 때문에 결정을 내리기가 어렵다.
(D) 안정적인 가치 패턴에 근거하여 결정이 도출된다.

해설 교수는 크게 Variable stage와 Static stage로 구분하고 있다. (D)는 21세 이후로 찾아오는 Static 단계로 자신만의 가치 체계를 기준으로 사물을 판단한다.

Actual Test 2

다음 교수와 학생의 대화의 일부를 듣고 물음에 답하시오.

🎧 스크립트

P Susan Smith speaking.
S Dr. Smith, my name is Jason Anderson. My roommate, Peter O'neil, is in your art history class. Uh-m... Art History 502.
P Yes.
S Well, he is sick and won't be in your class today. He asked me to bring his term paper to your office.
P OK. The paper is due by three o'clock.
S I have a class from one to two. I'll bring it to your office after my class.
P Well, I have a meeting this afternoon. So you can drop it off with the secretary of the art history department.
S OK. Oh, I almost forgot. I'm a Biology major. But my advisor told me that I need one more humanities course to graduate. I've noticed that you are teaching a course on landscape painters next semester. Could you tell me a little bit about it?
P Sure. Well, it's a course for non-art majors. We'll be looking at several different painters and examining their works. We'll also look at the history and politics of the era in which they lived.
S That sounds interesting. What else is required?
P There is no final exam. And there is only one required book. But each student has to give a major presentation on an individual painter at the end of the course.
S Hmm. It sounds good. Will you be in your office later today? I'd like to talk to you some more about it.
P Well, my meeting's scheduled to last all afternoon. Why don't you stop by tomorrow? Any time in the afternoon would be fine. My office is in the fine arts building right next to the library.
S Thanks. I'll do that.

교수 Susan Smith 입니다.
학생 Smith 교수님, 저는 Jason Anderson 이라고 합니다. 제 룸메이트 Peter O'neil이 교수님 미술사 수업을 듣고 있습니다. 어, 음, 미술사 502 수업이요.
교수 네.
학생 저, Peter가 오늘 아파서 수업에 참석하지 못할 것 같습니다. 제게 대신 기말 보고서를 교수님 사무실에 갖다 달라는 부탁을 했어요.
교수 그래요. 보고서 제출은 3시까지입니다.
학생 제가 1시에서 2시까지 수업이 있거든요. 수업 끝나고 교수님 연구실로 가져가겠습니다.
교수 글쎄요, 오늘 오후에는 회의가 있는데요. 그러면 미술사 학부 사람에게 맡겨 놓으세요.
학생 알겠습니다. 참, 깜박 잊을뻔 했어요. 저는 생물학을 전공하는데요. 지도 교수님께서 졸업을 하려면 제가 인문학부 수업을 하나 더 들어야 한다고 하셨어요. 제가 알기로는 교수님께서 다음 학기에 풍경화가에 관한 수업을 하시던데요. 그것에 관해 조금 말씀해주실 수 있으신가요?
교수 물론이에요. 음, 이 수업은 예술학부 전공자가 아닌 학생들을 위한 거예요. 몇 명의 화가들을 살펴보고 그들의 작품을 다룰 것입니다. 그리고 그들이 살았던 시대의 역사와 정치에 관해서도요.
학생 재미있을 것 같아요. 그밖에 필수 사항이 있나요?
교수 기말 시험은 없습니다. 그리고 필요한 건 오직 책 한 권이에요. 하지만 학생들은 강의 말에 한 화가에 관한 주요 발표를 해야 합니다.
학생 음... 좋아요. 교수님, 오늘 오후에 연구실에 계실 건가요? 그 수업에 관해 교수님과 말씀을 좀 더 나누고 싶은데요.
교수 글쎄요, 오늘 회의는 오후 내내 진행될 예정이에요. 내일 들르면 어떨까요? 오후에는 아무 때라도 괜찮아요. 내 연구실은 도서관 바로 옆 예술학부 건물에 있어요.
학생 감사합니다. 그럴게요.

1 학생이 교수에게 전화한 이유는 무엇인가?
(A) 수업에 참석할 수가 없다.
(B) 교수 연구실에 갖다 줄 것이 있다.
(C) 지난 수업 과제물을 제출하고 싶다.
(D) 교수의 강의 수강을 그만두고 싶다.

해설 룸메이트의 부탁을 받고 그의 기말 보고 자료를 교수 연구실에 갖다 주려고 한다.

2 다음 중 풍경화가에 관한 강의에 대해 옳은 것은 True에, 틀린 것은 False에 체크하시오.

	True	False
3학년과 4학년생을 위한 수업이다.		✓
몇 명의 화가들을 연구한다.	✓	
화가의 정치적 사상을 검토한다.		✓
화가의 개인사를 학습한다.		✓
비전공자를 위한 수업이다.	✓	
여러 가지 발표를 한다.		✓

3 교수가 설명하는 바에 따르면 수업에서 학생들에게 요구하는 것은 무엇인가? 정답 2개를 고르시오.
   (A) 풍경화를 그린다.
   (B) 구두로 보고한다.
   (C) 기말 시험을 치른다.
   (D) 책을 산다.

해설 (B)의 Oral Report는 곧 Major Presentation을 의미한다.

4 교수가 학생에게 제안하는 것은 무엇인가?
   (A) 회의 시작 전에 자신의 연구실로 오라.
   (B) 전공을 바꾸어라.
   (C) 교수와 내일 만나자.
   (D) 룸메이트와 수업에 관해 상의하라.

해설 학생은 교수에게 풍경화가를 주제로 한 강의에 관해 문의하고 싶다고 했다. 교수는 오늘 오후에 회의가 있으므로 내일 들르라고 이른다.

Dictation — Actual Test

Actual Test 1

① undergo a lot of intellectual changes
② in what is known as the variable category of
③ Variable
④ things aren't set in stone yet
⑤ This contrasts with the post-21 year period
⑥ It starts off with a stage
⑦ two fundamental kinds of principles
⑧ believes in Good and Evil
⑨ there is always a right and a wrong
⑩ a bit more complicated in the gray stage
⑪ the relativistic stage
⑫ according to time and place
⑬ where we have a stable set of values
⑭ the static category of ethical behavior

Actual Test 2

① is in your art history class
② won't be in your class
③ I'll bring it to your office
④ you can drop it off with the secretary
⑤ I've noticed
⑥ it's a course for non-art majors
⑦ of the era in which they lived
⑧ What else is required
⑨ has to give a major presentation
⑩ my meeting's scheduled to last
⑪ Any time in the afternoon

Vocabulary Review

다음 각 정의와 일치하는 단어를 골라 써 넣으시오.

1 variable   2 distinguish   3 relativism
4 migrating   5 pollutant   6 identification
7 undergo   8 potential   9 petition
10 require

1 상당히 자주 변하는
2 하나와 다른 하나를 구별하다
3 상황에 따라 진실도 변한다는 믿음
4 보통 새로운 먹이 공급 장소를 발견하거나 번식하기 위해 특정한 계절에 세계의 한 지역에서 다른 지역으로 이동하는 것
5 환경을 오염시키는 오염 물질
6 어떤 것이 존재한다는 것을 인식하는 행위; 다른 것과의 밀접한 관련
7 변화를 겪다
8 어떤 것에 대한 가능성을 갖는
9 공식적인 단체에 어떤 특정한 것을 요구하려고 많은 사람들이 서명한 문서
10 누군가에게 어떤 일을 하라고 요구하고, 그 일을 할 것을 기대하다

다음 구문을 사용하여 문장을 완성하시오.

1 fill in   2 made a commitment to
3 applied for   4 drop by
5 When it comes to

1 회원이 되시려면 지원서를 먼저 작성하셔야 합니다.
2 우리는 그가 교육 제도 개혁에 그의 일생을 바쳤다는 것을 안다.
3 비록 그 가능성은 거의 희박했지만, 그녀는 그 자리에 지원했다.
4 그는 내가 그를 만나기 위해 나중에 들릴 것인지 물었다.
5 화학 공업 분야에서는 귀사가 일류 기업에 속한다고 생각합니다.

CHAPTER 04
ORGANIZATION

Sample

교수 이동하는 동물들은 생존에 필요한 이상적인 환경을 찾습니다. 예를 들어, 음, 아프리카 영양은 해마다 싱싱한 목초를 공급받을 만한 곳을 따라 이주합니다. 날씨나 기타 조건들이 바뀌기 때문에 이동하는 경로도 다양하죠. 하지만, 결국은 모두 먹이를 위해서입니다. 알겠죠? 한편, 태평양 송어는 번식을 이유로 이동합니다. 이 물고기는 평생 딱 한 번 이동을 하는데, 자신이 태어난 작은 개울에서 큰 바다로 이동하여 짝짓기를 한 후, 결국 자신이 태어났던 그 작은 개울로 되돌아와 알을 낳고 죽습니다.

교수는 동물들이 이동하는 이유를 어떻게 설명하고 있는가?
(A) 아프리카의 강우 형태와 목초 성장을 설명하면서
(B) 대양에서 사는 송어의 생활 주기를 보여주면서
(C) 아프리카 영양과 태평양 송어의 이동 동기를 예로 들면서
(D) 이동하는 동물과 이동하지 않는 동물을 비교하면서

정답 (C)

Vocabulary Preview for Skill Check-up

다음 정의를 듣고 알맞은 단어를 고르시오.

1 colonize   2 audience   3 architect
4 meteorite 5 interpret 6 practical
7 wildlife   8 refuge   9 navigate
10 adept

1 establish a colony in a foreign country
  외국에 식민지를 건설하다
2 a group of people watching or listening to a performance
  공연을 듣거나 관람하는 사람들
3 a person who designs a building
  건물을 설계하는 사람
4 a piece of rock from the space fallen on the earth
  우주에서 지구로 떨어진 바위의 한 조각
5 give an explanation to
  ~에 대한 설명을 하다
6 related to actual use
  실질적인 사용과 관련된
7 living animals and other living things that are not domesticated
  살아있는 동물이나 그밖의 길들지 않은 생물들
8 a safe place from danger
  위험으로부터 안전한 장소
9 travel by a ship or a boat on water
  물 위를 배나 보트로 이동하다
10 proficient and skillful
   능숙하고 훈련이 잘 된

다음 단어를 이용하여 아래 문장을 완성하시오.

1 colonizing   2 audience   3 fascinated
4 adept   5 interpret 6 master
7 voluntary   8 celebrate 9 suspicious
10 desirable

1 그는 아프리카를 식민지로 만들고 수백만 아프리카 사람들을 노예로 만든 것은 서구 역사의 죄악이라고 생각한다.
2 연설자는 청중이 정신을 집중하여 자신의 연설에 주의를 기울이고 참여하도록 유도하여야 한다.
3 사람들은 그 건물이 기이한 각도로 기울어져 있다는 사실에 수세기 동안 매료되었다.
4 일단 단어나 구를 익히면, 그것을 사용하는 데 익숙해지도록 노력해야 한다.
5 그녀는 그 남자가 얘기한 내용을 반도 이해하지 못했다.
6 이 학교는 모든 학생들이 외국어를 하나 혹은 두 가지 정도 마스터할 것을 기대한다.
7 그는 (지금까지) 양로원에서 자발적으로 일해 왔다.
8 우리는 일요일에 모두 모여서 그의 여든 번째 생일을 축하해주었다.
9 모두들 Stephen이 제안한 새로운 아이디어에 회의적이었다.
10 통상적으로 이번 새 프로젝트는 고객에게 판매하기 쉬운 제품들을 생산해내는 것이 아니기 때문에 바람직하지 못하다.

Skill Check-up Organization of the Information Presented

1 교수는 인식의 변화를 어떻게 설명하고 있는가?
(A) 과거의 영화와 현재의 영화를 대조하면서
(B) (영화에) 사용된 특수 효과를 묘사하면서
(C) 인식의 변화라는 현상을 흥미로운 것으로 정의하면서

정답 (A)

해설 교수는 인식의 변화에 관해 얘기하겠다고 서두를 꺼낸 후, Lumiere 형제의 영화를 예로 들고 있다. 두 학생이 말한 boring 과 amazing 의 두 가지 반응은 영화를 보는 시각(즉, 과거와 현재의 눈)에 있다.

🎧 스크립트

P So, right... today, we're going to talk about changing perceptions ... well, at movies today, we expect to be blown away by special effects and action, I mean a lot of people... for sure... but was this always the case? Anyone seen a Lumiere brothers' film from around 1895?
S1 Yeah, it just showed a mother feeding a baby! It was so boring!
S2 You're looking at it through modern eyes. I'm sure at the time it seemed really amazing.

P Indeed. After all, just the fact that the pictures were moving was interesting enough for early film audiences.

교수 자, 좋아요. 오늘은 인식의 변화에 대해 이야기해 보겠어요. 에, 요즘은 영화를 보면서 특수 효과나 액션을 보고 기분전환이 되기를 기대하지요. 분명 많은 사람들이 그럴 겁니다. 그런데, 언제나 그러할까요? 1895년 즈음의 뤼미에르 형제의 영화를 본 사람이 있나요?
학생 1 네, 아이에게 젖을 주는 어머니의 모습만 보여주더라구요. 너무 지루했어요.
학생 2 그건 네가 요즘 눈으로 영화를 보고 있기 때문이야. 그 당시에는 그것도 아주 흥미롭게 보였을 거라고 생각해.
교수 맞아요. 아무튼, 그림이 움직인다는 사실만으로도 초기 영화 관객에게는 충분히 흥미로웠습니다.

---

2 교수는 Gehry의 조각적 건축에 대해 어떻게 설명하고 있는가?
(A) 그의 초고층 건물들이 세워진 도시들을 열거하면서
(B) 그의 스타일을 보여주는 자료들을 제공하면서
(C) 그가 다른 건축가들로부터 영감을 얻었다는 것을 강조하면서

정답 (B)

해설 교수는 Gehry의 예술적인 건축 양식을 설명하기 위해 그의 특징(곡선미를 살린 디자인)을 가장 잘 나타내는 작품 가운데 하나인 Guggenheim Museum을 예로 들고 있다.

🎧 스크립트

P Most of us probably don't think too much about the buildings we go into or walk past every day. But for an architect like Frank Gehry, a building has the potential to be more than just a house or an office — it can be a work of art. He is known for his sculptural approach to building design and building curvaceous structures. His most famous work, which shows the clearest expression of his style, is the Guggenheim Museum — I mean the one in Bilbao, Spain — which is an extraordinary combination of interconnecting shapes; right-angled blocks contrast with curved forms covered in titanium. And because of its complexity, some curved forms were designed with the aid of computers. He, in fact, names artists more frequently than other architects as his major influences.

교수 아마도 우리들 대부분은 우리가 매일 들어가는 건물들이나 스쳐 지나가는 건물들에 대해 깊게 생각하지 않을 것입니다. 그러나 Frank Gehry 같은 건축가에게 건물은 단순히 집이나 사무실 그 이상, 그러니까 예술 작품으로서의 가능성을 가지고 있었습니다. 그는 조각술에 가까운 기법을 접목시킨 건물 설계 방식과 곡선미를 살린 구조물을 짓는 것으로 유명하지요. 그가 설계한 가장 유명한 작품으로 그만의 스타일을 제일 잘 드러내는 작품은, 스페인 Bilbao에 건축된 구겐하임 박물관입니다. 이 건물은 직각의 벽돌들이, 티타늄으로 감싼 곡선미의 형상과 대조를 이루며 각 형태가 서로 완벽히 조화롭게 연결되어 있습니다. 그리고 이런 복잡함 때문에 일부 곡선 형상들은 컴퓨터의 도움을 받아 설계되었지요. 사실, 그는 자신에게 커다란 영향을 미친 인물들로 다른 건축가들이 아닌 예술가들의 이름을 더 자주 언급하고는 합니다.

---

3 교수는 고대 사회에서 운석이 사용되었음을 어떤 방식으로 보여주고 있는가?
(A) 무덤에서 발견된 고대의 칼을 예로 들면서
(B) 이집트에서 사용된 다양한 형태의 금속을 비교하면서
(C) 하늘에서 떨어지는 암석에 대한 고대 신화들을 묘사하면서

정답 (A)

해설 운석이 고대 왕의 무덤에서 단도의 형태로 발견된 예를 들고 있다. 신의 메시지로 인식되던 운석이 나중에 실생활에 사용되었음을 보여주는 증거이다.

🎧 스크립트

P Man has always been fascinated with rocks falling from the sky, what do we call these?
S Um, meteorites?
P Correct. In ancient times, meteorites were usually regarded as messages from God and people prayed to them for rain or things like that. But it turned out to be useless in bringing rain, so people began to use them for practical purposes. At some point, ancient cultures realized that there was metal in them and began to use them in their technology. Take a dagger for example... this one in particular was made of iron from meteorites and was found in King Tut's burial chamber! So we can see that though these rocks were often interpreted as a message from the Gods, they were used for very practical purposes.

교수 인류는 예로부터 하늘에서 떨어지는 돌에 관심을 가져왔습니다. 이것을 뭐라고 하죠?
학생 음, 운석인가요?
교수 맞아요. 역사적으로 볼 때 운석은 보통 신에게서 온 메시지로 여겨졌고 사람들은 비를 내려달라고, 혹은 그런 비슷한 이유로 운석을 향해 기도했습니다. 그러나 그것이 헛된 노력으로 판명이 나자, 사람들은 대신 운석을 실용적인 용도로 보기 시작했습니다. 어떤 점에서 보자면, 고대 문화는 이 우주 암석 안에 금속이 있다는 것을 깨닫고 그것을 그들의 기술에 사용하기 시작했던 것이죠. 한 예로 특히 이 단검, 운석에서 나온 철로 만들어졌고 투탕카멘(King Tut) 왕의 묘실에서 발견된 검이 있습니다. 이렇게 우리는 이 암석들이 종종 신의 메시지로 해석되기

4 교수는 현장학습의 중요성을 어떻게 강조하고 있는가?
   (A) 현장 학습이 수업 과정의 의무 사항이라고 설명하면서
   (B) 현장 학습 장소에서 볼 수 있는 것을 예시하면서
   (C) 은신처가 주로 콘크리트로 만들어졌음을 암시하면서

정답 (B)

해설 현장 학습이 의무가 아닌 자율이지만, 현장 학습을 통해 교실에서 배운 것을 실제에서 구체적으로 확인할 수 있다고 말한다.
(C)의 concrete 는 의미는 다르나 발음이 같은 것을 이용해 혼동을 조장하였다.

🎧 스크립트

S Professor, I wanted to get some more information about Saturday's field trip to the wildlife refuge.
P Sure... what do you need to know?
S Is it a requirement for the class?
P On the contrary, it's voluntary. But it will help, I think, make some of the abstractions we've been talking about more concrete. For example, we just read about the life of nocturnal birds, but we'll hopefully be able to see those birds while we're there.

학생 교수님, 야생동물 보호소로 가는 토요일 현장학습에 대해 좀 더 알고 싶은데요.
교수 좋아요, 무엇을 더 알고 싶나요?
학생 (현장학습이) 강의의 필수 사항인가요?
교수 그 반대예요. 자율이랍니다. 하지만, 내 생각에 (현장학습을 가면) 우리가 지금껏 이야기했던 추상적인 사항들을 보다 구체적으로 아는 데 도움이 될 거예요. 예를 들면, 우리는 그저 야생 조류의 생애에 관한 자료들만 읽었을 뿐이잖아요. 하지만 그곳에 가면 실제로 이런 새들을 볼 수 있을 거예요.

Skill Check-up Organization-Rhetorical Connection

1 교수가 이스터 섬의 식민지화를 언급한 이유는 무엇인가?
   (A) 폴리네시아 인들의 항해에 대한 그의 관점을 입증하려고
   (B) 폴리네시아 식민지화의 예를 제시하려고
   (C) 폴리네시아 인들의 배경을 제공하려고

정답 (A)

해설 강의의 주제는 폴리네시안 사람들의 탁월한 항해술이다. 교수는 그 탁월한 능력을 입증하기 위해 폴리네시아 사람들의 이스터 섬에 대한 식민통치를 근거로 들고 있다.

🎧 스크립트

P Navigating the vast ocean must be tough, right? Well, the Polynesians were very skilled at navigating the sea. They were so adept at navigation, in fact, that they could do it with just the stars to guide them. The Polynesians were able to go great distances in canoes hundreds of years before Europeans mastered long-distance sailing. They were actually able to reach and colonize Easter Island, which is clear across the Pacific from their original homes. They did it without sextants or compasses.

교수 광대한 대양을 항해하기란 무척 힘겨운 일일 겁니다. 그렇죠? 그런데 폴리네시아 사람들은 항해에 아주 능숙했습니다. 그들은 항해술에 대단히 숙련된 사람들이었기 때문에 실상 별의 길잡이 만으로도 항해가 가능했습니다. 이들은 유럽인들이 장거리 항해에 정통하기 앞서 수백 년 전에 이미 카누로 상당한 거리를 이동할 수 있었죠. 그래서 자기네들 고향에서 태평양 건너편에 있는 이스터 섬까지 도착해 그곳을 정복할 수 있었던 겁니다. 그것도 육분의나 나침반 없이 말이죠.

2 교수가 할렘 르네상스의 원인을 언급한 이유는 무엇인가?
   (A) 그 당시 유명한 작가들을 예를 들려고
   (B) 강의 주제에 관한 배경을 제공하려고
   (C) 강의 주제를 바꾸려고

정답 (B)

해설 강의의 주제는 Harlem Renaissance 가 미국 미술에 끼친 영향이라고 했다. 교수는 주제를 보다 명확히 주지시키기 위해 학생들에게 Harlem Renaissance 가 생겨난 계기를 설명하고 있다.

🎧 스크립트

P The years between 1920 and 1930 marked a flowering of the arts in African-American culture. What do we call this period of time?
S Wasn't it the 'Harlem Renaissance'?
P Exactly. But before we go into what we really have to focus on today, umm.. why would this have occurred then? Well... the economy was pretty good, for one. And African-Americans were beginning to celebrate their heritage and make more demands from an unjust society. This ultimately turned into a cultural movement. But to tie those two together, it was the good economy that spurred the greater consciousness of inequality. All right? Now take a look at the influences of the 'Harlem Renaissance' on American arts.

교수 1920년대와 1930년대는 아프리카계 미국인 문화 예술의 전

성기로 특징지어집니다. 이 기간을 뭐라고 할까요?
학생 할렘 르네상스가 아닌가요?
교수 맞습니다. 그런데 오늘 우리가 정말 중점적으로 다룰 내용에 앞서, 에, 그러면 이런 현상은 왜 일어났을까요? 음, 경제가 아주 낙관적이었다는 게 한 가지 이유가 되겠지요. 그리고 아프리카 계 미국인들이 자신들의 전통 의식을 수행하고 부당한 사회를 향해 보다 많은 것들을 요구하기 시작했다는 것도 이유가 되겠습니다. 이것이 마침내 문화적 운동으로까지 이어진 것입니다. 그러나 이 두 가지가 결합되기까지, 불평등이라는 대(大) 인식에 박차를 가한 것은 튼튼한 경제였습니다. 이해되나요? 자 이제, 미국 미술 분야에 있어 할렘 르네상스의 영향을 살펴보겠습니다.

3 교수가 설문 조사를 언급한 이유는 무엇인가?
(A) 대다수의 사람들이 신문을 어떻게 생각하는지에 관한 결론을 도출하기 위해
(B) 설문 결과가 대단히 신뢰할만한 것은 아님을 암시하기 위해
(C) 사람들이 지역 신문을 신뢰하는 이유를 소개하기 위해

정답 (C)

해설 최근의 여론 조사를 보면 사람들이 뉴스를 신뢰하지 않으면서 지역 뉴스의 출처는 신뢰한다고 한다. 교수는 사람들이 지역 뉴스의 출처를 신뢰하는 이유를 살펴보기 위해 지역 신문이 다루는 기사 내용들을 살펴볼 것이다.

🎧 스크립트

P A recent poll showed that most people, while responding that they "don't trust" what they read in national newspapers, also said that they did trust their local news sources.
S1 Well, that doesn't make any sense!
S2 It kinda does… the farther away the news source gets, the more suspicious people are of it.
P Yeah, that's pretty much what we can conclude from this. The other thing that we can conclude is that people don't realize their own biases. You know what I mean? They don't see that they are affected by the nearness of the news source. Then, why do most people trust their local news sources? I'd like to discuss a couple of reasons. First of all, we should carefully look at the materials they are dealing with in their newspapers… what do these newspapers usually talk about?

교수 에, 최근 조사를 보면 대부분의 사람들이 전국지(전국 단위의 신문)에서 읽은 내용들을 '신뢰하지 않는다'라고 응답한 반면에 지역 뉴스 소식통은 신뢰한다고 답했습니다.
학생1 음, 그건 말이 안 되는데요!
학생2 어느 정도는 말이 되는 것 같아요. 뉴스의 소식통이 멀어질수록 그 뉴스에 대한 의구심이 증가될 테니까요.
교수 네, 이 조사를 통해 충분히 그런 결론을 내릴 수 있습니다. 또 한 가지, 우리는 여기서 사람들이 자신의 편견을 깨닫지 못한다는 결론도 내릴 수 있습니다. 무슨 의미인지 알겠어요? 이들은 자신들이 뉴스의 출처에 근접해있음으로 인해 스스로 영향을 받고 있다는 사실을 알지 못하는 겁니다. 그러면, 대부분의 사람들이 지역 뉴스 소식통을 믿는 이유는 무엇일까요? 몇 가지 이유를 살펴보죠. 먼저 우리는 이들 신문이 다루고 있는 내용들을 주의 깊게 살펴보아야만 합니다. 이 신문들은 보통 어떤 이야기를 합니까?

4 교수가 금을 언급한 이유는 무엇인가?
(A) 체로키 족이 차지한 땅을 묘사하기 위해
(B) 미국 원주민들이 자신들 고향에서 내몰린 원인을 주지시키기 위해
(C) 미국-인디언 협정의 배경을 설명하기 위해

정답 (B)

해설 Cherokees인들이 강제 이주된 원인은 미국 인구가 증가하고 금광이 발견되면서 그동안 불모의 땅으로 여겨졌던 Cherokees의 땅이 미국에게도 가치 있는 곳으로 바뀌게 되었기 때문이다.

🎧 스크립트

P Let's look at the causes of the forcible removal of the Cherokees, a nation of Native Americans that lived in the state of Georgia for centuries. The population of that state began to increase rapidly over a relatively short period of time — there were six times the number of people there in 1830 than in 1790. In order to have room to build and farm there, settlers of European descent began taking what had been native lands, and forcing the Cherokee and other native people in the area farther and farther west. The path upon which the native Americans trod as they were forced from their homes was referred to as the Trail of Tears. The second thing that led to the Trail of Tears was the discovery of gold in the mountains there. Land that had not been seen as valuable was suddenly desirable, and again the natives were displaced.

교수 수세기 동안 조지아 주에 살아왔던 아메리카 인디언 국가 즉, 체로키 민족의 강제 이주 원인을 살펴봅시다. 조지아 주의 인구는 상대적으로 짧은 기간 동안 급격히 증가하기 시작했는데, 1830년대에는 1790년대에 비해 인구가 6배나 되었습니다. 때문에 그곳에 건물을 세우고 농사 지을 공간을 확보하기 위해 유럽 출신 개척자들은 원주민들의 땅을 차지하고 체로키 족과 다른 원주민들을 저 먼 서부지역으로 강제로 몰아냈습니다. 이들이 고향에서 강제로 쫓겨나면서 밟고 지나간 길을 눈물의 길이라고 부릅니다. 이들을 눈물의 길로 이끈 두 번째 원인은 이곳

산악지대에서 금광을 발견한 데 있습니다. 그때까지 전혀 가치가 없었던 땅이 갑자기 탐낼만한 가치 있는 땅으로 바뀌게 되면서 그렇게 또 원주민들이 추방되었습니다.

Exercise

1 A - (C) B - (D)　　2 A - (D) B - (B)
3 A - (B) B - (A)(C)　4 A - (C) B - (C)

Exercise 1
미술 역사 강의의 일부를 듣고 물음에 답하시오.

🎧 스크립트

P　Today's lecture is going to really narrow in on the French painter Edouard Manet, and in particular the way he heralds modern painting. At first, we'll have a quick look at his life and at some aspects of his paintings that made his work different from the work of earlier artists. Okay, so Manet painted in the 1860s through the 1880s. Manet's work was very controversial among critics because he chose subjects which were distinct from the old style. One of his famous paintings *Luncheon on the Grass* is an example. The painting of fully dressed men and a nude woman was not commonly acceptable at the time. Another of Manet's notable works is *Olympia*, a semi nude woman is wearing a few items of clothing and has a fully dressed servant next to her. The effect is the same as in *Luncheon on the Grass*. Despite such criticisms from older artists, a group of young painters expressed enthusiasm for Manet's work. In addition to the nude-fully clad conventions, Manet used an innovative technique, a rough sketch-like style, that further distinguished his work from realism. He also did black outlining of figures to draw viewers' attention to the surface of the picture plane. This is considered modern, too.

교수　오늘 강의는 프랑스 화가 에듀어드 마네, 특히 그가 어떻게 현대 회화의 도래를 알리게 되었는지에 초점을 맞추려고 합니다. 먼저 우리는 그의 삶과 그의 작품을 초기 예술가들의 작품과 구분 짓는 몇 가지 측면에 대해 간단히 살펴볼 것입니다. 자, 일단, 마네는 1860년부터 1880년대에 그림을 그렸지요. 마네의 작품은 비평가들 사이에 상당한 논란을 불러일으켰는데요, 이는 마네가 그 이전까지와는 다른 주제들을 택했기 때문입니다. 그의 유명한 작품 중 하나인 Luncheon on the Grass(풀밭 위의 점심 식사)가 그 예지요. 정장 차림의 남자들과 나체의 여성을 담은 이 그림은, 당시에는 보편적으로 납득되지 않는 그림이었습니다. 마네의 또 다른 유명한 작품으로 Olympia가 있습니다. 거의 나체 차림인 여성은 몇 가지의 아이템만 걸쳤고, 그녀 옆에는 옷을 다 갖춰 입은 하녀가 있습니다. 그 효과는 Luncheon on the Grass에서와 같았습니다. 기존 화가들의 비난에도 불구하고, 젊은 화가 집단은 마네의 작품에 열광하였습니다. 나체-정장 차림의 관례 외에도 마네는 그의 작품을 리얼리즘과는 현저히 구별되는 혁신적인 기술, 즉 거친 소묘 느낌의 스타일을 사용했습니다. 그는 또한 그림을 보는 사람의 주의를 끌기 위해 형체의 윤곽에 검은 테두리를 그렸는데, 이것 역시 (그의 작품이) 모던하다고 여겨지는 이유입니다.

어휘 narrow 좁히다, 좁게 하다　herald (사물, 일이) ~의 도래를 알리다　nude 벌거벗은, 나체의　acceptable 받아들일 수 있는　notable 주목할 만한, 뛰어난　enthusiasm 열광, 열중　clad 옷을 입은　convention (사회의) 관습, 풍습　innovative 혁신적인, 창조력이 풍부한　draw one's attention ~의 주목을 끌다

A　교수는 마네의 그림을 어떤 방식으로 설명하고 있는가?
(A) 마네와 모더니즘 사이의 관계를 정의하면서
(B) 마네의 작품에 대한 비평가의 설명을 제공하면서
(C) 마네 작품의 혁신적인 요소들을 나열하면서
(D) 마네의 그림과 19세기의 그림들을 대조하면서

해설 교수는 마네의 화풍이 당시에는 상당한 논란을 불러일으켰음을 주지시키면서 그런 논란의 계기가 된 그림(Luncheon on the Grass, Olympia)과 그만의 특징적인 스타일(rough sketch-like style, black outlining of figures)을 언급하고 있다.

B　마네의 작품은 어떤 면에서 현실주의 그림들과 구별되는가?
(A) 마네는 전경을 중요하게 생각했다.
(B) 현실주의 화가들은 인물에 검은 윤곽을 주었는데, 마네는 그렇게 하지 않았다.
(C) 마네는 형체와 물체를 뚜렷하지 않게(희미하게) 묘사했다.
(D) 마네는 논란이 될만한 주제를 택했다.

Exercise 2
경영학 수업에서의 토론의 일부를 듣고 물음에 답하시오.

🎧 스크립트

P　As we look at various global economies... uh... like I said earlier... something we notice is that climate can depress or boost economies. I mean the climate has an influence on economic growth and its stagnation. Anyone have any ideas about why this is?

S1　I can think of a few happenings in the rainy season. Hurricanes, floods, storms... there are some factors with a powerful impact on our life. Roads are sometimes swept by waves of the flood or communication facilities are blown away by hurricanes. Roads and communication networks are basically key elements of a country's economy. Consequently, natural disasters could result in stoppage or paralyzing of the country, and then influence other aspects of economy.

S2 I've heard of... I don't have any exact source... but I've heard that the tropical climate stagnates economies.

P Well, yes and no. Umm, we may say that there is a tendency of tropical cultures to have depressed or stagnated economies. The climate could interfere with growth, technological development and overall prosperity. However, there's no reason that climate should, on its own, prevent societies from developing at a rapid pace. But the fact is that the climate, for example in the tropical region as you mentioned, is part of the problem, in that it makes it possible for certain diseases to exist and thrive in tropical places. Even if people do not die from exposure to parasites and viruses, they are often weakened to the point where they cannot work, which has a massive and negative impact on the economy of these regions.

교수 다양한 세계 경제를 볼 때, 전에 말했던 것처럼... 우리가 주목하는 것은 기후가 경제를 침체시키거나 활성화시킬 수 있다는 것입니다. 그러니까 경제 성장이나 경기 침체에 기후가 영향을 미친다는 얘기예요. 왜 그런지 누구 아는 사람 있나요?

학생 1 우기에 발생하는 몇 가지 일들을 생각해볼 수 있을 것 같아요. 허리케인, 홍수, 폭풍처럼 우리 생활에 강력한 영향을 가진 몇 가지 요소들이 있습니다. 때때로 도로가 홍수에 휩쓸려 내려가고 통신 장비들도 허리케인 때문에 날아가잖아요. 도로나 통신 네트워크는 기본적으로 국가 경제의 중요 요소입니다. 결과적으로 보면, 자연 재해로 인해 국가 기능이 마비되고 다른 경제분야에도 영향을 미치게 되지요.

학생 2 제가 듣기로는... 정확한 출처는 잘 모르겠지만, 열대 기후도 경제를 침체시킨다고 하던데요.

교수 글쎄, 그렇다고 볼 수도 있고 아닐 수도 있습니다. 음, 어쩌면 열대 문화가 경기 침체나 부진을 가져오는 경향이 있다고 말할 수는 있을 겁니다. 기후가 경기 성장이나 기술 발전, 전반적인 번영을 방해하는 거죠. 그러나 기후 자체가 사회의 급속적인 발전을 저해하는 원인은 아니에요. 하지만, 예를 들어 학생이 언급한 열대 지방을 보면, 그 지역에 특정 질병이 출현하고 번성하는 데 기후가 일부 책임이 있음은 분명합니다. 사람들이 기생충이나 바이러스에 노출된다고 해서 반드시 죽는 것은 아니지만, (그것들 때문에) 종종 일하지 못할 정도로 몸이 쇠약해지는 경우가 있고, 이것이 이들 지역 경제에 상당히 부정적인 영향을 미치는 겁니다.

> **어휘** boost ~의 경기를 부양하다 stagnation 침체, 부진, 불경기 facility 설비, 시설 tropical 열대의, 열대 지방의 stagnate 침체하다, 정체하다 tendency 경향, 풍조, 추세 prosperity 번영, 번창, 융성 exposure (위험·공격 등에) 몸을 드러냄 parasite 기생충, 기생균 interfere with ~을 방해하다, ~와 충돌하다

A 교수가 열대 지방을 언급한 이유는 무엇인가?
 (A) 안정적인 구조물을 짓는 데 부정적인 영향이 있음을 보여주기 위해
 (B) 열대 지역 기후와 유럽 국가들의 기후를 비교하기 위해
 (C) 강의에 기후 사례 연구를 소개하기 위해
 (D) 기후가 경제에 커다란 영향을 미치는 이유를 제시하기 위해

해설 열대 기후가 사람들의 질병을 초래하여, 그 결과 노동력이 손실되고, 그것이 결국 경제에 부정적인 여파로 작용할 수 있음을 예로 들었다.

B 교수는 열대 문화에 대해 어떤 얘기를 하고 있는가?
 (A) 사회가 열대 지역일수록 그 사회의 경제 발전이 느리다.
 (B) 기후가 사람들의 경제 활동 참여를 방해할 수 있다.
 (C) 열대 지역의 사람들은 병들어 죽는 경향이 있다.
 (D) 기술 발달은 기후에 의해 가장 크게 영향을 받는다.

해설 교수는 열대 기후가 직접적으로 경제에 영향을 미치는지는 알 수 없으나 열대 지역의 기후가 병을 유발하여 사람들의 경제활동을 둔화시킬 수 있다고 말한다.

Exercise 3
농업학 수업에서의 대화의 일부를 듣고 물음에 답하시오.

🎧 스크립트

P The locust is an insect that, in large numbers, and at regular intervals, destroys huge areas of farmland, devouring the harvests. The locust plague is a worldwide issue now. It has occurred mainly in desert and scrub areas. It originated in Africa and has spread as far as western Asian countries such as India, Nepal, and China. The, um, the desert locusts normally increase in number when climate conditions are favorable... and as adults, they form swarms and travel great distances in search of food. They harm the crops in this way.

S1 What has been done to control the problem?

P Uh... for the method of controlling the

desert locust swarms, at present, some specialized insecticides are applied in small doses. They are sprayed directly to the insects by vehicle-mounted and aerial sprayers.
S2 The use of chemicals, I think, possibly, poisons the soil, and even animals or birds.
P Yes, many people have been concerned about it. This is why biological control has been available since the late nineties. The biological product... is a kind of fungus. It doesn't kill locusts quickly. The fungus typically takes two to three weeks to kill up to ninety percent of the locusts. But the advantage is very evident, though. It affects only locusts, allowing natural enemies of the insects to continue their work.

교수 메뚜기는 대규모로 움직이며 일정한 주기로 수확물을 먹어치워 큰 농장지역을 파괴하는 곤충입니다. 메뚜기의 이상 발생은 현재 세계적인 문제이며, 주로 사막이나 관목 숲에서 발생합니다. 이런 현상은 아프리카에서 최초 발생한 후, 인도, 네팔, 중국과 같은 서아시아 국가로 번져가고 있습니다. 에, 이 사막 메뚜기는 보통 기후 조건이 온화할 때 개체수가 증가하고, 성충이 되면 무리지어 먹이를 찾아 장거리를 이동하지요. 이들은 이런 방식으로 농작물을 훼손합니다.
학생1 이 문제를 해결하기 위해 어떤 조치가 이루어졌나요?
교수 에, 현재까지는, 이 사막 메뚜기 떼를 통제하는 방법으로 몇 가지 특수 살충제를 소량 적용시켜보았지요. 이 살충제들은 차량에 설치된 분사기나 항공 분사기를 이용해 곤충에 직접 살포됩니다.
학생2 제 생각에, 화학물질의 사용은 토양은 물론, 심지어 동물이나 조류들에게도 해로울 것 같은데요.
교수 네, 많은 사람들이 그 점을 염려했습니다. 그래서 19세기 후반부터 생물학적 방제를 이용하게 된 것입니다. 생물학적 생성물이란... 일종의 균입니다. 이 균이란 것은 메뚜기를 속히 제거하지는 못해서 메뚜기의 90% 가량을 죽이는 데 보통 2-3주가 걸리지요. 그래도 그 효과는 아주 확실합니다. 이 균은 오직 메뚜기에게만 영향을 주는 것이어서 천적은 아무런 해 없이 자기 일을 계속 할 수가 있지요.

어휘 locust 메뚜기 interval (장소, 시간의) 간격, 틈 devour 게걸스레 먹다, 탐식하다 harvest 수확, 추수 plague (유해 동물의) 이상(대량)발생 scrub 관목 덤불, 관목이 우거진 숲 swarm 무리, 떼 insecticide 살충, 살충제 dose (약의) 1회분, 복용량 aerial 공기의, 대기의, 기체의 in search of ~을 찾아서, ~을 구해서

A 교수는 메뚜기의 이상 발생 통제 방법을 어떻게 설명하는가?
(A) 그 방법의 장점을 나열하면서
(B) 그 방법이 환경과 동물에 미치는 영향을 비교하면서
(C) 살충제의 성공적인 사용 실례를 들면서
(D) 그 방법이 메뚜기 수에 어떤 식으로 작용되는지 알려주면서

해설 살충제를 이용한 방법은 그 역효과가 두드러진다.

B 다음 중 사막 메뚜기에 관해 언급된 것은 무엇인가? 정답 두 개를 고르시오.
(A) 서아시아 지역에 잠식해있다.
(B) 사막 메뚜기는 (다른 곳으로) 이동하지 않는다.
(C) 어떤 날씨는 사막 메뚜기의 수를 증가시킨다.
(D) 균(제거 방법)이 적용된 후 일주일 내에 죽었다.

해설 메뚜기는 아프리카에서 기원하여 일부 아시아 지역까지 이동했으며, 기후 조건이 좋을 경우 번식률이 증가한다고 했다.

Exercise 4

학생과 사서의 대화의 일부를 듣고 물음에 답하시오.

 스크립트

S Excuse me.
L How can I help you?
S I want to access the on-line database from my computer in my dorm room. But I can't get into it. Can you help me?
L Is this a new problem or have you experienced it before?
S Actually, this is the first time I have tried to access the database.
L Did you follow the directions on the screen?
S Yes, but it kept telling me I wasn't authorized to use the service.
L Ah... well, I think I know what has to be done with it... Did you get a password and user name from the Information Technology desk to use when you log on?
S Oh, I didn't know I needed to. I thought I could just use my e-mail name and password.
L The IT staff on the second floor will issue a new user name and password for you.
S Is the IT desk open now?
L Well, its hours are from 10 am to 5 pm. Sorry, but it's not open till tomorrow morning. But you are welcome to use the library computers for the time being.
S That'll save me. Thanks.

학생 실례합니다.
사서 뭘 도와드릴까요?
학생 기숙사 방에서 제 컴퓨터로 온라인 데이터베이스에 들어가고 싶은데 들어갈 수가 없어요. 도와주실래요?
사서 이런 문제가 처음 접하는 일인가요, 아니면 전에도 있었던 일

인가요?
학생 사실, 데이터베이스에 들어가 보려고 한 건 이번이 처음이거든요.
사서 화면에 나타난 지시사항을 잘 따랐나요?
학생 네, 그런데 자꾸 서비스를 사용할 권한이 없다고 해요.
사서 음, 그래요. 어떻게 해야 할지 알겠네요. Information Technology(정보 기술) 데스크에서 로그인에 필요한 비밀번호와 사용자 이름을 발급받으셨어요?
학생 이런, 그런 게 필요한지 몰랐는걸요. 그냥 제 이메일 이름과 비밀번호를 쓰면 되는 줄 알았어요.
사서 2층에 가시면 IT 직원이 학생에게 사용자 이름과 비밀번호를 새로 발급해 줄 거예요.
학생 지금 IT 창구가 문을 열었나요?
사서 글쎄요, (운영) 시간은 오전 10시부터 오후 5시까지예요. 죄송합니다. 내일 아침에야 열리겠군요. 하지만 임시로 도서관 컴퓨터를 사용할 수는 있어요.
학생 천만다행이네요. 감사합니다.

> 어휘 authorize 권한을 부여하다, 위임하다 issue (면허증 등을) 내주다, 발행하다 log on (컴퓨터에) 접속하다, 사용 개시하다

A 사서는 어떤 방식으로 학생이 자신의 문제점을 이해하도록 돕고 있는가?
(A) 학생에게 IT창구의 직원에게 문제를 설명하도록 지시함으로써
(B) 학생에게 문제점을 적어서 아침에 제출하라고 요청함으로써
(C) 학생이 알맞은 정보를 사용하지 않았다는 것을 지적함으로써
(D) 학생의 컴퓨터가 업데이트되어야한다는 것을 알려줌으로써

해설 사서는 컴퓨터 접속 장애의 원인이 될 만한 몇 가지 가능성들을 하나하나 짚어보다가 결국, 학생이 잘못된 정보를 사용하여 접속을 시도하려 했음을 알아냈다.

B 이제 여자는 무엇을 할 것인가?
(A) 내일 IT창구가 문을 열 때까지 기다릴 것이다.
(B) 새로 받은 비밀번호와 사용자 이름으로 다시 시도할 것이다.
(C) 도서관 컴퓨터를 이용할 것이다.
(D) 자신이 데이터베이스에서 찾고자 하는 정보가 무엇인지 사서에게 이야기할 것이다.

해설 개인적으로 컴퓨터 자료를 활용하려면 IT 데스크에서 개인 아이디와 비밀번호를 새로 발급받아야 하지만 지금 당장 신청할 수는 없다. 학생은 임시로 도서관 컴퓨터를 사용할 것이다.

Dictation Exercise

Exercise 1

① narrow in on the French painter
② he heralds
③ the work of earlier artists
④ controversial among critics
⑤ which were distinct from
⑥ fully dressed men and a nude woman
⑦ has a fully dressed servant next to her
⑧ is the same as in
⑨ the nude-fully clad conventions
⑩ black outlining of figures

Exercise 2

① various global economies
② climate can depress or boost
③ Anyone have any ideas about why this is
④ think of a few
⑤ with a powerful impact on our life
⑥ swept by waves of the flood
⑦ are blown away
⑧ could result in stoppage or
⑨ I've heard of
⑩ the tropical climate stagnates
⑪ overall prosperity
⑫ on its own
⑬ at a rapid pace
⑭ it makes it possible for
⑮ do not die from exposure to
⑯ often weakened to the point

Exercise 3

① The locust is an insect
② at regular intervals
③ devouring the harvests
④ mainly in desert and scrub areas
⑤ has spread as far as
⑥ they form swarms
⑦ in search of food
⑧ are applied in small doses
⑨ poisons the soil
⑩ biological control has been available
⑪ is a kind of fungus
⑫ two to three weeks to kill up to
⑬ allowing natural enemies of the insects

Exercise 4

① access the on-line database
② I can't get into it

③ follow the directions on the screen
④ I wasn't authorized to use the service
⑤ get a password and user name
⑥ I didn't know I needed to
⑦ The IT staff on the second floor will issue
⑧ are from 10 am to 5 pm
⑨ it's not open till
⑩ That'll save me

Actual Test

1 1 - (B) 2 - (C) 3 - (B) 4 - (A)
2 1 - (B) 2 - (C) 3 - (D) 4 - (D)

Actual Test 1

음악 역사 수업에서의 토론의 일부를 듣고 물음에 답하시오.

🎧 스크립트

P   When we talk about the definition of music, we often recall John Cage, one of the most important and controversial musicians of the 20th century. He is possibly best known for his piece 4′33″. He performed the piece first in 1952. All the audience did was see a player sit at the piano and lift the lid of the piano. Some time later, without playing any notes, he closed the lid. A while after that, again he lifted the lid. And then again, having played nothing, he closed the lid. The piece was finished without a note being played.

S1 Wait a second... he didn't play a single note?

P   Nope. He was completely silent. Now what do you suppose he was doing?

S1 Maybe he was trying to prove that he thought his audience was stupid to pay for tickets for a concert that had no music?

P   (laughing) Not exactly, but. . .

S2 Well, to me, he was making an important point. The audience was forced to sit there and listen to all the sounds in the auditorium. It really made them think about listening, which is an important part of music.

P   Exactly. For Cage, listening was the important part of music. That is to say, John meant to let the audience expect unexpected sounds. He regarded that listening intently in silence. That was how John Cage defined music. He was a person who tried to put his concept of music into practice.

교수 우리가 음악의 정의에 대해 이야기할 때면 종종 20세기에 가장 영향력을 지녔으며 많은 논란을 불러일으킨 음악가 가운데 한 명인 John Cage를 떠올리곤 합니다. John Cage는 아마도 4'33" 이라는 작품으로 가장 잘 알려져 있을 텐데요. 그는 1952년에 처음으로 이 작품을 연주했습니다. 이 때 관중들이 한 일은 피아노 앞에 앉아 피아노 뚜껑을 들어 올리는 연주자를 본 것뿐이었습니다. 그리고 얼마 후에, 그 연주자는 아무것도 연주하지 않고는 다시 뚜껑을 닫았습니다. 또 잠시 후에 연주자는 뚜껑을 들었다가, 이번에도 역시 아무것도 연주하지 않고 뚜껑을 닫았습니다. 이 작품은 한 음도 연주하지 않은 채로 끝났습니다.

학생1 잠깐만요. 한 개 음도 연주하지 않았다고요?

교수 그래요. 그는 전혀 소리를 내지 않았습니다. 자, 여러분은 그가 무엇을 했던 거라고 생각하십니까?

학생1 아마도 음악을 연주하지도 않는 콘서트에 돈을 지불할 만큼 자기 관객들은 어리석을 거라는 자신의 생각을 입증하려고 한 건가요?

교수 (웃음) 그렇진 않아요. 하지만...

학생2 글쎄요. 제가 볼 때는, 그는 중요한 요소를 지적한 거 같아요. 관객은 그곳에 앉아 강당 내의 모든 소리를 들을 수밖에 없었을 거예요. 그 때문에 관객들은 음악의 중요한 부분인 '듣는다는 것'에 관해 생각하게 되었을 거고요.

교수 맞습니다. Cage에게 듣기는 음악의 중요한 부분이었어요. 말하자면, John은 관객들로 하여금 예기치 않은 소리를 기대하도록 이끌어 가고 싶었던 겁니다. 그는 침묵 속에서 그렇게 할 수 있을 거라고 생각했습니다. 그것이 John Cage가 음악을 정의한 방식이었죠. 그는 자신의 발상을 직접 실행하려고 한 사람이었습니다.

1 교수가 4' 33"을 언급한 이유는 무엇인가?
  (A) 침묵이 음악만큼 가치있다는 자신의 견해를 뒷받침하기 위해
  (B) 청취가 음악의 중요 부분이라는 John Cage의 개념을 소개하기 위해
  (C) 음악과 시간이 밀접하게 연관되어 있다는 증거를 제공하기 위해
  (D) 1950년대의 중요 음악 작법의 예를 들기 위해

해설 교수는 John Cage 의 4'33' 이라는 작품을 통해 그가 궁극적으로 청취자들에게 전달하려는 의미가 무엇인지 얘기하고 있다.

2 교수의 중심 견해는 무엇인가?
  (A) Cage의 작품을 음악으로 분류해서는 안 된다.
  (B) Cage의 실험은 젊은 음악가들에게 모델이 되었다.
  (C) 음악은 단순히 연주 이상의 그 무엇이다.
  (D) 음악은 그 음악을 듣는 사람만이 정의할 수 있다.

해설 교수는 Cage가 시도한 playing이 빠진 형태의 음악을 언급함으로써 학생들로 하여금 음악의 본질적 요소가 무엇인지를 생각하게 하고 있다.

3 교수가 John Cage에 대해 말한 것은 무엇인가?
(A) Cage는 아마 피아노 연주자로 가장 잘 알려져 있을 것이다.
(B) 그는 무대에서 작품 4'33"을 공연하면서 피아노를 한 음도 연주하지 않았다.
(C) Cage는 작곡을 할 때 노트를 사용했다.
(D) 그는 음악을 정의하는 데 여러 가지 방법이 있음을 보여주려고 했다.

해설 John Cage는 실제 연주가 되지 않는 피아노 곡 4'33"을 선보임으로써 청중과 비평가들로부터 많은 논쟁을 불러일으켰다.
(A) - Cage는 그의 실험 정신을 시도한 것으로써 유명한 것이지 피아노 연주가로써 유명하다는 언급은 없다.

4 Cage의 작품에 대한 교수의 의견은 어떠한가?
(A) Cage의 작품이 관객들로 하여금 음악에 대해 다르게 생각하도록 했으므로 긍정적인 입장이다.
(B) 중립적인 입장이며 학생들의 의견을 듣고 싶어 한다.
(C) 작곡가가 속임수를 사용했기 때문에 부정적이다.
(D) 학생들의 의견을 듣고 자신의 의견을 바꿨다.

해설 교수는 Cage의 4'33"은 청중들이 음악의 본질, 즉 listening이 무엇인지를 생각하게 만든 가치 있는 시도였다고 생각하고 있다.

Actual Test 2
두 학생 간의 대화를 듣고 물음에 답하시오.

🎧 스크립트

S1 Hey Marie, come in, how can I help you?
S2 I just got the rough draft of my essay back from my professor and she basically said I need to rewrite the whole thing!
S1 That's pretty stressful, huh? What did she say the problem was?
S2 Almost everything! She said I didn't use enough sources to support my claims, that my thesis statement was confusing, and that my writing had significant grammatical errors in it. I don't know how I'm going to get it fixed in time to hand it in next Friday. Would you help me?
S1 Well, if you want I could help you on the weekend, but I think the writing center is a better option because you need to fix this problem quickly.
S2 What can I get from the writing center, then?
S1 Umm, they can show you the places where you need more evidence, and uh, help you figure out where to get it. The center's tutors can help with the thesis and grammar problems, too. They're really fast and extremely professional.
S2 What if they don't know anything about my paper's topic?
S1 Well, I think your problem is not the information; it's more how your essay is organized and written. I guarantee they can help.
S2 Umm… I've got to visit the center to get help from them. The center, let's see, where's it located?
S1 It's in the humanities building.

학생 1 안녕, Marie. 들어와. 내가 도와줄 거 있어?
학생 2 방금 교수님으로부터 내가 쓴 에세이 초고를 돌려받았는데 기본적으로 원고 전체를 다 다시 써야 한다고 해서.
학생 1 스트레스 받겠다. 뭐가 문제라고 하시니?
학생 2 거의 다! 내 주장을 뒷받침할만한 자료도 충분히 사용하지 않았고 주제문도 모호한데다 글에는 상당히 큰 문법적 오류도 있대. 금요일까지 내야 하는데 제시간에 제출하려면 어떻게 수정해야 할지 모르겠어. 도와줄 수 있니?
학생 1 글쎄, 네가 원하면 주말에 널 도와줄 수는 있어. 하지만 문제점들을 빨리 수정해야 할 테니까 내 생각엔 작문 센터가 더 좋을 거 같아.
학생 2 그럼, 작문 센터에서 어떤 걸 고칠 수 있지?
학생 1 음, 증거 자료가 더 필요한 부분을 제시해 줄 거야. 그리고 음, 그런 자료를 어디서 얻을 수 있는지도 알려 줄 테고. 센터 강사들이 주제문 수정이나 문법적 오류를 잡아내는 것도 도와주셔. 정말 빠르고 아주 전문적인 분들이지.
학생 2 그런데 그 사람들이 내가 정한 논문 주제에 관해서 지식이 없으면 어떡해?
학생 1 글쎄, 내 생각에 네 문제는 (논문 주제에 관한) 정보는 아닌 것 같아. 에세이가 얼마나 잘 짜여 있고 잘 썼는가 하는 게 더 중요하다고 봐. 그들이 도움이 될 거라고 장담해.
학생 2 음… 센터에 가서 도움을 받아야겠다. 어디 보자, 센터가 어디 있어?
학생 1 인문학 건물에 있어.

1 남자는 자신의 제안을 어떤 식으로 설명하는가?
(A) 그의 친구에게 에세이의 논제에 관해 더 열심히 작업할 것을 권하면서
(B) 작문 센터와 그 자신이 줄 수 있는 도움을 비교하면서
(C) 그녀가 쓰고 있는 주제에 관해 그들(작문 센터 강사들)이 잘 알고 있을 것이라고 설득하면서
(D) 그녀의 지난 에세이 결과를 설명하면서

해설 남자는 2가지 선택안을 제시하면서 자신은 주말에나 시간을 낼 수 있으므로 보다 빠르고 정확한 도움을 줄 수 있는 Writing center를 찾아보라고 권한다.

2 여자가 남자를 찾아 간 이유는 무엇인가?
(A) 자신의 과제에 내려진 평가에 대해 불평하려고

(B) 자신의 과제 내용에 관해 상의하려고
(C) 남자가 자신의 과제를 도와줄 수 있는지 물어보려고
(D) 남자도 비슷한 문제를 겪었었는지 확인하려고

3 다음 중 교수가 지적한 문제가 <u>아닌</u> 것은 무엇인가?
(A) 논문의 진술 방식을 이해하기 어렵다.
(B) 전체적으로 문법적 오류가 있다.
(C) 기본적으로 주장하고 있는 것들에 대한 근거가 충분하지 않다.
(D) 작문의 대부분은 잘못된 주장을 하고 있다.

해설 논리적 근거(즉, 정보)가 부족하고, 설명하는 문장들이 이해하기 어려우며, 문법상의 오류가 많다고 지적당했다.

4 대화에 따르면, 작문 센터의 강사들은 어떠한가?
(A) 논문 자료 조사를 돕는다.
(B) 몇 가지 좋은 문법책을 추천해 줄 수 있다.
(C) 모두 작문 경험이 풍부하다.
(D) 구조적 문제를 지적하는 데 능숙하다.

해설 Writing center에서는 문법상의 오류나 에세이의 구조 수정 등에 관한 도움을 준다.

Dictation — Actual Test

Actual Test 1

① the definition of music
② performed the piece first in 1952
③ did was see a player
④ without playing any notes
⑤ A while after that
⑥ he closed the lid
⑦ He was completely silent
⑧ was stupid to pay for
⑨ was forced to sit there
⑩ all the sounds in the auditorium
⑪ meant to let the audience
⑫ listening intently
⑬ tried to put his concept of music into practice

Actual Test 2

① the rough draft of my essay back
② I need to rewrite
③ my thesis statement was confusing
④ significant grammatical errors in it
⑤ get it fixed in time to hand it in

⑥ need to fix this problem quickly
⑦ figure out where to get it
⑧ help with the thesis
⑨ What if they don't know
⑩ how your essay is organized and written
⑪ where's it located

Vocabulary Review

다음 각 정의와 일치하는 단어를 골라 써 넣으시오.

1 controversial	2 distinct	3 criticism
4 climate	5 rapid	6 negative
7 destroy	8 evident	9 authorize
10 guarantee		

1 공공연히 논쟁을 야기하는
2 본질이나 특성에서 어떤 것과 차이가 있는
3 평가 또는 가치 판단
4 특정 장소에서의 장기간에 걸친 날씨 조건
5 짧은 기간 안에 행해진
6 비난, 부정, 또는 거부하는
7 어떤 것을 망치거나 돌이킬 수 없는 해를 끼치다
8 명백히 눈에 띄는
9 ~할 권리를 주다
10 어떤 것에 대해 보증하다, 또는 확신을 하다

다음 구문을 사용하여 문장을 완성하시오.

| 1 that is to say | 2 tried to | 3 figure out |
| 4 in time | 5 were forced to | |

1 그는 자발적으로 고아원에서 일한다. 즉, 그는 보수를 받지 않고 일한다.
2 무척 힘들었지만 그래도 그녀는 그 프로젝트를 혼자서 끝내려고 했다.
3 그는 교수가 뭐라고 말하는 지 이해할 수 없어서 투덜거렸다.
4 두 회사는 시간 안에 해결책을 내놓았다.
5 많은 시골 사람들이 일자리가 부족하여 도시로 이주해야만 했다.

Progress Test

3 1 - (A) 2 - (D) 3 - (B) 4 - (A) 5 - 번역참조
4 1 - (C) 2 - (B) 3 - (A) 4 - (C) 5 - (A)

Progress Test 3

생물학 수업에서의 대화를 듣고 물음에 답하시오.

🎧 스크립트

P Let's pick up today with the mass

extinction of the dinosaurs. This has been a source of controversy in the scientific community. What caused this extinction? Now, as you might guess, millions upon millions of animals died. But I want you to keep in mind the concepts, not so much the numbers. In trying to find answers, scientists have proposed a number of theories. One type of theory suggests that there was a cataclysmic event like a meteor collision. Another type holds disease accountable. And a third type suggests that it was the rise of a mammal that preyed on dinosaur eggs that led to their demise. The meteor or cataclysm theory was given a boost in credibility by the discovery of the iridium layer. The presence of this chemical element in the soil points to a massive impact from space, which would have caused a major, though temporary, change in climate. This killed off the dinosaurs.

S But why would other species have survived? They needed a stable climate and sunlight too, right?

P Right! And let me tell you, this is a major flaw in the theory. Some suggest that because other animals were smaller they were better equipped to survive. Others feel that this is not a convincing explanation and are searching for a more plausible theory to explain their disappearance. So we're still not really sure what happened.

교수 오늘은 공룡의 집단 멸종에 대해 이야기해 봅시다. 이 주제는 그동안 과학계에서 논란이 되는 소재였지요. 무엇이 공룡을 멸종시킨 걸까요? 자, 여러분도 아시겠지만, 수백만 동물이 죽었습니다. 그러나 저는 여러분들이 마음속에 숫자보다는 개념을 떠올렸으면 합니다. 문제의 해답을 찾으려는 시도를 통해 과학자들은 여러 이론들을 제시했습니다. 그 이론 중의 하나는 유성의 충돌 같은 대격변이 있었다는 것이지요. 다른 이론에서는 그럴듯한 질병들을 원인으로 내세웁니다. 그리고 세 번째 이론에서는 공룡의 알을 먹이로 하는 포유류가 등장했기 때문에 멸종할 수밖에 없었다고 말합니다. 운석, 즉 대격변 이론은 이리듐 층을 발견함으로써 신빙성을 획득하였습니다. 토양층에 이 화학 물질이 존재한다는 것은 우주로부터 커다란 영향이 있었음을 암시하는 것이며, 이는 비록 일시적이긴 하나 커다란 기후 변화를 초래하였습니다. 그리고 이 때문에 공룡들이 죽었다는 겁니다.

학생 그러면 다른 종들이 살아남을 수 있었던 이유는 뭔가요? 그들 역시 안정적인 기후나 햇빛이 필요했을 텐데요, 안 그런가요?

교수 맞아요! 한 가지 말씀드릴 건, 이게 바로 이 이론의 두드러진 결점이라는 거죠. 물론 다른 동물들은 (공룡보다 덩치가) 작았기 때문에 생존에 더 적합했던 거라고 주장하는 사람들도 있습니다. 하지만 또 다른 이들은 이것으로 확실하게 설명되는 것은 아니라며 집단 멸종을 설명할 보다 타당한 이론을 찾고 있지요. 그래서 사실 우리는 여전히 (그 시대에) 무슨 일이 있었는지 확실히 알지 못합니다.

1 이 대화의 주된 화제는 무엇인가?
(A) 공룡 멸종을 둘러싼 논쟁
(B) 공룡 멸종의 원인이 된 포유동물의 역할
(C) 집단 멸종에 있어서의 우주 물체의 영향
(D) 공룡 생존에 있어서의 기후 변화의 영향

해설 교수는 지금껏 밝혀진 공룡 멸종의 원인을 크게 세 가지로 분류하여 설명한다. 첫 번째 운석의 낙하, 두 번째 질병, 세 번째 공룡 알을 먹이로 삼는 포유동물의 등장이 그것이다. (B), (C), (D)는 강의 내용의 일부일 뿐 전체 주제를 아우르지 못한다.

2 교수가 운석을 논한 이유는 무엇인가?
(A) 공룡과 운석은 아무 관련이 없다는 것을 주장하기 위해
(B) 운석 이론이 반증되었음을 지적하기 위해
(C) 운석의 영향으로 질병이 발생했음을 나타내기 위해
(D) 운석 이론이 지금까지는 가장 믿을만한 이론임을 설명하기 위해

해설 지구상에서 발견된 iridium의 흔적을 통해 학계에서는 meteors가 지구 기후에 커다란 영향을 미친 것으로 보고 있다. 단, 이 기후 변화가 병원 물질을 일으키는 원인 (C)이라는 전제는 없다.

3 교수는 운석 이론의 영향을 어떻게 강조하고 있는가?
(A) 여러 과학자들의 의견들을 요약함으로써
(B) 기후 변화가 어떻게 공룡들을 죽게 했는지를 설명함으로써
(C) 교수 자신이 이 이론을 가장 신뢰한다고 말함으로써
(D) 다른 이론의 타당성을 도외시함으로써

4 교수가 요약한 바에 따르면 다음 중 공룡 멸종의 원인으로 가능하지 <u>않은</u> 것은 무엇인가?
(A) 광범위한 빙하기의 도래
(B) 천적으로서의 포유동물의 역할 증대
(C) 외계 암석의 영향
(D) 공룡에게 영향을 준 주요 전염병

해설 교수가 언급한 공룡 멸종의 원인은 1) 운석 2) 질병 3) 천적의 등장이다.

5 강의에서 교수는 대격변 이론을 설명하고 있다. 다음 중 이 이론과 관련이 있는 것에 체크하시오.

	Yes	No
이리듐 층을 증거로 제시하였다.	✓	
외계 물체의 영향으로 멸종이 야기되었다.	✓	
공룡은 방사선 때문에 생존하지 못했다.		✓
기후 변화가 공룡 멸종을 야기했다.	✓	
운석은 공룡을 죽인 바이러스를 들여왔다.		✓

해설 대격변 이론은 운석과 관련되어 있다. 방사선이 방출되었다는 언급은 없다.

Progress Test 4

학생과 상담원과의 대화의 일부를 듣고 물음에 답하시오.

🎧 스크립트

S   Hi. I'm an exchange student from Germany. I was told that I should come to this office to get information about campus housing.
C   Yes, you've come to the right place. Where are you staying right now?
S   With a cousin who lives in a town about an hour from the college. But I'd like to be on campus.
C   An hour's far away! And you have a couple of options. One is to live in the dormitory. You would share a room with another student and there is a common bathroom, laundry room, and TV room.
S   Is there a kitchen?
C   If you live in the dorms, you have to sign up for a meal plan at the cafeteria.
S   I'd prefer to cook for myself to save money, actually.
C   Okay, well then another on-campus housing option is to live in a co-op. You would have a roommate, and a laundry room, just like the dorm, but there is a common kitchen. Residents sign up to cook, clean, and do other chores around the house. It's significantly less expensive than the dorm.
S   And I still get to live with and meet other students, right?
C   Yep! Should I sign you up for a room in a co-op?

학생 안녕하세요, 전 독일에서 온 교환학생인데요, 교내 숙소에 관한 정보를 얻으려면 여기로 가라고 하더군요.
상담원 맞아요, 제대로 찾아오셨어요. 지금은 어디에서 지내나요?
학생 학교에서 한 시간 정도 떨어진 마을에 사촌과 함께 살고 있어요. 그런데 전 학교에서 지내고 싶어요.
상담원 한 시간이라면 상당히 머네요! 두어 가지 선택안이 있어요. 하나는 기숙사에서 사는 거예요. 다른 학생과 방을 공유해야하고 공용 욕실, 세탁실, 그리고 TV 룸이 있어요.
학생 부엌은 있나요?
상담원 기숙사에 살게 되면 식당의 급식을 신청해야 해요.
학생 사실, 전 직접 음식을 만들어 먹고 돈을 절약하는 쪽이 더 좋은데요.
상담원 좋아요, 그럼 Co-op(협동조합) 방식으로 살 수 있는 방법을 선택할 수 있어요. 기숙사처럼 다른 학생과 방을 함께 써야 하고, 세탁실도 있지요. 그리고 공용 부엌이 있어요. 거주자들은 요리하고 집 주변을 청소하는 등 기타 여러 일들을 하겠다고 서명해야 합니다. 기숙사보다는 훨씬 덜 비싸요.
학생 그리고 여전히 다른 학생들과 함께 살고 만나기도 하는 거고요, 맞나요?
상담원 네. Co-op(협동조합)의 방으로 등록해 드릴까요?

1 학생이 사무실을 찾아온 이유는 무엇인가?
(A) 현재 학교 밖에서 살고 있는 자신의 주거 상황에 대해 불평하기 위해
(B) 타 학교 학생을 만나지 못하는 것에 대한 염려를 표시하기 위해
(C) 학교 내에서 살 집을 찾기 위해
(D) 급식을 신청할 충분한 돈이 없다는 것을 나타내기 위해

해설 학생은 통학 시간이 오래 걸리기 때문에 기숙사 생활을 하고 싶어 한다.

2 상담원은 두 번째 선택 사항인 Co-op을 어떻게 설명하는가?
(A) 현재로서는 학생이 사촌과 함께 살아야 한다고 제안하면서
(B) 기숙사와 어떻게 다른지 보여주면서
(C) 기숙사와 비교할 때 어떤 점을 이용할 수 없는 것인지 지적하면서
(D) Co-op 방식으로 살 경우 학생이 얻게 될 이점을 언급하면서

해설 두 번째 안은 첫 번째 안과 거의 유사하나, 식사 해결 방식만 다르다. 식사를 직접 해결하는 것(두 번째 안)이 학생이 원하던 것이므로 (C)의 not available 은 부적절한 답이 된다.

3 기숙사에서 학생에게 제공하지 않는 것은 무엇인가?
(A) 공용 부엌
(B) 공용 TV 룸
(C) 세탁실
(D) 공용 욕실

해설 공용 부엌은 두번째 안에 해당한다.

4 학생이 기숙사에서 살고 싶어 하지 않는 이유는 무엇인가?
(A) 룸메이트와 함께 방을 쓰고 싶지 않다.
(B) 기숙사가 너무 시끄러울 것을 염려한다.
(C) 자기 식사를 스스로 준비하고 싶다.
(D) 학교에서 너무 멀리 떨어져있을까 봐 걱정이다.

해설 학생은 생활비 절감을 위해 기숙사 식당에서 밥을 사먹는 것보다 직접 요리를 해 먹기를 원한다.

5 다음 중 Co-op에서 제공되지 않는 것은 무엇인가?
(A) 독방
(B) 공용 부엌
(C) 협동 업무
(D) 세탁실

해설 Co-op 에서도 방은 룸메이트와 공유해야 한다.

Dictation — Progress Test

Progress Test 3

① with the mass extinction of
② a source of controversy in
③ a number of theories
④ like a meteor collision
⑤ the rise of a mammal
⑥ preyed on
⑦ was given a boost in credibility
⑧ points to a massive impact
⑨ change in climate
⑩ killed off
⑪ this is a major flaw in the theory
⑫ they were better equipped to survive
⑬ searching for a more plausible theory
⑭ we're still not really sure

Progress Test 4

① I'm an exchange student from
② to get information about
③ you've come to
④ lives in a town about an hour from
⑤ An hour's far away
⑥ You would share a room
⑦ sign up for a meal plan
⑧ I'd prefer to cook for myself
⑨ is to live in a co-op
⑩ do other chores
⑪ It's significantly less expensive than the dorm
⑫ sign you up for a room in a co-op

5 다수의 것들이 그룹으로 모인 것
6 더 이상 존재하지 않음
7 어떤 것의 최후 혹은 죽음
8 우주에서 지구 대기권으로 들어오면서 빛을 내며 타버리는 소립자
9 대단히 파괴적인 방식으로 나타나는 변화
10 알을 낳지 않고 새끼를 낳는 동물, 특히 그 암컷

다음 구문을 사용하여 문장을 완성하시오.

1 kill off   2 preyed on   3 pointed out
4 are searching for   5 prefer to

1 그 단체는 "나무의 (성장에 해가 되는) 딱정벌레 알을 죽일만한 충분한 자금이 없습니다." 라고 말했다.
2 고양이는 쥐를 잡아먹고 딱정벌레는 진드기를 잡아먹는다.
3 그는 내 글의 오류를 지적했다.
4 인터넷을 통해 어떤 정보를 찾을 때는 다양한 포털 사이트를 이용하는 것이 좀 더 도움이 될 거예요.
5 이렇게 해도 괜찮은지 아니면 모임을 취소하는 것이 더 좋은지 알려주세요.

Vocabulary Review — Progress Test

다음 각 정의와 일치하는 단어를 골라 써 넣으시오.

1 flaw   2 plausible   3 dormitory
4 resident   5 mass   6 extinction
7 demise   8 meteor   9 cataclysmic
10 mammal

1 사물의 결함이나 약점, 또는 사람에게 바람직하지 못한 성품
2 사실일 수도 있으나 확실하지 않은
3 대학에서 제공한 학생들의 거처
4 특정 장소에서 사는 것, 또는 특정 장소에서 사는 사람

CHAPTER 05
INFERENCE / STANCE

Sample

학생 교수님의 심리학 101수업은 제가 다음 학기에 들어야하는 102 수업의 선수 과목인데, 정원이 꽉 찼어요. 어떻게 수강할 수 없을까요?
교수 김 교수의 강의는 시도해 봤나요? 그 과목은 지금쯤 열려 있을 겁니다.
학생 그것도 생각은 해봤습니다만... 김 교수님 수업은 제 (수업) 스케줄과 맞지 않아요.
교수 아니면, 가능성이 없기는 하지만, 다른 분반을 열어달라고 청원할 수도 있지요. 50명이 청원을 하면 대학에서는 법적으로 새 강좌를 개설하도록 되어 있으니까요.
학생 50명이요, 음... (약간 회의적이다. 그렇게 많은 사람의 청원을 받기는 어려울 것 같다)
교수 그럼, 학생은 이번 학기 전 시간 수업을 듣는 거죠? 그러면, 등록 대기자 명단에 이름을 올려놓으세요. 그럼 아마 더 많은 기회가 있을 거예요.
학생 (기대감에 들떠서) 아, 그건 어떻게 하죠?

대화로부터 추론할 수 있는 것은 무엇인가?
(A) 학생은 (교수의) 수업을 듣지 않을 것이다.
(B) 교수는 다른 분반을 개설할 것이다.
(C) 학생은 김 교수의 수업을 듣는 것을 고려하고 있다.
(D) 학생은 대기자 명단에 자신의 이름을 올려놓을 것이다.
정답 (D)

Vocabulary Preview — for Skill Check-up

다음 정의를 듣고 알맞은 단어를 고르시오.

1 innate 2 breed 3 alumni 4 term
5 insulate 6 transparent 7 deposit 8 amnesia
9 traumatic 10 instruction

1 not established but born with
  (후천적으로) 형성된 것이 아니라 타고난
2 a special type of an animal
  동물의 특별한 유형
3 people who used to be students of a school, college, or university
  학교, 전문대, 또는 종합 대학의 학생이었던 사람들
4 a limited period of time that a school, or university divides the year into
  학교나 대학에서 일 년을 나누는 한정된 시간 단위
5 protect from outside influences like heat, wind, noise etc.
  열, 바람, 소음 등의 외부 영향으로부터 차단하다

6 can be seen through
  ~을 통과하여 볼 수 있다
7 a sum of money given as security for temporary use
  일시적 사용에 대한 담보로 주어진 얼마간의 돈
8 partial or total loss of memory
  일부 혹은 완전한 기억력 상실
9 related to a shocking or upsetting experience causing psychological damage
  심리적 피해를 일으키는 충격적인 또는 근심스러운 경험과 관련된
10 a message that explains how something is to be done
   어떤 것이 어떻게 진행되어야 하는지를 설명하는 메시지

다음 단어를 이용하여 아래 문장을 완성하시오.

1 transferred 2 deposit 3 susceptible
4 telescope 5 traumatic 6 transparent
7 repressed 8 instructions 9 innate
10 amnesia

1 당신이 런던으로 이동할(전근갈) 것이라는 얘기 들었어요.
2 이 집에 대한 임대차 계약에 서명한 후에 얼마간의 돈을 보증금으로 치러야 한다.
3 특히, 노인들이 그런 질병에 취약하다.
4 망원경으로 달이나 별을 보는 것은 그녀의 취미 중의 하나이다.
5 자신이 사랑하는 개가 죽은 것은 그의 나이에는 충격적인 경험이었다.
6 잠자리의 날개는 거의 투명하다.
7 그는 너무 오랫동안 자신의 감정들을 억눌러서 자신을 표현하는 방법을 거의 잊은 것처럼 보였다.
8 당신은 이 완벽한 설명서로 오븐 사용법을 쉽게 배울 수 있습니다.
9 어떤 사람들은 타고난 성선설을 믿지만, 나는 아니다.
10 그 자동차 사고의 희생자는 기억상실에 걸려서 자신의 어린 시절을 기억하지 못했다.

Skill Check-up Inference

1 강의를 듣고 추론할 수 있는 것은 무엇인가?
(A) 역행성기억상실보다 일부기억상실이 더 심각하다.
(B) 정신은 종종 특정한 기억을 지움으로써 정신적 외상을 받은 피해자를 보호할 것이다.
(C) 기억상실은 정신치료를 통해 비교적 쉽게 치료될 수 있다.
정답 (B)

해설 역행성 건망증은 과거의 모든 기억을 잃는 것이고 일부 기억상실로 고통스러운 기억만을 잃어버리는 증상이다.

🎧 스크립트

P You know, in the movies, it seems amnesia is always a complete loss of memory, right? Well, this kind of amnesia is actually for real and is known as retrograde amnesia; you just don't remember anything in the past... right? But by far the most common form of amnesia is called lacunar amnesia, the... uh... it's, it's a repressed memory, it's like you can't remember a specific moment or sometimes a traumatic event. You know what's interesting, though? Your mind does this for your benefit! Amazing, isn't it? Anyway, if a person recognizes this has happened, he should get help through some type of psychosocial therapy.

교수 여러분도 아시겠지만, 영화에서 기억상실증은 언제나 기억을 완전히 잃어버리는 것으로 보입니다. 맞죠? 네, 실제로 이런 종류의 기억상실이 존재하는 것은 사실이며 이것은 역행성 기억상실로 알려져 있습니다. 과거에 일어난 일을 아무것도 기억하지 못해요, 그렇지요? 그러나 현재까지 기억 상실증의 가장 흔한 종류는 일부기억상실로, 에, 기억이 억압되는 것이라 할 수 있습니다. 그것은 특정한 순간이나 때때로 충격이 큰 사건을 기억하지 못하는 것 같은 것입니다. 흥미로운 건 무엇인지 아시나요? 이런 일부기억상실은 스스로를 이롭게 하기 위해 마음이 시킨 일이란 겁니다. 놀랍지 않습니까? 어쨌든 이런 일이 생긴 것을 알게 되면, 그 사람은 심리사회 치료법 같은 것을 통해 도움을 받아야 합니다.

2 대화로부터 추론할 수 있는 것은 무엇인가?
(A) 여자는 다른 수업을 듣고 있다.
(B) 교수는 일반적으로 자신의 집무 시간을 지키지 않는다.
(C) 남자는 언제 교수를 방문해야 하는지를 몰랐다.

정답 (C)

해설 남자는 교수를 몇 번 찾아가 보았지만 그 때마다 문이 잠겨 있어 문제를 해결하지 못했다고 한다. 즉, 교수를 언제 찾아가야 만날 수 있을지 알지 못했다는 얘기이다.

🎧 스크립트

S1 Man, I'm really worried about this physics assignment for tomorrow.
S2 What do you mean? You don't understand the instructions?
S1 Not at all. I heard she explained what she wanted in class... uh, but I was sick on that day, so I missed the lecture.
S2 Hmm... well, why don't you go talk to the professor?
S1 That's what I did several times, but the door was locked.
S2 Check out the syllabus, the office hours are listed there. Or... isn't Cindy Preston in your class? You could just go across the hall and talk to her.
S1 Cindy is nice... but, I think I'll check the hours first.

학생1 이런, 내일 내야하는 이 물리학 숙제 정말 걱정돼.
학생2 무슨 소리야? 지침서를 이해 못하는 거야?
학생1 전혀. 수업 시간에 교수님께서 원하는 바가 무엇인지 설명하는 것은 들었어. 어, 근데 그날 아파서 강의를 놓쳤거든.
학생2 흠..., 그러면 교수님께 가서 직접 여쭤보지 그래?
학생1 몇 번 해 봤어. 근데 (교수님 연구실) 문이 잠겨있더라고.
학생2 수업 계획서를 확인해 봐. 거기에 집무 시간이 나와 있어. 아니면, Cindy Preston이 같은 수업을 듣지 않니? 저기 강당에 가서 그 애한테 말해 봐.
학생1 Cindy가 좋은 애이기는 하지... 그런데 교수님 시간을 먼저 확인해 볼게.

3 남자가 다음과 같이 말할 때 그 의미는 무엇인가?

S Maybe Rico is just one smart dog!

(A) 그는 강아지들이 똑똑하다고 생각한다.
(B) 그는 Rico가 예외적으로 똑똑한 거라고 생각한다.
(C) 그는 연구 대상이 된 개들이 너무 적었다고 생각한다.

정답 (B)

해설 just one smart dog이라는 표현은 일반적으로 다른 개들은 Rico 처럼 인간과의 의사소통에 능하지 못하다고 생각한다는 얘기이다.

🎧 스크립트

P Well... we think now that there's some innate ability of dogs to learn human language. As you know this dog, Rico, a border collie in Germany, has been able to learn and remember a large number of words. Rico, in fact, knows over 200, and seems to be able to understand what his owner means... even if he doesn't know the word!
S Maybe Rico is just one smart dog!
P But, while Rico had the biggest vocabulary of dogs studied in this research project so far, many of the other breeds of dogs involved exhibited large vocabularies, too. Dogs seem to have evolved to communicate well with humans.

교수 음, 우리는 이제 인간의 언어를 배우는 선천적인 능력을 가진 개들이 있다고 생각합니다. 여러분도 알다시피, 이 개, 독일 태생의 북잉글랜드산 콜리종 목양견인 Rico는, 수많은 단어를 학습한 후 다시 기억해냅니다. 실제 Rico는 200 단어 이상을 알고 있으며, (주인이 말을 하면) 그 단어는 이해하지 못할지라도 주인이 무슨 말을 하는지는 이해하고 있는 것처럼 보입니다.
학생 아마 Rico는 유일하게 똑똑한 강아지이겠지요.
교수 그런데, 물론 지금까지 이 연구 프로젝트에서 연구한 개들 가운데 Rico가 가장 많은 단어를 습득하기는 했지만, 그 밖에 이 연구에 참여한 많은 다른 종들의 개들도 단어를 많이 습득했습니다. 개들은 아마도 인간과 의사소통을 잘 하는 쪽으로 진화해오고 있는 것 같아요.

4 여자는 다음에 무엇을 할 것으로 보이는가?
(A) 방을 예약하기 위해 돈을 예치할 것이다.
(B) 그 장소를 빌리기 위해서 돈을 지불하는 일에 대해 교수와 상의해 볼 것이다.
(C) 남자에게 (예약이) 가능한 방이 있는지 물어볼 것이다.

정답 (A)

해설 남자가 321호 방이 사용 가능하다고 하고 예치금을 지불해야 한다고 했을 때 이의를 제기하지 않고 사용할 시간을 알려주고 있으므로 (B)나 (C)와 같은 상황은 있을 수 없다.

🎧 스크립트

S1 Hi there. Who do I talk to about reserving a room for a student group meeting?
S2 I can help you with that here. What's the group?
S1 It's for a literary magazine.
S2 All right... and I'm assuming you're all students?
S1 Umm... well, we have several professors and a few alumni...
S2 Well, the majority of participants need to be students for us to rent you the room.
S1 That's no problem, then.
S2 Okay. Room 321 is available. I just need you to fill out this form and the group has to put a deposit on the room. And is this a one-time thing or...?
S1 We'll need it Monday nights, between 7 and 9 p.m.

학생 1 안녕하세요. 학생 동호회 모임에 쓸 방을 예약하려면 누구에게 이야기해야 하나요?
학생 2 제가 여기서 도와드릴 수 있어요. 무슨 모임인가요?
학생 1 문학잡지 모임이에요.
학생 2 좋아요. 그런데 모두 학생이시죠?
학생 1 음... 저, 교수님 몇 분과 동문 몇 명이 있는데요.
학생 2 글쎄요. 참석자 가운데 다수가 학생이어야만 저희가 방을 제공해드릴 수가 있는데요.
학생 1 그럼 문제될 것 없겠군요.
학생 2 좋아요. 321호실을 사용하실 수 있습니다. 이 양식을 작성해 주시고, 방에 보증금을 거셔야 합니다. 그런데 모임은 일회성인가요, 아니면...?
학생 1 저희는 월요일 저녁 7시에서 9시 사이에 필요해요.

Skill Check-up   Stance

1 등록 문제에 관해서 남자의 태도는 어떠한가?
(A) 수업에 들어갈 수 없을지도 몰라서 낙담해 있다.
(B) 그는 학생 수가 많은 것이 불만이다.
(C) 네트워크 시스템이 느린 것에 화가 나 있다.

정답 (A)

해설 수강 신청을 계속 시도하고 있으나 이미 정원이 꽉 찬 상태라 신청이 어렵다. 네트워크 시스템 자체에 대한 불만을 토로하지는 않는다.

🎧 스크립트

S1 Are you trying to register?
S2 Trying! Every class I try and get into is full. I don't know what I'm going to do.
S1 That's the hard part about being a freshman. We have to register last. But don't get too mad. Just keep trying.
S2 Why bother?
S1 People change their schedules around a lot and sometimes spots open up.
S2 Great... so basically, I have to sit in front of my computer trying to get into classes until the term starts?
S1 As I said, it's hard being a freshman. But it shouldn't be that bad.

학생 1 수강신청하려고 하는 거니?
학생 2 하고는 있지! 내가 들어가려고 하는 강의는 다 찼어. 뭘 어떡해야 할지 모르겠네.
학생 1 1학년이 제일 힘든 점이 그거지. 우리가 제일 마지막에 등록해야 하니까 말이야. 그래도 너무 열 받지 말고 계속 해 봐.
학생 2 왜 그래야 하지?
학생 1 사람들이 (수업) 일정을 많이들 바꾸기 때문에 간혹 자리가 나거든.
학생 2 좋아. 그러니까 근본적으로 내가 계속 컴퓨터 앞에 앉아서 학기가 시작될 때까지는 수업에 들어가려고 계속 시도를 해야 한단 말이네?
학생 1 말했잖아, 신입생 노릇도 힘들다고. 그래도 그렇게 나쁘지는 않아.

2 남자가 다음과 같이 말할 때 그 의미는 무엇인가?

S I was there only for a semester, so...

(A) 그는 모든 학점을 옮겨서는 안 된다고 알고 있다.
(B) 그는 학점 수에 문제가 없을 거라고 확신한다.
(C) 그는 학교로부터 공식적인 성적표를 얻을 수 있을지 확신할 수 없다.

정답 (B)

해설 예전 학교에서는 겨우 한 학기만 수강했을 뿐이므로, 학점 이수의 최대 가능 조건인 36시간 이상은 넘지 않을 것이라는 의미이다.

🎧 스크립트

S Hi. I wanted to try and get some credits transferred from my previous school.
C Okay, sure. But we can't accept more

than thirty six credit hours from other colleges.
S I was there only for a semester, so...
C All right, then. I have to see an official transcript from your old school so we can verify that the classes are comparable to ours, and... that should be provided by five o'clock tomorrow. Then it takes about four weeks for the transfer to go through.
S I'll have my old school send my transcripts right away.
C Okay... anything else you want me to do for you?

학생 안녕하세요. 전에 다니던 학교에서 받은 학점을 옮기고 싶은데요.
사무원 네, 그럼요. 그런데 타 대학에서 받은 학점을 36학점 이상 대체할 수는 없습니다.
학생 전 그곳에서 한 학기만 다녔어요. 그러니까...
사무원 그러면 괜찮습니다. 그 학교 수업이 저희 학교 수업과 대체할 수 있는 것인지 확인해 봐야 하니까 학생이 다닌 예전 학교에서 보낸 공식 성적표를 봐야 합니다. 그리고... 내일 5시까지는 준비되어야 해요. 그런 다음 학점을 옮기기까지 4주 정도 걸릴 거예요.
학생 예전 학교에서 제 성적표를 바로 보내게 할게요.
사무원 좋아요. 또 달리 도와드릴 게 있나요?

3 Eden 프로젝트에 대한 교수의 태도는 어떠한가?
  (A) 아주 중요한 환경 정화 장소라고 생각한다.
  (B) 누구나 방문해보고 싶어하는 장소가 될 것이라고 생각한다.
  (C) 프로젝트 규모나 사용 자재들 때문에 흥분해있다.

정답 (C)

해설 교수는 Eden 건축물의 크기나 규모, 독특한 외장재의 사용을 언급하며 긍정적인 평가를 내리고 있다.

🎧 스크립트

P Okay... now let's talk about the Eden Project. This project we originally conceived as a large-scale environmental complex. Although relatively new, the project has quickly become one of the most popular visitor attractions in the United Kingdom.
Well... like I said... it's distinctive primarily for its size and scope. The complex includes two giant, transparent domes and it covers over 124 acres. The project took two years to construct and it's ongoing. Additionally, as we'll, uh, see from this film, rather than using glass, the usual material in greenhouse construction, project architects used this special material... I mean... foil, a transparent and lightweight covering, instead. It has excellent insulating properties, and is a, uh, a lot lighter, and is not as, uh, susceptible to damage by the sun.

교수 좋아요. 자, 에덴 프로젝트에 관해 얘기해봅시다. 우리는 원래 이 프로젝트를 대규모의 환경 복합 건물로 생각했지요. 그러나 비교적 신축임에도 불구하고, 이 단지는 빠르게 영국에서 가장 인기 있는 관광명소 중의 하나가 되었습니다.
음, 제가 말했던 것처럼 이 단지는 우선 그 규모나 영역에 있어 차별되어 있습니다. 이 복합 건물은 두 개의 거대하고 투명한 돔을 포함하고 있는데 124에이커의 면적을 차지합니다. 이 단지를 건설하는 데 2년이 걸렸으며 지금도 (건설이) 진행 중이지요. 더욱이 에, 이 필름을 통해서도 보게 되겠지만 온실 건조에 쓰이는 일반적 재질인 유리를 사용하는 대신, 건축가들은 이 특별한 물질, 그러니까 투명하고 가벼운 외피인 포일(금속 박편)을 사용했습니다. 이 물질은 단열효과가 굉장히 탁월하고, 어, 훨씬 가볍고, 그리고 음, 태양에도 쉽게 손상되지 않습니다.

4 남자가 다음과 같이 말할 때 그 의미는 무엇인가?

S You mean you can actually see the thermal radiation? I never used one of those radio telescopes...

(A) 교수의 말을 제대로 들은 것인지 확신하지 못하고 있다.
(B) 그 이미지가 어떻게 보인다는 것인지 궁금하다.
(C) 교수가 이야기한 것을 믿지 못한다.

정답 (B)

해설 학생은 전파 망원경을 사용해 본 경험이 없다. 그래서 교수가 그 모습을 보여주겠다고 한다.

🎧 스크립트

P You may have looked through an optical or reflecting telescope at the... moon, for example... But sometimes radio telescopes... are used to pick up the naturally occurring radio signals... coming from distant galaxies.
S Why use a radio telescope instead of a reflecting one?
P Well, we use this kind of telescope to measure the... the thermal radiation from different galaxies, which is not visible with a reflecting scope.
S You mean you can actually see the thermal radiation? I never used one of those radio telescopes.
P Here... let's take a look at some images provided by radio telescopes to see what I mean.

Inference / Stance

교수 여러분은 광학 망원경이나 반사 망원경을 통해, 예를 들면... 달을 본 적이 있을 겁니다. 그런데 때로는 먼 은하계에서 오는 자연 발생적인 전파 신호를 잡아내기 위해 전파 망원경을 사용하기도 합니다.
학생 반사 망원경 대신 전파 망원경을 사용하는 이유는 뭔가요?
교수 그러니까, 다른 은하로부터 오는 열복사 에너지 수치를 재기 위해 이런 종류의 망원경을 사용하지요. 이것은 반사 망원경으로는 보이지 않으니까요.
학생 그 말은 실제로 열복사 에너지를 눈으로 볼 수 있다는 말인가요? 전 그런 전파 망원경을 사용해 본 적이 없어서요.
교수 여기, 전파 망원경으로 찍은 몇 가지 이미지들을 보면 제 말을 이해할 수 있을 겁니다.

Exercise

1 A - (C) B - (D) 2 A - (B) B - (B)
3 A - (D) B - (A) 4 A - (C) B - (D)

Exercise 1
칼로리와 장수의 관계에 관한 토론의 일부를 듣고 물음에 답하시오.

🎧 스크립트

P For a certain period of time, rats in the lab had their caloric intake severely restricted... in other words, they didn't eat much! The important thing here, however, is energy intake must be minimized, but sufficient quantities of minerals, vitamins, and other important nutrients must be ingested. Anyway, we got a result from the experiment, that the rats' life expectancy increased by 33 percent when their caloric intake was restricted. Obviously weighing less... their aging processes slowed and fewer diseases appeared compared to a group of rats with a normal diet. More research was done and it showed these same results occurred in other animals, too.
S1 I'm sure it's probably the same thing with humans! Being overweight increases the risk of many diseases and health conditions.
S2 No way. Our bodies need energy to keep them going. We get the energy from food, so without enough food we can't manage a healthy life. Worse than that, not eating enough would cause health problems and increase mortality, if anything.
P Well, the result of the experiment might be applied to other animals, too. Actually there are those who claim that as long as humans ingest enough nutrients in a very low calorie diet, they can live longer. Well, next class we'll look at those studies, but we've run out of time today. Come and pick up your exams on your way out.

교수 일정 기간 동안, (연구자들은) 실험실 쥐들의 열량 섭취를 엄격히 제한하였습니다. 말하자면, 많이 먹지 못하게 한 거죠. 그러나 여기서 중요한 것은 에너지 섭취는 최소화시켰지만 미네랄이나, 비타민, 그리고 다른 중요한 영양분은 충분히 섭취하게 했다는 것입니다. 어쨌든, 우리는 이 실험을 통해 쥐의 열량 섭취를 제한할 경우 그들의 수명이 33퍼센트 증가했다는 결과를 얻었습니다. 분명한 것은 체중이 덜 나감으로써, 정상적인 식사를 한 쥐들과 비교했을 때 이들의 노화 과정이 느려지고 발생하는 질병의 수도 더 줄어들었습니다. 더 많은 실험을 한 결과 다른 동물들에게서도 이와 똑같은 결과가 나왔습니다.
학생 1 인간도 아마 같은 결과를 보일 거라고 확신해요! 비만은 여러 질병과 건강 문제의 위험을 높이니까요.
학생 2 그렇지 않아요. 우리의 신체는 계속 활동하려면 에너지를 필요로 하는데, 이 에너지를 음식에서 얻잖아요. 음식을 충분히 섭취하지 않고는 건강한 삶을 지속해나갈 수 없어요. 그것보다 더 나쁜 것은, 충분히 먹지 않으면 건강상에 문제가 생기고 사망률도 높아진다는 거예요.
교수 그래요. 이 실험 결과는 아마 다른 동물들에게도 적용될 수 있을 겁니다. 사실 인간도 칼로리 섭취량을 최소화한 상태에서 필요 영양분만 충분히 섭취한다면 장수할 수 있다고 주장하는 사람들도 있으니까요. 그럼, 이들 연구 내용은 다음 시간에 살펴보도록 하고, 오늘은 시간이 다 됐습니다. 나가는 길에 여기 와서 시험지를 가져가세요.

어휘 intake 섭취량 restricted 제한된, 한정된 sufficient 충분한, (~하기에) 족한 nutrients 영양분, 영양소 ingest (음식물을) 섭취하다 life expectancy 평균 수명 mortality 사망률 be applied to ~에 적용되다, 적합하다

A 토론으로부터 추론할 수 있는 것은 무엇인가?
(A) 학생들은 교수의 의견에 반대한다.
(B) 다른 동물들에게서는 다른 결과가 나타났다.
(C) 인간에게는 (쥐에게 한 것과) 같은 실험을 하지 않았다.
(D) 교수는 이 실험이 사망률을 높인다는 데 동의한다.

해설 실제로 인간에게도 같은 원리가 적용된다고 주장하는 사람들이 있다. 그러나 인간에게도 동일한 실험이 행해졌다는 언급은 없다.

B 칼로리 섭취량을 줄이는 것에 대해 사실이 아닌 것은 무엇인가?
(A) 수명이 길어진다.
(B) 질병 수가 적게 나타난다.
(C) 다른 동물들도 비슷한 결과를 보인다.
(D) 더 많이 동기부여가 되는 것으로 증명되었다.

해설 동기 유발같은 심리 상태에 대한 언급은 없다.

Exercise 2

바나나에 관한 강의의 일부를 듣고 물음에 답하시오.

🎧 스크립트

P Modern bananas and plantains originated in the southeast Asian and western Pacific regions. But the origin of bananas is traced back to Malaysia. So the, uh, the history of the banana is... the history of global exploration and trade, in a sense. The movement of people and goods across the world, the uh, fact that the world has uh, become smaller, helps explain how this exotic fruit from the tropics has come to be a common part of the Western diet. The tree... which is actually the world's biggest, uh, biggest herb plant... has its origins in Malaysia, and was brought to India by travelers. From there, it was transported to other parts of Asia and then, uh, on to the Mediterranean. Eventually, this tropical fruit reached Africa. Traders of slaves, ivory, and spices then introduced the banana to Africa, where it grew very well in the climate. The banana trade followed the slave trade to the new world, then, and banana plantations sprang up all over South and Central America. And so by the 1800s, bananas had come to North America So, uh, having looked at the uh, history, let's uh, focus a bit more on the economic and societal impact in South America of this fruit. More specifically, I mean, we will take a look at the importance of bananas production for export, and developments in banana trade, including prices and consumption in the markets.

교수 현대의 바나나, 혹은 바나나의 일종은 동남아시아 태평양 서부지역에서 기원한 것입니다. 하지만 바나나의 최초 기원은 말레이시아로 더듬어 올라가죠. 그래서 에, 일면 바나나의 역사는 에, 세계 탐험이나 세계 무역의 역사이기도 합니다. 사람들과 상품이 세계 곳곳으로 이동하는 것, 음, 세계가 점점 작아지고 있다는 사실로 이 열대의 이국적인 과일이 어떻게 서양 식탁에서 일상적인 먹거리가 되게 되었는지를 설명할 수 있을 겁니다. 이 바나나 나무, 세계에서 가장 크죠, 이 거대한 식용 식물인 바나나 나무는 말레이시아에 기원을 두고 있는데 여행자들에 의해 인도로 옮겨갔지요. 그리고 거기에서 아시아, 그리고 지중해의 다른 지역으로 운반되었습니다. 그리고 마침내 이 열대 과일은 아프리카까지 도달했죠. 노예나 상아, 향료의 무역상들이 바나나를 아프리카에 소개했고, 그곳 기후에서 아주 잘 자라났습니다. 그러니까 바나나 무역은 노예무역을 따라 신세계로 따라왔다가 그 나무가 중남미 전역에서 싹을 틔우게 됩니다. 그렇게 해서 1800년대에 이르러 바나나가 북미로 오게 됩니다. 자, 에, 바나나의 역사를 살펴보았으니 이번에는 이 과일이 남미 경제 및 사회에 미친 영향에 보다 초점을 맞추어 볼까 합니다. 좀 더 구체적으로는, 그러니까, 시장에서의 가격 및 소비 부분을 포함해 수출용 바나나 생산의 중요성 및 바나나 무역의 발전에 대해 살펴보겠습니다.

어휘 plantain〔식물〕바나나의 일종 exotic 외국산의; 이국적인 herb 식용(식물)풀, 초본 ivory 상아 plantation 대규모 농원 societal 사회의, 사회 활동의 consumption 소비(량), 소비(액) trace back 더듬어 올라가다 spring up (식물이) 나다, 싹이 트다, (갑자기) 나타나다, 발생하다

A 강의의 일부를 다시 들으시오.

P So the, uh, the history of the banana is... the history of global exploration and trade, in a sense. The movement of people and goods across the world, the uh, fact that the world has uh, become smaller, helps explain how this exotic fruit from the tropics has come to be a common part of the Western diet.

교수가 다음과 같이 말할 때 그 의미는 무엇인가?

P So the, uh, the history of the banana is... the history of global exploration and trade, in a sense.

(A) 바나나는 전문가들이 무역에 대해 토론할 때 사용하는 대체 용어이다.
(B) 바나나의 보급은 문화 및 무역 확대와 동시에 일어났다.
(C) 바나나는 무역 전쟁을 가져온 원인이다.
(D) 바나나는 인도와 지중해 식물 생태의 결과이다.

해설 바나나의 역사는 곧 세계 탐험의 역사, 세계 무역의 역사이고 그것이 결국 문화의 세계화로 이어지게 되었음을 지적하고 있다.

B 교수는 다음에 무엇에 관해 토론할 것인가?

(A) 북미 요리에 수용된 바나나
(B) 바나나가 남아메리카에 영향을 미친 방법
(C) 착오로 나무라고 불리게 된 다른 종류의 식용 식물
(D) 바나나가 최초로 북아메리카에 오게 된 방법

해설 교수는 바나나의 이동 역사에 대해 설명한 다음, 바나나가 남아메리카에 미친 경제적, 사회적 영향을 살펴보겠다고 한다.

Inference / Stance   57

Exercise 3
두 학생의 대화의 일부를 듣고 물음에 답하시오.

🎧 **스크립트**

S1 I'm having a hard time integrating my sources into this paper. I want to make sure I do it right. Well, actually, I'm worried about plagiarism. To develop my idea I need to refer to some articles, but I don't know what the rules are about using them.

S2 I've actually been leading a workshop on avoiding plagiarism at the writing center.

S1 Great! I'm trying to use this article as a basis for the claim that college tuition is too expensive, Okay? But I'm not sure I'm making it clear that I got the info from an article, that it's not my idea.

S2 Hmmm... let me take a look at it... Okay, yeah, I see your point. It's not clear at all. In fact, if I read this, I wouldn't realize you were citing an article.

S1 Well, how can I make it clearer? I don't want to plagiarize!

S2 Well, you must give citations when using other's ideas and identify your sources. Even if you paraphrased some ideas in your own words, it's certain that they are not your own ideas. For example, rather than paraphrasing here, I would use a direct quote from the article. The quote marks will make it very clear that it's someone else's idea.

S1 Okay, that makes sense.

학생 1 내가 찾은 자료들을 내 논문에 통합해 넣어야 하는데 아주 어려워. 제대로 하고 있는지 모르겠어. 음, 실은 표절하게 될까봐 걱정이거든. 내 이론을 전개하려면 몇몇 자료들을 인용해야 하는데 이런 걸 사용할 때 어떤 규칙이 있는지 모르겠어.

학생 2 실은 내가 작문 센터에서 표절하지 않는 방법에 관한 워크샵을 하고 있어.

학생 1 굉장하다! 내가 '대학 등록금이 너무 비싸다'는 주장의 근거로 이 자료를 사용하려고 하거든, 이해돼? 그런데 이게 내 생각이 아니라 자료에서 인용한 정보라는 걸 분명히 밝히고 있는 것인지가 확실하지 않아.

학생 2 음... 어디 좀 보자. 그래, 음, 네 말이 무슨 말인지 알겠어. 전혀 분명하지 않네. 사실 이걸 읽고 있어도 네가 어떤 자료를 참고하고 있는지 전혀 모르겠어.

학생 1 그럼, 어떻게 밝혀야 할까? 난 표절하고 싶지 않아!

학생 2 글쎄, 다른 사람의 생각을 사용할 때는 그것을 인용해서 출처를 보여줘야 해. 설사 네가 어떤 개념들은 네 말로 다시 고쳐 썼다고 해도 그게 네 아이디어가 아닌 건 분명하니까 말이야. 예를 들어 여기, 이걸 다른 말로 바꿔 쓰는 것보다는 차라리 자료에서 직접 따다가 인용 부호를 넣고 써 봐. 인용부호가 있으면 그게 다른 사람의 아이디어라는 게 아주 분명해지거든.

학생 1 알았어. 그거 말이 되네.

어휘 integrate 통합하다, 합병하다 plagiarize 표절하다 citation 인용, 인용문 paraphrase 바꾸어 쓰다, 바꾸어 말하다 quote 인용 부호, 인용문(구)

A 여자에 대해 추론할 수 있는 것은 무엇인가?
(A) 그녀의 충고는 회의적이다.
(B) 여자는 동일한 문제를 해결하기 위해 워크샵에 참여했다.
(C) 그녀는 남자의 논문을 어떻게 도울지 확신히 알지 못한다.
(D) 그녀의 제안은 아마 효과가 있을 것이다.

해설 여자는 표절에 관한 연구 모임을 하고 있어서 이에 대한 적절한 대처 방법을 알고 있다.

B 대화의 일부를 다시 들으시오.

S1 I'm having a hard time integrating my sources into this paper. I want to make sure I do it right. Well, actually, I'm worried about plagiarism. To develop my idea I need to refer to some articles, but I don't know what the rules are about using them.

S2 I've actually been leading a workshop on avoiding plagiarism at the writing center.

여자가 다음과 같이 말할 때 그 의미는 무엇인가?

S2 I've actually been leading a workshop on avoiding plagiarism at the writing center.

(A) 그녀는 자신이 도울 수 있다고 확신한다.
(B) 남자가 워크샵에 가면 도움을 받을 수 있다.
(C) 그녀는 (남자가) 작문 센터에 가는 것이 더 좋다고 생각한다.
(D) 남자는 여자로부터 도움을 기대해서는 안 된다.

해설 자신이 표절에 관한 연구 모임을 하고 있으므로 표절을 해결할 구체적인 방법을 제시할 수 있다는 암시이다.

Exercise 4
교수와 학생의 대화의 일부를 듣고 물음에 답하시오.

🎧 **스크립트**

S Professor, I've missed two weeks of class, but I've been in the hospital.

P I knew you must have been sick, since you never missed a class before. Sounds serious.

Are you feeling all right?

S I'm still a little weak, but I'm going to be back in class this week... but... um.. I know it's the last week of the semester, so...

P Yeah. We'll just mainly be reviewing for the final. Are you worried about the final exam?

S Well, not exactly, I mean, there was a homework assignment that I had to hand in, that's due in two weeks. I know each student is allowed one or two extensions with no loss of credit if there is a medical reason why he can't meet the deadline. I'd like to get an extension on the project. I'm really behind in all of my classes and I don't think there's any way I can get everything done in two weeks.

P Hmm, I don't know about the extension, it'll only give you a few extra days.

S I don't think I can complain about that.

P You know, finishing the project is one important thing but what grade you're getting is another thing you should consider... hmm... well... why don't we do this? I'll give you a couple of extra days... and in addition... I think I could allow a few more days even after the final exam to hand in the project. How does that sound? And you let me know how the work goes.

S Sure, I shouldn't have a problem. And I can't tell you how much I appreciate this.

학생 교수님, 제가 지난 두 주간 수업에 들어오지 못했어요. 병원에 있었거든요.

교수 학생이 한 번도 수업에 빠진 적이 없어서 틀림없이 아픈 건 줄 알았어요. 심각한 것 같은데, 괜찮은가요?

학생 지금도 여전히 좀 기운이 없긴 하지만, 이번 주에는 수업에 들어가려고요. 그런데, 음... 이번 주가 이번 학기 마지막인 걸로 아는데, 저...

교수 맞아요. (이번 주 수업 시간에는) 기말 시험을 대비해 주로 복습을 하게 될 거예요. 기말 시험이 걱정되나요?

학생 음, 그게 아니고요. 실은 제가 2주 안에 제출해야 하는 과제가 있어요. 제가 알기로는 건강상의 이유로 학생이 마감일을 지키지 못하면 학점을 손해 보지 않고 한두 번은 마감 기한 연장이 허용된다고 하던데요. 그래서 이번 숙제의 제출 기한을 연장해 주셨으면 합니다. 수업에 모두 뒤처져서 2주 안에 전부 다 해낼 방법이 없어요.

교수 글쎄, 기한 연장에 대해선 잘 모르지만, 겨우 며칠을 더 주는 것뿐일 텐데요.

학생 그걸 불평할 처지는 아닌 것 같아요.

교수 학생도 알다시피, 과제를 해내는 것도 중요하지만 어떤 점수를 받게 될지도 생각해봐야 하는 문제에요. 흠... 글쎄요, 이러면 어떨까요? 기간을 며칠 더 줄게요. 그리고 기말 시험이 끝나고도 프로젝트 제출 기한을 며칠 더 늘려줄 수 있을 것 같아요. 어때요? 그리고 일이 어떻게 진행되어 가는지 내게 보고해줘요.

학생 그러겠습니다. 문제없어요. 그리고 정말 감사합니다.

> **어휘** assignment 숙제, (연구) 과제 extension (날짜의) 연기, 연장 deadline 최종 기한 behind ~보다 뒤떨어져, 뒤늦어 consider 고려하다, 숙고하다 be in the hospital 병원에 입원해 있다

A 대화의 일부를 다시 들으시오.

S I'd like to get an extension on the project. I'm really behind in all of my classes and I don't think there's any way I can get everything done in two weeks.

P Hmm, I don't know about the extension, it'll only give you a few extra days.

교수가 다음과 같이 말할 때 그 의미는 무엇인가?

P Hmm, I don't know about the extension, it'll only give you a few extra days.

(A) 예전에는 과제 제출 기한을 연장해 준 적이 없다.
(B) 과제 제출 기한을 연장해 주면 어떤 문제가 발생할지 확신하지 못한다.
(C) 그 정도의 기한 연장이 학생에게 과제를 끝내기에 충분한 시간이 될지 확신하지 못한다.
(D) (기한 연장을 해주는 것이) 다른 학생들에게 공평한지 아닌지 모르겠다.

해설 마감 기한을 연장해 주는 제도가 있다고 해도 며칠에 불과할 뿐이므로 실제 학생이 과제를 마치는 데 도움이 될지 미지수라는 의미가 담겨 있다.

B 대화를 듣고 추론할 수 있는 것은 무엇인가?
(A) 학생은 과제 제출 기한을 연장하지 못할 것이다.
(B) 교수는 학생이 언제든 과제를 마치는 대로 제출해도 좋다고 허락할 것이다.
(C) 교수는 학생에게 마지막 주에는 수업에 참석하라고 요구하지 않을 것이다.
(D) 학생은 학기가 끝난 후에도 과제를 계속할 수 있을 것이다.

해설 기말 시험이 끝난 후에도 며칠 더 기일을 준다고 했으므로, 학생은 학기가 끝난 후(D)에도 과제를 계속 진행하게 될 것이다.

Dictation   Exercise

Exercise 1

① rats in the lab
② severely restricted

③ energy intake must be minimized
④ other important nutrients must be ingested
⑤ the rats' life expectancy
⑥ their aging processes slowed
⑦ these same results occurred in
⑧ the risk of many diseases
⑨ need energy to keep them going
⑩ we can't manage
⑪ increase mortality
⑫ enough nutrients in a very low calorie diet
⑬ but we've run out of time today

Exercise 2

① originated in
② the origin of bananas is traced back to
③ goods across the world
④ this exotic fruit from the tropics
⑤ has its origins in
⑥ was brought to India by travelers
⑦ it was transported to
⑧ where it grew very well in the climate
⑨ sprang up all over
⑩ focus a bit more
⑪ including prices and consumption in the markets

Exercise 3

① integrating my sources into this paper
② I need to refer to
③ leading a workshop on avoiding
④ as a basis for the claim
⑤ I'm making it clear that
⑥ It's not clear at all
⑦ I wouldn't realize you were citing an article
⑧ identify your sources
⑨ some ideas in your own words
⑩ rather than paraphrasing here
⑪ a direct quote from

Exercise 4

① it's the last week of the semester
② We'll just mainly be reviewing
③ that's due in two weeks
④ one or two extensions with no loss of credit
⑤ why he can't meet the deadline
⑥ behind in all of my classes
⑦ it'll only give you a few extra days
⑧ I'll give you a couple of extra days
⑨ let me know how the work goes

Actual Test

1 1 - (C) 2 - (B) 3 - (B) 4 - (D)
2 1 - (B) 2 - (A) 3 - (B) 4 - (D)

Actual Test 1

경제학 강의의 일부를 듣고 물음에 답하시오.

 스크립트

P Obesity has dominated the media over the past several years as the average weight of westerners continues to increase. There're some real economic implications here. Anyone want to throw some out?

S Well, being overweight causes a lot of health problems. So there's more money being spent on medical treatments, right? And people miss work because of those health problems. I think I read somewhere that billions are lost by this.

P It's true. According to a recent study, the impact of obesity on health is as great as that of smoking or drinking. Some diseases such as diabetes, heart diseases, and high cholesterol have been proved to have relation to obesity. So it is sure that those diseases caused by obesity are recognized as one of the major health problems nowadays. However, one economist recently suggested that there are some positive economic benefits to the obesity epidemic, too. He claims that we're missing the fact that our economy is uniquely poised to make it easier to dominate the global weight-loss market. This is what we call a niche economy. A niche is a specialized market, remember? You need another example of these markets?... I guess not...

In response to the obesity problem, hundreds of billions of dollars in revenue from new businesses such as clinics and gyms have been generated. And these can be exported to other countries, all of which adds strength to the economy.

교수 서양인들의 평균 체중이 계속 증가하자 지난 몇 년간은 비만이 미디어를 장악했습니다. 이것은 사실 경제와도 밀접한 연관이 있지요. 누가 여기에 대해 말해 볼래요?

학생 음, 비만은 여러 건강상의 문제를 일으킵니다. 그래서 의료 치료에 지출되는 돈도 늘어나겠지요? 그리고 사람들은 그런 건강상의 문제로 직장에 나가지 못합니다. 이런 이유로 수십억의 손실이 있었다고 어딘가에서 읽은 것 같습니다.

교수 맞아요. 최근 한 연구에 따르면, 건강에 대한 비만의 영향은 흡연이나 음주만큼 크다고 합니다. 당뇨나 심장병, 고(高) 콜레스테롤 같은 일부 질병들은 비만과 관련이 있는 것으로 입증되기도 했고요. 따라서 비만에 의해 유발되는 이런 질병들이 요즘 주요한 건강 문제의 하나로 인식되는 것은 분명합니다. 그러나 한 경제학자는 최근의 비만 만연 풍조가 경제에 긍정적인 영향을 미치기도 한다는 의견을 제기했습니다. 그가 주장하는 바에 따르면, 우리는 우리 경제가 세계 체중 감량 시장을 보다 쉽게 장악할 준비가 되어 있다는 사실을 간과하고 있다는 것입니다. 이것을 틈새시장 경제라고 하는데요, 틈새시장이란 특수 시장입니다, 기억하나요? 이런 시장 형태의 다른 예가 더 필요한가요?... 아닐 것 같군요...

비만 문제와 관련하여 병원, 체육관에 이르는 신규 사업에 수천억 달러의 수익이 생성되었습니다. 게다가 이들 사업은 타국에 수출하는 것도 가능하고 이 모든 것은 경제에 활력을 불어 넣지요.

1 비만에 관해 추론할 수 있는 것은 무엇인가?
(A) 주로 언론이나 대중들은 비만을 무시한다.
(B) 비만에 대한 경향이 서서히 역전되고 있다.
(C) 최근 비만에 대한 광범위한 연구가 진행되었다.
(D) 비만과 건강 문제와의 관련은 과장된 것이다.

해설 최근 몇 년간 비만의 증가 추세가 계속되어 이에 대한 염려가 제기되고 있으나 일부 경제학자들은 비만과 경제학적 상관관계의 긍정적 측면을 제시하고 있다. 이를 볼 때 비만에 대한 연구가 활발히 진행되었음을 알 수 있다.

2 건강 문제와 비만에 관해 학생이 의미하는 것은 무엇인가?
(A) 의사들은 이 문제를 충분히 심각하게 생각하지 않는다.
(B) 경제적으로 커다란 손실을 낳는다.
(C) 사람들의 생산성에 거의 영향을 미치지 않는다.
(D) 전반적인 국가 경제 쇠퇴(원인)의 일부일 뿐이다.

해설 학생은 비만을 통해 파생되는 여러 가지 문제(당뇨병, 심장 질환 등)를 언급하면서, 이것이 노동력 손실을 초래함으로써 결국 경제 활동 부진을 초래한다고 생각한다.

3 대화의 일부를 다시 들으시오.

P This is what we call a niche economy. A niche is a specialized market, remember? You need another example of these markets?... I guess not...

교수가 다음과 같이 말할 때 그 의미는 무엇인가?

P You need another example of these markets?... I guess not...

(A) 다른 예를 들고 싶지 않다.
(B) 학생들 모두 이 시장이 무엇인지 이해하고 있다고 확신한다.
(C) 그는 다른 예를 들어야 하는지 아닌지 확신하지 못한다.
(D) 그는 학생들이 모두 이 시장이 무엇인지를 이해하고 있는지 알고 싶어 한다.

해설 틈새시장에 대한 다른 설명이 더 필요 없을 것 같다, 즉 학생들이 이미 틈새시장의 개념을 알 것으로 생각되기 때문에 바로 본론으로 들어가겠다는 의미이다.

4 교수가 체중 감량 산업에 대해 말한 것은 무엇인가?
(A) 국가 경제에 부정적인 영향을 주고 있다.
(B) 건강 관리 산업을 주요 수익 모델로 삼고 있다.
(C) 건강 관련 문제를 줄이고 비만자들의 생산성을 향상시켰다.
(D) 적어도 비만 관련 문제로 인해 손해 본 만큼의 돈을 벌어 들인다.

해설 비만 인구가 많아짐에 따라 체중 감량(weight-loss)을 원하는 사람들의 수도 비례하여 증가하였다. 즉, 체중 감량을 내건 새로운 사업이 증가함으로써 새로운 재원을 창출하게 된다.

Actual Test 2
컴퓨터 실습실에서 일어난 대화의 일부를 듣고 물음에 답하시오.

🎧 스크립트

S Excuse me. Can you help me?
L Are you having a mechanical problem?
S Well, I'm just having problems accessing my professor's website.
L I'm sorry.
S It worked yesterday! I think I've got the address right, I'm able to link to things on other websites... I even shut down the computer and tried again. But it won't let me link to the article that I'm supposed to download and summarize for class on Monday.
L Hmm... yeah. I see that. Has anyone in your class mentioned having problems getting to the articles before?
S I don't think so...
L Well, sometimes a homepage server becomes overloaded due to heavy demand

Inference / Stance 61

or the articles you wanted have so many images that it has a problem with display. In both cases, all you have to do is wait and try again, I guess.
S But actually, all the other articles that the professor handed out have been photocopied.
L Ah, I see. Then the link to the article isn't working. Look, all you have to do is just type the web address of the article up here in the address box. Links often don't work, but you can usually get through by going straight to the source.
S Uh oh! I'm not sure of the exact address, but I'll try to find it. I really need to get this article for class.
L Well, I've done all I can. Why not get in touch with your professor? That's all the advice I can give at this point.

학생 실례합니다. 저를 좀 도와주실 수 있나요?
직원 기계적인 문제가 있나요?
학생 교수님의 웹사이트에 접속이 잘 안 돼요.
직원 안타깝군요.
학생 어제는 됐거든요. 주소도 맞고, 다른 웹사이트에는 접속이 돼요. 컴퓨터를 껐다가 다시 해보기까지 했어요. 그런데도 이 자료에는 접속이 안 되네요. 그 자료들을 다운받아서 월요일 수업 시간까지 요약을 해야 하거든요.
직원 흠.... 네, 알겠어요. 예전에도 반 학생 중에 또 누가 이 자료를 다운받는 데 문제가 있다고 한 적이 있나요?
학생 없는 거 같아요.
직원 저, 가끔 과도한 접속 때문에 홈페이지 서버가 과부하가 되거나 학생이 원하는 자료에 이미지가 너무 많아서 화면에 표시하는 데 문제가 생긴 것일 수 있어요. 두 가지 경우 모두, 기다렸다가 다시 해보는 수밖에 없습니다.
학생 그렇지만 사실, 교수님이 나눠주신 다른 자료들은 모두 복사했는걸요.
직원 아, 알겠어요. 그 자료로 연결이 안 되는 거네요. 그러면, 주소창에 그 자료의 웹 주소를 직접 입력해 넣어 보세요. 연결이 안 되는 경우 자료 소스로 직접 접근하면 접속이 가능하기도 하거든요.
학생 아, 네. 정확한 주소는 모르지만, 찾아볼게요. 수업 때문에 이 자료가 정말 필요하니까요.
직원 자, 제가 할 수 있는 건 다 한 것 같군요. 교수님과 직접 연락해 보지 그래요? 제가 이 시점에서 할 수 있는 충고는 그게 답니다.

1 실습실 직원에 관해 추론할 수 있는 것은 무엇인가?
(A) 어려운 컴퓨터 코드를 작성하는 데 유능하다.
(B) 해결책을 제시해 주지만 현재로서는 도움이 안된다.
(C) 그는 실험실에서 일한 지 며칠밖에 되지 않았다.
(D) 그는 전에도 이 학생이 자료를 다운받는 일을 도와왔다.

해설 남자는 웹페이지에 접근이 안되는 여러 가지 이유들을 점검해가면서 여자가 접속할 수 있는 방안을 찾아주고 있다. 그러나 결국 문제가 해결되지 않아서 여자가 필요로 하는 문서를 다운로드하지 못했다.

2 학생에 관해 추론할 수 있는 것은 무엇인가?
(A) 그녀는 컴퓨터 사용 초보자가 아니다.
(B) 그녀는 자신이 정확한 웹사이트 주소를 쳤는지 확신하지 못했다.
(C) 그녀는 전에 웹사이트 접속을 시도해 본 적이 없다.
(D) 그녀는 숙제 때문에 컴퓨터를 사용하는 일이 불편하다.

해설 학생이 자료를 다운받지 못하는 이유는 웹사이트 접속 상의 문제이지 사용 방법을 모르기 때문이 아니다.

3 실습실 직원이 다음과 같이 말할 때 그 의미는 무엇인가?
L Has anyone in your class mentioned having problems getting to the articles before?
(A) 그는 학생이 집중하지 않고 있다고 생각한다.
(B) 그는 이 문제가 (일시적이 아닌) 지속적인 것이라고 생각한다.
(C) 그는 학생이 왜 그 자료를 필요로 하는지 혼란스럽다.
(D) 그는 자신이 학생을 도와줄 수 있을 것이라고 생각하지 않는다.

해설 학생이 웹사이트의 정확한 주소를 알고 있으며 여러 차례 재시도해 보았다고 하니까 다른 학생들도 이와 비슷한 종류의 문제를 겪었냐고 묻고 있다. 일시적인 현상이 아닐 거라고 생각하는 것이다.

4 학생이 다음에 할 행동은 무엇일까?
(A) 다른 컴퓨터를 이용해 그 자료에 접속해 볼 것이다.
(B) 도서관에서 그 자료를 인쇄물 형태로 얻을 것이다.
(C) 필요한 자료를 하드 카피(인쇄) 형태로 찾을 것이다.
(D) 교수에게 그 자료에 직접 연결할 수 있는 정확한 웹 주소를 물어볼 것이다.

해설 필요한 문서에 직접 엑세스할 수 있는 정확한 주소를 알아야 한다. 교수에게 확인하는 것이 가장 확실한 방법이다.

Dictation Actual Test

Actual Test 1

① Obesity has dominated the media
② the average weight of westerners
③ being spent on medical treatments
④ billions are lost by this
⑤ is as great as that of
⑥ have been proved to have relation to obesity
⑦ is uniquely poised to make it easier
⑧ A niche is a specialized market

⑨ hundreds of billions of dollars in revenue from
⑩ all of which adds strength to

Actual Test 2

① Are you having a mechanical problem
② accessing my professor's website
③ I'm able to link to things on
④ it won't let me link to the article
⑤ Has anyone in your class mentioned
⑥ becomes overloaded due to heavy demand
⑦ it has a problem with display
⑧ the link to the article isn't working
⑨ type the web address of the article up here
⑩ get through by going straight to the source
⑪ Why not get in touch with

Vocabulary Review

다음 각 정의의 맞게 알맞은 단어를 골라 써 넣으시오.

1 obesity 2 nutrients 3 exotic
4 restricted 5 sufficient 6 plagiarism
7 cite 8 extension 9 consumption
10 mortality

1 평균 체중보다 더 많이 나감
2 동물의 성장에 필요한 물질
3 세계의 다른 장소에서 온
4 아주 작은 혹은 제한된 범위, 양, 정도 등
5 어떤 일을 의도된 대로 충분히 할 수 있는
6 다른 사람의 아이디어나 작품을 사용해서 마치 자신의 것인 양 꾸미는 것
7 어떤 것을 참조하다
8 일정 기간의 추가
9 필요를 충족시키기 위해 물건을 사는 행위
10 일부 지역 또는 특정 상황에서의 사망률

다음 구문을 사용하여 문장을 완성하시오.

1 is poised to   2 having a hard time
3 in response to   4 get through
5 be traced back

1 정부는 석유 수입 관세를 낮출 준비가 되어 있다.
2 아이들은 낱말 맞추기 퍼즐을 하느라 애를 먹고 있다.
3 너의 제안에 대한 답장으로 나는 너에게 이메일을 보낸다.
4 나는 쓰기만 빼고는 모든 것을 마칠 수 있었다.
5 일부 공포증들은 어린 시절의 경험으로 거슬러 올라간다.

CHAPTER 06
FUNCTION

Sample

학생 1 McEwan 교수님 수업 훌륭하지 않니?
학생 2 글쎄, 잘 모르겠어. 난 그 강의에서 배우는 게 그다지 많지 않은 것 같거든.
학생 1 그래? 난 교수님 강의가 멋지다고 생각하는데. 특히 슬라이드를 이용한 강연이 좋더라.
학생 2 그게 문제야. 그거 때문에 노트필기를 제대로 할 수가 없잖아.
학생 1 흠… 지난번 논문 말이야, 내가 논문 주제 때문에 애먹었던 것 기억나? 내가 교수님 연구실로 찾아갔더니 몇 시간이나 도와주셨잖아.
학생 2 어, 그랬지!
학생 1 정말 내가 장담하건대, 교수님께서 어떻게 하면 제대로 노트할 수 있는지도 기꺼이 보여주실 거야. 아주 좋은 분이셔.

대화의 일부를 다시 들으시오.

S1 Hmmm… remember the last paper, I had a lot of trouble doing my thesis? He helped me for a couple of hours when I visited him in his office.
S2 Yeah, right!

여자가 다음과 같은 말을 한 이유는 무엇인가?

S1 Hmmm… remember the last paper, I had a lot of trouble doing my thesis?

(A) 강의 노트가 리포트를 쓰는 데 아주 중요하다는 것을 나타내기 위해
(B) 남자에게 교수님 도움을 청하도록 격려하기 위해
(C) 지난번 자신이 쓴 과제의 완성도가 좋지 않았음을 강조하기 위해
(D) 남자에게 자신과 같은 실수는 하지 말라고 부탁하기 위해

정답 (B)

Vocabulary Preview   for Skill Check-up

다음 정의를 듣고 알맞은 단어를 고르시오.

1 incompatible 2 permit   3 regular
4 convenience   5 ancient   6 sewage
7 gene   8 offspring 9 embody
10 survive

1 not in harmony
   조화롭지 않은
2 allow someone to do something
   누군가 어떤 일을 하도록 허락하다
3 happening at fixed intervals
   일정한 간격으로 일이 일어나는
4 something very useful or suitable for you
   당신에게 대단히 쓸모 있고 적합한 어떤 것
5 belong to a time early in history
   역사적으로 초기에 속하는
6 dirty water from houses
   가정에서 발생하는 더러운 물
7 the part of a cell as a unit of heredity
   유전 형질의 한 개체로서의 세포의 한 부분
8 children of a person or young of an animal
   사람의 자식이나 동물의 새끼
9 represent an idea in bodily form
   어떤 개념을 구체적인 형태로 제시하다
10 continue to live in spite of all the difficulties
   모든 어려움에도 불구하고 계속 생존하다

다음 단어를 이용하여 아래 문장을 완성하시오.

1 regular   2 permit   3 sewage   4 common
5 proposed 6 ancient   7 prevent 8 public
9 provide   10 survive

1 우리 회사는 모든 직원에게 정기적인 버스 편을 제공한다.
2 우리 형은 절대 내가 형의 디지털 카메라를 사용하는 것을 허락하지 않을 것이다.
3 이 강은 산업 폐수로 오염되었다.
4 영어가 국제 사회의 공통어라는 점에는 누구나 동의한다.
5 위원회는 우리에게 Jefferson Industries를 매점하라고 제안하면서 매매가 끝나면 우리 회사의 주가가 올라갈 거라고 확신시켰다.
6 그들은 고대 중국의 위대한 지도자들의 몇몇 묘실을 발견했다.
7 경찰은 발생할지도 모를 테러 공격을 막기 위해 서울의 보안을 강화했다.
8 이 새 박물관은 다음달에 일반인들에게 개방될 것이다.
9 그 신부는 가난한 빈민층에게 먹을 것을 제공해 주는 것으로 잘 알려져 있다.
10 나는 그녀가 어떻게 하루에 한 끼만 먹고 버틸 수 있는지 모르겠다.

Skill Check-up   Function-Purpose

1 여자가 다음과 같이 말하는 이유는 무엇인가?

S2 How much do you have to pay for the tickets?

(A) 남자가 벌금을 얼마나 내야하는지 물어보기 위해
(B) 남자에게 주차 위반 딱지를 피할 수 있는 방법을 조언해 주기 위해
(C) 남자에게 또다른 통학 수단을 제안하기 위해

정답 (C)

해설 여자는 주차 위반 범칙금이 많을 것이므로 주차가 필요 없는 다른 방안

을 생각해 보라고 권한다. 여자가 한 말의 뒷부분의 의미에 유념하자.

 스크립트

S1 I can't believe I got another parking ticket!
S2 Oof! Again? Isn't this your third time getting the ticket?
S1 Fourth, actually. I tried to get a permit at the parking service... but they only have a limited number.
S2 How much do you have to pay for the tickets? I mean, since you can't get the permit this semester, you should do something. Well how about a campus bus? It's free.
S1 Hmm... I hadn't thought about that. Does it run regularly?
S2 Yeah, like every 10 minutes. And it goes all over campus.
S1 Well, maybe I'll try it. It's better than paying all these tickets!

학생 1 주차 위반 딱지를 또 뗐어!
학생 2 이런, 또? 딱지 뗀 게 이번이 세 번째 아니야?
학생 1 네 번째지, 정확히는. 주차 서비스 센터에서 허가를 얻으려고 했는데, 한정된 수만 허가를 해 준대.
학생 2 주차 위반 딱지 때문에 물어야 할 벌금이 얼마니? 그러니까 내 말은, 네가 이번 학기에는 허가를 못 받았다니까 뭔가 다른 대책을 세워야 할 거 아냐. 음... 학교 버스는 어때? 그건 무료인데.
학생 1 흠... 그 생각은 안 해봤어. 정기적으로 다니니?
학생 2 그래, 10분 간격이나, 뭐 그런 식으로. 그리고 학교 곳곳을 다 다녀.
학생 1 그럼, 버스를 타고 다녀봐야겠다. 벌금 내는 거 보다 나을 테니까.

2 남자가 다음과 같이 말한 이유는 무엇인가?

S Come on!

(A) 교수의 말을 믿지 못하겠다는 것을 표현하기 위해
(B) 자신이 들은 내용을 정정하기 위해
(C) 그런 사실은 상식이라는 것을 설명하기 위해

정답 (A)

해설 바로 뒤이어 학생은 '로마인들이 실내 화장실을 사용했었냐'고 되묻고 있다. 기원전 800년경에 로마인이 이미 실내 수도 시설을 갖추고 있었다는 말에 대한 놀라움의 표현이다.

스크립트

P We think that indoor plumbing is just a modern convenience. But the Romans had it as far back as 800 B.C.
S1 Come on! They had indoor toilets?
P Yep. In fact, public lavatories and the homes of the rich had constantly running water beneath the toilets to wash away the waste.
S2 Yeah, I heard that Rome today still uses part of the ancient sewage system.
P That's right. The Cloaca Maxima was the main drainage tank in ancient Rome and is still in use.

교수 우리는 보통 실내 배관이 현대 시설이라고 생각하지요. 하지만 로마인들은 기원전 800년에 벌써 이 시설을 사용했습니다.
학생 1 그럴리가요! 실내 화장실이 있었다고요?
교수 네. 실제로, 공중 화장실이나 부유층 집에는 화장실 아래쪽에 오물을 씻어버릴 수 있도록 계속 물이 흐르도록 했지요.
학생 2 네, 요즘도 로마에서는 고대에 쓰던 하수 체계를 이용한다는 얘기를 들었어요.
교수 맞습니다. Cloaca Maxima는 고대 로마의 주요 배수 탱크였는데, 오늘날도 여전히 사용되고 있습니다.

3 상담원이 다음과 같은 말을 한 이유는 무엇인가?

A It's kind of a common problem. You really have to talk to her first.

(A) 문제 해결을 위해 여자가 할 수 있는 일을 제안하기 위해
(B) 여자의 문제점을 룸메이트에게 직접 얘기해야 한다는 것을 암시하기 위해
(C) 자신이 기숙사에서 발생하는 대부분의 문제들을 이해하고 있다는 것을 보여주기 위해

정답 (B)

해설 학생이 불만스러워 하는 부분은 일상적으로 일어나는 문제점이므로 룸메이트와의 대화를 통해 해결해 보라고 권하고 있다. 즉, 방을 옮기는 게 급선무가 아니라는 지적이다.

스크립트

A Can I help?
S Yeah, it's my roommate. She's up all night, making tons of noise, but I'm an early riser. So I'm not getting any sleep. And she brings her friends all the time... I mean... we're, like, totally incompatible. I just want to move to another room or something.
A It's kind of a common problem. You really have to talk to her first.
S I tried several times and... that's not the only thing.
A Well?
S I asked for a non-smoker on the housing form. But she smokes! I mean... that's something I can't really stand.
A Hmm... the housing form is supposed to

prevent these problems. There must have been a mix-up. Let me try and find you another room.

상담원 도와드릴까요?
학생 네, 제 룸메이트 때문에요. 그녀는 밤새도록 잠도 안자고 아주 시끄럽게 굴어요. 전 일찍 일어나는 사람이거든요. 그래서 통 잠을 잘 수가 없어요. 그리고 그녀는 친구들도 자주 데려와요. 제 말은, 그러니까 우리는 전혀 맞지가 않아요. 다른 방으로 옮기거나 뭐 그러고 싶어요.
상담원 그것은 (다른 학생들도 많이 겪는) 일반적인 문제예요. 먼저 룸메이트랑 이야기를 해보세요.
학생 여러 번 해봤어요. 그리고 그게 전부가 아니에요.
상담원 그러면요?
학생 주거 신청서에 제가 비흡연자를 신청했는데 그녀는 담배를 피운다구요! 그건 정말 참을 수 없어요.
상담원 흠... 주거 신청서는 그런 문제들을 막기 위한 것인데, 뭔가 혼선이 있었던 것 같습니다. 제가 다른 방을 알아 봐 드리겠습니다.

4 교수가 다음과 같은 말을 하는 이유는 무엇인가?

P Cool, huh?

(A) 그 이론에 자신이 동의하고 있음을 표현하기 위해
(B) 학생들을 토론에 참여하도록 유도하기 위해
(C) 밈(문화구성요소)과 유전자가 서로 관련이 있음을 확신시키기 위해

정답 (A)

 스크립트

P When animals procreate, they pass on their genes to their offspring, right? Well, interestingly, science writer Richard Dawkins proposed that cultural ideas do the same thing. He called these ideas memes.
S It kinda sounds like the word "gene."
P Yeah, right. That was Dawkins' point. Just like, er... genes exist to provide strong characteristics for the next generation, so memes embody cultural ideas, like religion, rights, and so on, that make a culture stronger. Cool, huh? But just like all genes don't survive, not all memes survive to be passed on.

교수 동물은 번식을 하면서 자손에게 그들의 유전자를 전달합니다, 맞죠? 에, 흥미롭게도, 과학 저자인 Richard Dawkins는 문화적 개념도 이와 똑같은 역할을 한다고 주장했습니다. 그는 이것을 밈(문화구성요소)이라고 명명했습니다.
학생 유전자(Gene)라는 단어와 발음이 비슷하게 들리는데요.
교수 맞아요. 그건 Dawkins이 의도했던 겁니다. 마치 유전자가,

에… 다음 세대에게 강력한 특성을 제공하기 위해 존재하는 것처럼, 밈(문화구성요소)도 문화를 보다 확고하게 만드는 종교나 권리 같은 문화적 개념들을 구체화시킨다는 거죠. 흥미롭죠? 하지만 모든 유전자가 다 생존하지 못하는 것처럼, 모든 밈(문화구성요소)이 살아남아 (다음 세대로) 전달되는 것은 아닙니다.

Exercise

1 A - (A) B - (B)   2 A - (C) B - (C)
3 A - (A) B - (D)   4 A - (B) B - (C)

Exercise 1
White Noise에 관한 수업에서의 대화의 일부를 듣고 물음에 답하시오.

스크립트

P So, noise can really disrupt sleep. Cars, neighbors, barking dogs. But noise can also solve many people's sleep problems. I'm talking about white noise. So... what is white noise? Is it a particular frequency of sound? Actually, white noise is a combination of all the sound frequencies in equal amounts. If you took all kinds of sounds that you can hear around you and combined them together, you would have white noise. Why do we use the adjective "white" in this case? It's because it works in the same way white light works. Just like the color white is made up of all the colors in the light spectrum.
S I know that it sounds kinda like a "whoosh", like waves crashing in the ocean.
P Good... so, the result of the sound combination is... this whooshing sound. And then, how does it work? Here is one way to think about it. Suppose there are two kinds of sound, for example, a man is singing a song while listening to music. You may distinguish the two sounds. And now, there are a hundred kinds of sound in equal amounts, and you may not distinguish one from the others. So when you try to sleep, it would be better if there is white noise, that is, a combination of all the sound frequencies than just two or three different kinds of sounds, not to make you distinguish one

from others. Now, this sound has some real proven benefits in helping people relax. Because it incorporates all sound frequencies, from high to low, it cancels out a lot of other noises, making people sleep easier.

교수 자, 소음은 수면을 방해합니다. 차 소리, 이웃집 소음, 개 짖는 소리 등등 말입니다. 그러나 소음은 또 많은 사람들의 수면 장애를 해결할 수도 있습니다. 제가 얘기하고 있는 건 White Noise라는 겁니다. 그렇다면, White Noise란 뭘까요? 특별한 주파수의 소리인가요? 사실, White Noise는 같은 양의 소리 주파수들을 모두 조합한 것을 일컫습니다. 여러분이 주변에서 들을 수 있는 모든 종류의 소리를 모아서 그것들을 조합하면, 그것이 바로 White Noise가 됩니다. 그런데 왜 이 경우에 형용사 White를 쓰는 걸까요? 그것은 백색광이 작용하는 방식과 같은 방법으로 이루어지기 때문입니다. 가지각색의 모든 빛이 조합하였을 때 백색광이 만들어지는 것처럼 말이지요.

학생 바다에서 나는 파도 소리처럼 '쉭' 하는 소리로 들리는 것이라고 알고 있어요.

교수 맞습니다. 그러니까, 그 모든 소리가 조합한 결과는 바로 이런 '쉭' 하는 소리인 겁니다. 그러면, 그것은 어떻게 작용할까요? 여기 한 가지 생각할 수 있는 방법이 있습니다. 두 가지 종류의 소리가 있다고 해봅시다. 예를 들어, 한 남자가 음악을 들으면서 노래를 부르고 있습니다. 여러분은 이 두 소리를 구분할 수 있을 겁니다. 자, 이제 백 가지 종류의 소리가 동일한 양으로 존재한다고 가정해 봅시다. 여러분은 (그 많은 소리 가운데) 하나를 다른 것으로부터 (일일이) 구별하지 못할 것입니다. 그렇기 때문에 만약 여러분이 잠을 자려고 한다면, (주변에) White Noise가 있는 것이 더 낫겠지요. 말하자면 그냥 두세 가지 소리보다는 모든 소리의 주파수들이 혼합되어서 당신이 소리 하나하나를 다른 것과 구분해내지 못하도록 말이죠. 자, 이 소리(White Noise)는 사람들을 편안하게 하는 데 실제 도움이 된다는 것이 증명되었습니다. 이것이 높은 주파수에서부터 낮은 주파수까지 모든 소리의 주파수를 통합하고 있기 때문에 여러 다른 소음들을 배제하고 사람들이 쉽게 잠들 수 있도록 한다는 것입니다.

어휘 disrupt 혼란시키다, 분열시키다 frequency 진동수, 주파수 adjective 형용사의 spectrum 범위, 스펙트럼, 분광 whoosh 획하고 움직이는 소리 proven 증명된, 입증된 incorporate 통합시키다, 혼합하다

A 대화에서 빛의 스펙트럼이 언급된 이유는 무엇인가?
 (A) White Noise를 만드는 것과 빛에 있어서의 백색광을 만드는 것의 유사함을 비교하기 위해
 (B) 학생들에게 유사한 예를 생각해보도록 하기 위해
 (C) 소음이나 색상에서 '하얗다' 라는 단어가 사용된 이유를 설명하기 위해
 (D) 일반적인 White Noise의 한 가지 유형을 제시하기 위해

해설 교수는 white noise가 다른 소음과 구별되는 원리를 white light가 생성되는 원리와 비교하여 설명하고 있다.

B 대화의 일부를 다시 들으시오.

P But noise can also solve many people's sleep problems. I'm talking about white noise. So... what is white noise? Is it a particular frequency of sound? Actually, white noise is a combination of all the sound frequencies in equal amounts.

교수가 다음과 같이 물어본 이유는 무엇인가?

P So... what is white noise?

 (A) 학생들이 읽기 자료를 읽었다는 것을 확인하기 위해
 (B) White Noise의 정의를 내리기 위해
 (C) 수면장애에 대한 자신의 의견을 주기 위해
 (D) White Noise가 만드는 소리를 묘사하기 위해

Exercise 2
역사 수업에서의 대화의 일부를 듣고 물음에 답하시오.

 스크립트

P Over, uh, over the past 30 years, the Huichol Indians of Mexico have migrated to Mexican cities in order to make money. And... and... that's... how their, uh, unique arts were introduced to the rest of the world. The most common artworks that we see are um, are bead and yarn paintings, depicting, which uh, show the sacred worlds of Huichol culture. The uh, most common themes in these paintings are creation — we see deer and corn, two symbols of fertility and renewal for the Huichol — and the spirit world, which is, uh, often represented by the peyote flower. You know what peyote is, right? It's a hallucinogenic drug used in Huichol rituals. The Huichol thought the peyote was a divine gift from the Gods. They believed through peyote's hallucinogenic effects, enlightenment and shamanic powers can be achieved. Are you familiar with the word 'hallucinogenic' or 'hallucinate'?

S It's... I mean... if you hallucinate, you see things that are not really there, either because you are ill or because you have taken a drug.

P Here you go! Okay, everyone? All right! ... So, it's said peyote gave the Huichol an opportunity to see the spirit world. So uh, elements of this world are often depicted in the colorful and intricate yarn and bead paintings.

교수 지난, 에, 지난 30년 동안 멕시코의 Huichol 인디언은 돈을 벌기 위해 멕시코 도시로 이주하였습니다. 그리고 그렇게, 음… Huichol 인디언의 독특한 예술품들이 세상으로 소개가 되었습니다. 현재 우리가 접하는 가장 흔한 수공예품은 구슬이나 직물로 된 그림으로, Huichol 문화의 종교 세계를 그대로 보여주고 있습니다. 이들 그림에 나타난 가장 흔한 주제는 신의 천지창조입니다. 우리는 (이 그림들에서) 사슴이나 곡물을 보는데, 이 두 가지는 Huichol 문화에서 다산과 부활을 상징합니다. 그리고 또 다른 주제는, 보통 Peyote 꽃으로 상징되는 신의 세계입니다. Peyote가 무엇인지는 알고 있죠? Peyote는 Huichol의 종교적인 의식에 사용되는 환각제로 Huichol 인들은 그것을 신이 준 선물이라고 생각했습니다. 이들은 Peyote의 환각 효과를 통해 개화되거나 주술적인 힘을 얻을 수 있다고 믿었습니다. 여러분은 이 '환각 유발의'나 '환각을 일으키게 하다'와 같은 단어를 잘 알고 있나요?

학생 그건, 그러니까… 우리가 아프거나, 아니면 약을 복용했기 때문에 '환각을 일으키는' 상태가 되면 실제로는 거기 존재하지 않는 것을 볼 수 있게 된다는 뜻이에요.

교수 맞아요! 자, 모두 이해되죠? 좋습니다! 그러니까 Peyote는 Huichol 인들이 신의 세계를 접할 수 있는 기회를 제공한 거라고 합니다. 그래서 에, 이 세계의 요소들이 종종 화려한 색상의 복잡한 직물이나 구슬 그림으로 묘사되는 거죠.

어휘 migrate 이주하다, 이동하다　artwork 수공예품, 예술 작품　bead 구슬, 유리알　yarn 직물 짜는 실, 방적사　sacred 신성한, 성스러운　fertility 비옥, 다산, 풍부　renewal 부흥, 부활　divine 신의, 신성의　intricate 얽힌, 복잡한

A 대화의 일부를 다시 들으시오.

> S It's… I mean… If you hallucinate, you see things that are not really there, either because you are ill or because you have taken a drug.
> P Here you go! Okay? everyone? All right!…

교수가 다음과 같은 말을 한 의미는 무엇인가?

> P Here you go! Okay? everyone? All right!…

(A) 학생이 설명을 계속할 수 있도록 격려하기 위해
(B) (학생의 설명은) 대부분의 사람들이 오해하고 있는 것과 같다는 것을 암시하기 위해
(C) 학생의 답이 맞았다는 것을 표현하기 위해
(D) (자신은) 학생들 모두가 그 내용을 이해하기를 원한다고 암시하기 위해

해설 교수는 학생이 내린 정의에 대해 첨삭 없이 바로 다음 설명으로 넘어가고 있다.

B 교수가 멕시코 도시들로 이주한 이주자들을 언급한 이유는 무엇인가?
(A) 그 도시가 (Huichol 인디언들의 본래 거주지와) 가장 가까웠음을 암시하기 위해
(B) 수공예품이 그 당시에는 가치 있는 것이었음을 알려주기 위해
(C) 수공예품이 널리 알려지게 된 최초의 원인을 들기 위해
(D) Huichol 문화의 쇠락에 대한 염려를 표현하기 위해

해설 Mexican City로 이주함으로써 Huichol Indians 문화가 처음 세상에 소개되었다.

Exercise 3

두 학생의 대화의 일부를 듣고 물음에 답하시오.

🎧 **스크립트**

S1 Why do you look so upset?
S2 Man! That was a killer, wasn't it?
S1 Actually, I didn't think it was so bad. I feel like I did pretty well.
S2 Oh… but I think… I failed this exam… I studied nonstop for the past two weeks but the exam was so hard.
S1 You know, I've heard this all before. Didn't you think you were going to fail the last one, but you still got an A?
S2 Well, yeah, I did, but… this time I'm serious… There were four to five questions I wasn't sure about and definitely more than five questions I had no idea. I'm too worried… just can't sit back and wait until I get the exam back.
S1 Well, I shouldn't take your prediction seriously… but… well… I was going to go to see the TA tomorrow… I got some questions to ask on the exam… and if you feel like going together… maybe you can ask about the questions… what do you think?
S2 No, what if I hear from her that I failed the exam? That's the last thing that I want to hear.
S1 No way. That can't be! You can just ask about the questions you weren't sure about, and I'm sure she will give you, at least what is right or wrong. Then, you might be relieved at your answers.
S2 Oh-uh, well…

학생 1 왜 그렇게 근심스러운 얼굴이니?
학생 2 세상에! 정말 심했어, 안 그래?

학생 1 글쎄, 난 그렇게 나빴다고 생각하지는 않아. 난 꽤 잘한 것 같거든.
학생 2 그래… 하지만 난… 아무래도 이번 시험 망친 것 같아. 지난 두 주 동안 정말 쉬지 않고 공부만 했는데도 이번 시험은 너무 어려웠어.
학생 1 너도 참, 예전에도 다 듣던 말이야. 너 지난번에도 시험을 망쳤다고 하더니 A 받은 거 기억 안 나?
학생 2 음, 그래, 그랬어. 하지만… 이번엔 진짜야. 답이 확실하지 않은 것이 네다섯 개는 되고 다섯 문제는 전혀 모르겠더라고. 너무 걱정이 돼서 시험 성적이 나올 때까지 가만히 앉아서 기다릴 수가 없어.
학생 1 글쎄, 네 말을 심각하게 받아들이지는 않지만, 음, 내가 내일 조교를 찾아갈 거거든. 시험에 관해 몇 가지 물어볼 것이 있어서 말이야. 너도 같이 가서 그 문제들에 관해 물어보면 어때? 어떻게 생각해?
학생 2 싫어, 낙제했다는 얘기라도 들으면 어떻게 해? 그런 말은 정말 듣고 싶지 않아.
학생 1 말도 안 돼. 그럴 리 없잖아! 너는 그냥 네가 확신하지 못하는 문제들을 물어보면 되는 거야. 그러면 적어도 그녀가 뭐가 맞고 뭐가 틀렸는지는 알려 줄 거야. 그럼 너도 네가 쓴 답안들에 대해 안심할 수 있을 테지.
학생 2 음, 글쎄…

> **어휘** killer 매우 힘든 일, 굉장한 것 nonstop 쉬지 않고, 연속적으로 prediction 예언, 예측 TA 조교 (= Teaching Assistant) relieve 안도케 하다, 긴장을 덜다

A 여자가 자신이 답하지 못한 문제의 개수를 말한 이유는 무엇인가?
(A) 자신이 시험을 얼마나 못 봤는지를 강조하기 위해
(B) 시험이 너무 어려웠다는 것을 불평하기 위해
(C) 시험 문제가 그다지 많지 않았다는 것을 지적하기 위해
(D) 시험이 그다지 어렵지는 않았다는 것을 암시하기 위해

> **해설** 답을 전혀 모르거나 답이 불확실한 문제가 많았으므로 이번 시험은 틀림없이 망칠 거라고 생각한다.

B 대화의 일부를 다시 들으시오.

> S2 Oh… but I think… I failed this exam… I studied nonstop for the past two weeks but the exam was so hard.
> S1 You know, I've heard this all before. Didn't you think you were going to fail the last one, but you still got an A?

남자가 다음과 같은 말을 한 의미는 무엇인가?

> S1 Didn't you think you were going to fail the last one, but you still got an A?

(A) 이번 시험의 난이도와 대조하기 위해
(B) 두 시험의 유사성을 설명하기 위해
(C) 수업의 시험 수에 대해 불평하기 위해
(D) 여자의 시험 성적이 (예전과 마찬가지로) 좋을 것임을 예상하기 위해

> **해설** 여자는 지난번에도 시험 성적을 걱정했으나 결과는 A 였다. 따라서 이번 시험에 대한 걱정도 크게 염려하지 않는다는 말이다.

Exercise 4

학생과 상담원과의 대화의 일부를 듣고 물음에 답하시오.

 스크립트

S I want to apply to grad school for history next year, but I'm not sure what my chances are.
C Our graduate admissions committee requires the GRE to measure the student's general intellectual ability and the possibility of success in graduate school. Thus, the students willing to apply to grad school have to obtain the best scores they can. And now, well, looking at your transcript, I wouldn't think you would have much of a problem with your grades. I mean you have enough to get into some of the nice schools…
S But do you think I could get into a top school? Is there any other things I should be concerned about?
C It will be better if you have three or four recommendations, and those recommendations should come from faculty members. And I advise you to try to obtain research experience.
S Oh, I see.
C And, well, is there any extracurricular activities you have been involved in?
S I've worked on the student newspaper since my freshman year. And I'm the president of the history club. But will that be enough?
C What are you talking about? It's better to have one or two activities that you are very involved in instead of doing five or six things that you can't really give your full attention to.
S Really? Oh, good. That makes me feel a lot better.

학생 저 내년에 역사 대학원에 진학하고 싶은데, 제가 그럴 가능성이 있는지 모르겠어요

상담원 우리 대학원 입학 위원회에서는 학생의 전반적인 학업 능력과 대학원에서의 성공 가능성을 측정하기 위해 GRE 시험 성적을 요구하고 있습니다. 그러니까 대학원에 진학하려는 학생들은 가능한 최상의 성적을 얻는 게 좋지요. 그런데 학생의 성적표를 보니까 성적에는 별 문제가 없을 것 같군요. 충분히 여러 좋은 학교에 들어갈 수 있을 거예요.

학생 그러면 상위 학교에도 들어갈 수 있을까요? 제가 고려해야 할 다른 사항들은 없는지요?

상담원 추천서를 서너 장 받아오면 더 좋겠네요. 물론 그 추천서는 교수님들께 받아와야 합니다. 그리고 학생의 연구 부분에서 경험을 쌓아두라고 권하고 싶군요.

학생 네, 알겠어요.

상담원 그리고 음, 참여하고 있는 과외활동이 있나요?

학생 전 1학년 때부터 학생 신문사에서 일해왔습니다. 그리고 역사 동아리의 회장이고요. 그런데 이 정도로도 충분할까요?

상담원 무슨 말이에요? 전력을 기울이지 못하는 일을 대여섯 개 하는 것보다는 학생이 열중할 수 있는 한두 개 활동 분야를 갖고 있는 게 더 좋지요.

학생 정말요? 그거, 다행이에요. 훨씬 안심이 되네요.

어휘 committee 위원회 measure 평가하다, 측정하다, 재다 graduate school 대학원 transcript 성적 증명서, 사본 recommendation 추천(장) faculty (대학) 교수단 field (활동, 연구) 분야 extracurricular 정규과목 이외의, 과외의

A 여자가 과외활동을 언급하는 이유는 무엇인가?
(A) 남자에게 과외활동을 하라고 설득하기 위해
(B) 대학원에 지원하려면 과외 활동을 하는 것이 중요하다는 것을 나타내기 위해
(C) 남자가 어떤 과외활동을 했는지 알아보기 위해
(D) 남자가 충분한 입학 자격을 갖추고 있는지 보기 위해

해설 여자는 대학원 입학 자격 요건을 하나씩 열거하면서 남자가 해당되는지를 짚어나가고 있다. 과외 활동 경력도 이 중 하나이므로 이것 역시 대학원 입학 시 중요 사항이 된다는 뜻이다.

B 대화의 일부를 다시 들으시오.

S I've worked on the student newspaper since my freshman year. And I'm the president of the history club. But will that be enough?

C What are you talking about? It's better to have one or two activities that you are very involved in instead of doing five or six things that you can't really give your full attention to.

여자가 다음과 같은 말을 한 이유는 무엇인가?

C What are you talking about?

(A) 남자가 또 다른 활동을 하고 있는지 물어보기 위해
(B) 남자가 자신의 질문에 대답하지 않았다는 것을 말하기 위해
(C) 남자가 하고 있는 활동만으로도 충분하고 단언하기 위해
(D) 그녀가 남자의 답에 실망했음을 표현하기 위해

해설 다양한 분야에서의 활동보다 집중적인 한두 가지 활동이 보다 효율적일 수 있다는 말을 하고 있다.

Dictation Exercise

Exercise 1

① noise can really disrupt sleep
② I'm talking about white noise
③ a particular frequency of sound
④ all the sound frequencies in equal amounts
⑤ the adjective "white" in this case
⑥ waves crashing in the ocean
⑦ distinguish the two sounds
⑧ in equal amounts
⑨ some real proven benefits in helping
⑩ it incorporates
⑪ from high to low

Exercise 2

① have migrated to
② unique arts were introduced to
③ bead and yarn paintings
④ show the sacred worlds of
⑤ two symbols of fertility and renewal
⑥ represented by the peyote flower
⑦ a divine gift from the Gods
⑧ things that are not really there
⑨ you are ill or
⑩ you have taken a drug
⑪ an opportunity to see the spirit world
⑫ depicted in the colorful and intricate yarn

Exercise 3

① That was a killer
② I studied nonstop for the past two weeks
③ I've heard this all before
④ four to five questions I wasn't sure about
⑤ can't sit back and wait until
⑥ shouldn't take your prediction seriously

⑦ That's the last thing that I want to hear
⑧ That can't be
⑨ at least what is right or wrong
⑩ you might be relieved

Exercise 4

① apply to grad school for
② Our graduate admissions committee
③ to measure the student's general intellectual ability
④ obtain the best scores they can
⑤ I wouldn't think
⑥ I should be concerned about
⑦ should come from faculty members
⑧ any extracurricular activities
⑨ better to have one or two activities
⑩ involved in instead of
⑪ you can't really give your full attention to

Actual Test

1 1 - (D) 2 - (C) 3 - (B) 4 - (B)
2 1 - (C) 2 - (A) 3 - (B) 4 - (C)

Actual Test 1

봉독(벌독)용법에 관한 강의의 일부를 듣고 물음에 답하시오.

🎧 스크립트

P Umm... most of us try to avoid bee stings, right? But believe it or not, many people are currently turning to bee stings... umm... do I intentionally want to get stung by a bee? Oh.. no! But, the fact of the matter is, if you could imagine the chronic pain of rheumatoid arthritis... a bee sting barely hurts. Actually people suffering from rheumatoid arthritis are willing to be stung by bees or injected with bee venom. Oh, yeah!... ah... it's called uh, apitherapy... Apitherapy is the medical use of honeybee products... it has been practiced since ancient times. In the modern world honeybee venom has found wide uses in treating arthritis and other inflammatory and degenerative disease. Well... the apitherapy most commonly refers to use of bee venom, called bee venom therapy (BVT) to help with rheumatoid arthritis... you know the problems on joints, such as elbow or knee... While it isn't widely endorsed by the medical community, the studies that have been done on the therapy indicate that it is, uh, in fact, pretty effective. Why is this? Well, we don't... we're not sure, but we do know that among the 18 active substances in bee venom, several are extremely potent anti-inflammatories. The anti-inflammatory substances that are believed to be responsible for the beneficial effects seen when they are allowed to sting patients with severe rheumatoid arthritis and some other neurological syndromes. Uh, we haven't been very successful at isolating these chemicals, but why bother... when administering them via the bee sting seems to really work for a lot of people?

교수 음, 우리들 대부분은 벌침을 피하려고 하겠죠? 그러나 믿기 힘들겠지만, 벌침에 의지하는 사람들도 많이 있습니다. 음, 제가 의도적으로 벌에 쏘이려고 하는 걸까요? 아, 아닙니다. 그러나 문제는, 만약 여러분이 류머티즘 관절염의 만성적 고통을 상상할 수 있다면 벌침의 고통은 사실 아무것도 아니라는 데 있습니다. 실제로 류머티즘 관절염을 앓고 있는 사람들은 벌에 쏘이거나 벌의 독침을 맞으려고 하지요. 네, 그렇습니다. 그리고 에, 이것을 Apitherapy(봉독요법)라고 하는데, 이는 꿀벌 소산물의 의학적인 사용을 일컫습니다. 이 방법은 고대부터 사용되어 왔지요. 현재 꿀벌 독은 관절염과, 기타 염증을 일으키는 질병이나 퇴행성 질병에 널리 사용되고 있습니다. 자, Apitherapy는 가장 일반적으로는 류머티즘 관절염 치료를 위한 벌 독 치료, 즉 BVT라고 불리는 벌 독의 사용을 의미합니다. 류머티즘 관절염이란 팔꿈치나 무릎 같은 관절 부분에 생긴 문제들이죠. 물론 의학계에서는 일반적으로 이 방법을 신임하지 않지만, 이 치료법을 연구한 결과 실제 이 방법이 대단히 효과적인 것으로 나타났습니다. 왜 그럴까요? 글쎄요, 현재 우리는, 확신할 수는 없지만, 벌 독에 들어 있는 18가지 활성물질 가운데 몇 가지가 대단히 강력한 항염증 물질을 포함하고 있는 것으로 알고 있습니다. 이 항염증 물질이 류머티즘 관절염이나 다른 신경성 증후군으로 고통스러워하는 환자들에게 벌침을 놓았을 경우 효과를 보인 원인으로 받아들여지고 있습니다. 에, 물론 지금껏 이 물질을 성공적으로 분리해 내지는 못했지만, 벌침만으로도 많은 사람들에게 효과를 나타냈다면 굳이 그럴 필요가 있을까요?

1 이 강의는 주로 무엇에 관한 것인가?
(A) 류머티즘 관절염과 그 증상
(B) 벌침과 류머티즘 관절염의 고통

(C) 벌독의 구성 요소와 효과
  (D) 벌침 치료법과 그 효과

해설 민간요법의 하나인 벌침이 류마티스 관절염을 앓고 있는 환자들에게 효력을 보이는 것으로 나타났다.

2 다음 중 Apitherapy(봉독요법)에 관해 사실인 것은 무엇인가?
  (A) 벌독을 이용하여 관절염을 치료하는 최근 요법이다.
  (B) 가장 대중적인 류머티즘 관절염 치료법의 하나가 되었다.
  (C) 봉독요법은 관절 문제에 효과가 있는 것으로 증명되었다.
  (D) 봉독요법의 부정적 효과가 나타날 수 있기 때문에 (의학계에서) 인정받지 못했다.

해설 봉독요법이 여러 효과를 인정받고는 있다.

3 강의의 일부를 다시 들으시오.

> P Umm... most of us try to avoid bee stings, right? But believe it or not, many people are currently turning to bee stings, umm... do I intentionally want to get stung by a bee? Oh... no! But, the fact of the matter is, if you could imagine the chronic pain of rheumatoid arthritis... a bee sting barely hurts.

교수가 다음과 같이 말한 이유는 무엇인가?

> P do I intentionally want to get stung by a bee? Oh... no!

  (A) 이 치료법이 특이하다는 것을 인정하기 위해
  (B) 벌침에 대한 사람들의 태도를 간략히 설명하기 위해
  (C) 벌침을 이용한 봉독요법이 정말 고통스러움을 강조하기 위해
  (D) 벌침 치료에 대한 자신의 개인적인 의견을 주기 위해

해설 교수 자신을 포함한 대부분의 사람들은 일부러 벌에 쏘이는 일은 하지 않지만 류머티즘 관절염을 앓고 있는 환자들은 벌침의 고통을 감수하고라도 치료를 위해서는 벌에 쏘이는 쪽을 택할 거라는 것을 강조하고 있다.

4 교수가 다음과 같은 말을 한 의미는 무엇인가?

> P Uh, we haven't been very successful at isolating these chemicals, but why bother... when administering them via the bee sting seems to really work for a lot of people?

  (A) 사람들을 치료하는 데 효과적인 화학 물질을 사용하여 발명된 약은 없다.
  (B) 벌침 요법은 류머티즘 관절염 환자들을 치료하는 데 충분히 효과적이다.
  (C) 류머티즘 관절염에 효과적인 화학 물질에 대한 연구가 더 많아져야 한다.
  (D) 화학물질의 정체를 성공적으로 밝혀낼 때까지 벌침 치료가 이용되어서는 안 된다.

해설 치료의 직접적 원인이 되는 물질을 분리하지는 못했지만 류머티즘 관절염을 앓고 있는 환자들에게 적용시켜 본 결과 효과가 있음이 입증되었다.

Actual Test 2

교내 의료 센터에서 일어난 대화의 일부를 듣고 물음에 답하시오.

🎧 스크립트

N What can I do for you?
S I'm coughing a lot.
N Oh, okay... you'll just have to wait a bit. Have you visited the student health center before?
S Uh-uh. This is my first semester at the college.
N Okay. And we don't charge the students for their visit. Can I see your ID?
S Umm... wait. Oh! Great, well... how about other IDs?
N I'm sorry?
S Like my social security number.
N Well, is there anything else that can verify that you're a student here? Our health services are free to the students only.
S Oh, I have my license. Will my driver's license work?
N That will be fine. If the doctor prescribes medicine for your cough, you'll have to pay for it. You can get it for a discount at the campus pharmacy, though.
S Okay... is there anything else I need to do?
N Yes. Just fill out this questionnaire asking you about your medical history, any other health concerns, those kinds of things.
S Okay. Should I come back after my class, which starts in thirty minutes?
N I'll have the doctor see you as soon as possible.

간호사 무엇을 도와드릴까요?
학생 제가 기침을 좀 많이 해서요.
간호사 네, 알겠습니다. 잠깐 기다리셔야 합니다. 전에 학생 의료 센터에 방문한 적이 있나요?
학생 저, 전 이번이 대학 첫 학기예요.
간호사 좋아요. 학생들이 (병원을) 방문할 경우에는 진료비를 청구하지 않습니다. 신분증을 보여주시겠어요?
학생 네, 잠깐만요. 이런, 다른 신분증은 안 되나요?
간호사 네(어떤 거요)?
학생 사회보장번호 같은 거요.

간호사	글쎄요, 학생 신분임을 입증할 수 있는 다른 것은 없나요? 저희 진료 서비스는 학생에게만 무료거든요.
학생	아, 면허증이 있어요. 제 운전면허증은 될까요?
간호사	됩니다. 의사 선생님께서 기침 증세에 맞게 처방전을 써주시면 약값은 지불하셔야 합니다. 하지만 그것도 학교 약국에 가시면 할인 받으실 수 있어요.
학생	알겠습니다. 더 필요한 게 있나요?
간호사	네. 학생의 병력이나 다른 건강 문제 같은 것을 묻는 이 질문지를 작성해 주세요.
학생	네. 수업 끝나고 다시 와야 할까요? 수업이 30분 후에 시작하거든요.
간호사	가능한 한 빨리 진찰받도록 해드릴게요.

1 간호사가 학생증을 요구한 이유는 무엇인가?
 (A) 그가 병원에 온 적이 없다는 것을 입증하기 위해
 (B) 그가 신분증이 있는지 없는지 물어보기 위해
 (C) 그가 무료 진찰을 받을 자격이 있는지 확인하기 위해
 (D) 기록을 위해 그의 개인 정보를 얻기 위해

해설 학생들은 진료비가 무료라고 했다. 무료 진료 혜택을 받으려면 학생 신분을 증명할 수 있어야 한다.

2 간호사가 학교 약국에 대해 말한 것은 무엇인가?
 (A) 학생들이 처방전을 받으면 할인된 가격으로 약을 제공한다.
 (B) 병원 옆에 위치해 있다.
 (C) 약을 무료로 제공한다.
 (D) 학생들은 (의무적으로) 학교 약국을 이용해야 한다.

해설 처방전을 받아 교내 약국으로 가면 할인 혜택을 받을 수 있다.

3 대화의 일부를 다시 들으시오.

 N What can I do for you?
 S I'm coughing a lot.

학생이 다음과 같이 말한 이유는 무엇인가?

 S I'm coughing a lot.

 (A) 몸 상태가 좋지 않은지 그 이유를 설명하기 위해
 (B) 사소한 병세가 있음을 의미하기 위해
 (C) 자신이 제대로 된 장소를 찾아왔는지 확인하기 위해
 (D) 절차가 긴 것에 대해 불평하기 위해

해설 간호사가 학생에게 진료 예약을 했는지 묻자 학생은 기침을 많이 해서 왔다고 한다. 즉, 감기 증후를 발견하여 찾아왔다는 얘기이다.

4 대화의 일부를 다시 들으시오.

 S umm... wait... Oh! Great, well... how about other IDs?
 N I'm sorry?

간호사가 다음과 같은 말을 한 의미는 무엇인가?

 N I'm sorry?

 (A) 다른 신분증은 안 된다는 것을 나타내기 위해
 (B) 남자에게 다시 말해달라고 부탁하기 위해
 (C) 남자에게 신분증을 자세히 설명해 달라고 요구하기 위해
 (D) 남자에 대한 자신의 느낌을 표현하기 위해

해설 학생이 다른 ID를 내겠다는 말에 I'm sorry?라며 반문하고 있다. 뒤에 이어지는 학생의 대답(Like my social security number.)을 보면, 학생 신분증 외에 구체적으로 어떤 신분증이냐는 물음이다.

Dictation **Actual Test**

Actual Test 1

① avoid bee stings
② want to get stung by a bee
③ the chronic pain of
④ are willing to be stung
⑤ injected with bee venom
⑥ called bee venom therapy
⑦ on joints, such as elbow or knee
⑧ While it isn't widely endorsed
⑨ extremely potent anti-inflammatories
⑩ when they are allowed to sting patients
⑪ at isolating these chemicals
⑫ when administering them via the bee sting

Actual Test 2

① I'm coughing a lot
② This is my first semester at the college
③ we don't charge the students for their visit
④ Like my social security number
⑤ are free to the students only
⑥ prescribes medicine for your cough
⑦ You can get it for a discount
⑧ fill out this questionnaire
⑨ which starts in

Vocabulary Review

다음 각 정의에 알맞은 단어를 골라 써 넣으시오.

1 relax   2 sacred   3 endorse   4 verify
5 prescribe   6 disrupt   7 avoid   8 cancel
9 depict   10 therapy

1 덜 경직되거나 견고해지다
2 신성한 것으로 믿거나, 종교와 관련된
3 당신이 지지하거나 승인함을 확신시키다
4 과학적 실험을 통해 어떤 것이 사실임을 확인하다
5 어떤 약이나 치료법을 써야 하는지 써주다
6 어떤 것이 작동되지 못하게 하거나 계속되지 않게 하다
7 어떤 것 또는 누군가로부터 멀리 떨어지다
8 예정된 일을 취소하거나 연기하다
9 글이나 그림으로 설명하다
10 정신적·육체적 질병을 가진 사람에 대한 특별한 치료

다음 구문을 사용하여 문장을 완성하시오.

1 involved in   2 instead of   3 enough to
4 suffering from   5 familiar with

1 당신은 얼마나 많은 차가 그 충돌 사고에 관련되어 있는지 아는가?
2 한국 사람들은 왜 우리 가족이나 우리 형처럼 '나의' 라는 말 대신에 '우리' 를 쓰는지 궁금하다.
3 눈이 올만큼 춥지는 않다.
4 리포터는 그 지역의 거주자들이 현재 물 기근을 겪고 있다고 말했다.
5 나는 우리 회사의 우편 체계에 대해 익숙하지 않아 걱정이다.

Progress Test

5 1 - (D) 2 - (B) 3 - (D) 4 - (A) 5 - (C)
6 1 - (B) 2 - (D) 3 - (A) 4 - (C) 5 - (A)

Progress Test 5

산파에 관한 토론의 일부를 듣고 물음에 답하시오.

🎧 스크립트

P The role of the midwife in attending and assisting with labor is an ancient practice seen in almost all cultures. However, by the mid-19th century, more and more women began to use primarily male doctors rather than female midwives to attend their births. There were a number of reasons for this change. Does anyone have any thoughts on what these might be?

S1 Well, I know that death in childbirth was a lot more common in the past than it was today, and those days maybe, uh... the belief was spread that it was less dangerous to give birth in a hospital with a doctor than at home with a midwife.

S2 I'll bet it was more about money. As it became more... uh... more profitable to be a doctor, they probably wanted less competition and possessed all the information related to the childbirth exclusively.

P Actually, you're both right. By the mid-19th century, as doctors learned more about the causes of disease like childbed fever, which was one of the leading causes of death in childbearing women, and the need to wash their hands and sterilize instruments, mortality declined. Of course, passing this information on to midwives would have had the same effect for midwifery practices. But doctors, as Mike said, were competitive, and wanted to increase their business, which is basically what happened. Now, let's look at the particular ways in which scientific understanding increased during this time.

교수 임산부를 돌보거나 분만을 돕는 산파의 역할은 고대 모든 문화에서 볼 수 있는 의학 풍토의 하나입니다. 그러나 19세기 중반에 이르러서는 점점 더 많은 여성들이 분만 시 여자 산파보다 남자 의사들을 선호하기 시작했습니다. 이같은 변화에는 여러 이유가 있었습니다. 이런 현상이 일어난 이유에 대해 누구 아는 사람 있나요?

학생 1 네, 과거에는 분만 시 유아의 사망률이 지금보다 훨씬 더 높았다고 알고 있어요. 그리고 그 당시에는 집에서 산파의 도움으로 아이를 낳는 것보다는 병원에서 의사가 함께 하는 것이 덜 위험하다는 믿음이 팽배했었죠.

학생 2 제가 보기엔 분명 돈과 관련이 있는 것 같아요. 의사라는 직업이 점점 더 돈벌이가 되자 의사들은 아마도 경쟁자가 줄어들기를 원했을 테고, 그래서 출생과 관련한 정보들을 자기들만이 독점하게 된 거죠.

교수 네, 둘 다 맞습니다. 19세기 중반에 이르러 의사들은 임신 여성의 주요 사망 원인의 하나였던 산욕열 같은 질병이 발생하는 원인을 알게 되었고, 손을 씻거나 의료 도구 소독의 필요성을 인식하게 되었죠. 그 결과, 사망률도 줄어들었습니다. 당연히, 이런 정보를 산파들에게도 전달한다면 산파 시술시에도 같은 효과를 불러왔을 겁니다. 하지만 Mike가 말했듯이 의사들은 경쟁적으로 자신들의 사업을 번창시키고자 했습니다. 기본적으로 이렇게 된 겁니다. 자, 이제 이 시기에 과학적 지식이 증가한 특정 분야들을 살펴봅시다.

1 **토론은 주로 무엇에 관한 것인가?**
(A) 산파보다 의사를 활용할 때 생기는 이점
(B) 세계의 산파술 비교

(C) 임산부들이 걸릴 수 있는 질병의 종류들
(D) 19세기에 여성 산파의 수가 감소한 이유

해설 고대에는 산파가 출산을 돕는 일이 관행이었으나 19세기 중반부터 그 역할이 의사(주로 남자 의사)들에게로 넘어간 배경에 대해 얘기하고 있다.

2 토론의 일부를 다시 들으시오.

P However, by the mid-19th century, more and more women began to use primarily male doctors rather than female midwives to attend their births. There were a number of reasons for this change. Does anyone have any thoughts on what these might be?

교수가 다음과 같은 말을 한 의미는 무엇인가?

P Does anyone have any thoughts on what these might be?

(A) 교수는 그 이유가 무엇인지 확신하지 못한다.
(B) 교수는 학생들이 참여하기를 바란다.
(C) 교수는 그 이유가 명확하다고 생각한다.
(D) 교수는 학생들이 알고 있다고 생각하지 않는다.

해설 교수는 산파의 역할 축소라는 화두를 던져놓고 그 이유를 밝힘에 있어 학생들의 참여를 유도하고 있다.

3 토론의 일부를 다시 들으시오.

S1 Well, I know that death in childbirth was a lot more common in the past than it was today, and those days maybe, uh... the belief was spread that it was less dangerous to give birth in a hospital with a doctor than at home with a midwife.

S2 I'll bet it was more about money. As it became more... uh... more profitable to be a doctor, they probably wanted less competition and possessed all the information related to the childbirth exclusively.

학생들에 관해 추론할 수 있는 것은 무엇인가?
(A) 그들은 같은 의견을 공유하고 있다.
(B) 그들 모두 교수에 의견에 동의하지 않는다.
(C) 둘다 이유가 무엇인지 확신하지 못한다.
(D) 그들은 (산파 수 감소) 원인에 대한 의견이 서로 다르다.

해설 두 학생은 산파의 수가 감소하게 된 이유에 대해 서로 다른 의견을 내놓고 있다. 교수는 학생들의 참여를 유도했을 뿐 이 단계에서는 아직 특정 의견을 제시하지 않았다.

4 교수의 말에 따르면, 의사들이 정보 공유를 꺼린 이유는 무엇인가?
(A) 산파들과 경쟁하고 싶지 않았다.
(B) 산파들(의 존재)을 알지 못했다.
(C) 산파가 (그 정보를) 이해하지 못할 거라고 생각했다.
(D) 정보가 이미 알려져 있다고 생각했다.

해설 의사들은 자신들이 습득한 정보를 산파들과 공유할 경우 소득이 줄어들게 될 것을 염려했다.

5 교수가 소독된 의료 기구에 대해 언급한 이유는 무엇인가?
(A) 의사들이 사용하기 전에 산파가 사용한 것의 예를 들기 위해
(B) 아주 최근까지도 병원에서 의료 기구를 소독하는 것이 흔치 않은 일이었음을 보여주기 위해
(C) 사망률을 낮추게 된 방법의 예를 들기 위해
(D) 여성들이 산욕열을 일으킨 일반적인 원인이 소독된 의료 기구 때문임을 나타내기 위해

해설 산욕열의 원인 발견, 위생 및 의료 기구 소독 등에 관한 중요성을 인식함에 따라 산모의 사망률이 감소하게 되었다.

Progress Test 6
교수와 학생의 대화를 듣고 물음에 답하시오.

 스크립트

S Hi, Professor Jackson. I had an appointment with you today.
P Sure, Janie, come on in. What can I do for you?
S Well, I've decided to apply for an internship this summer at Starmark Publishing... if I get it, it will be a really good experience.
P Terrific. Starmark is a big company. Not only is it well-known, which can help you get a job when you graduate, but if you enjoy working there, they will probably be able to find a position for you.
S That's kind of what I'm hoping. But anyway, the reason I wanted to talk to you was to see if you would mind writing me a recommendation for the internship. I need two references. I thought it would be good to have one from an English professor.
P Absolutely. Is there a form I need to fill out or something?
S No, not really. They just want a letter talking about why I'd be good for the job. I've got the hiring person's name and address.
P Okay. And you know what else would help

me? A copy of your résumé, so I can mention some of your professional accomplishments, extracurricular activities, that kind of thing.

S Sure, no problem. I can email those to you when I get home.

학생 안녕하세요, Jackson 교수님. 오늘 교수님과 약속을 했었는데요.
교수 그럼요, Janie. 어서 들어와요. 무엇을 도와줄까요?
학생 저, 제가 이번 여름에 Starmark 출판사의 인턴제에 지원하기로 결정을 했습니다. 만약 그렇게 된다면 아주 좋은 경험이 될 것 같아서요.
교수 좋죠. Starmark는 아주 큰 회사잖아요. 유명한 회사라 학생이 졸업한 후 취직을 할 때도 도움이 될 거예요. 뿐만 아니라 거기서 일하는 게 마음에 든다면 아마 그 회사에서 (인턴제가 끝난 후) 학생을 위해 자리를 마련해 줄 수도 있을 거예요.
학생 저도 그랬으면 좋겠어요. 그런데, 제가 오늘 교수님을 찾아뵌 이유는 교수님께서 그 인턴제에 제 추천서를 써주실 수 있는지 여쭤보려고요. 추천서 두 장이 필요한데 하나는 영어과 교수님께 받으면 좋을 것 같아서요.
교수 물론이에요. 내가 작성해야 할 양식이나 뭐 그런 것이 있나요?
학생 아뇨, 그렇지는 않습니다. 그 회사에서는 그냥 제가 그 임무에 적합한 이유가 무엇인지에 관해 쓴 거면 된다고 합니다. 저한테 고용주의 이름과 주소가 있어요.
교수 좋아요. 그리고 나한테 있으면 도움이 될 게 뭔줄 알죠? 학생의 이력서가 필요해요. 그걸 봐야 내가 학생이 성취한 내력이나 과외 활동들 같은 것을 언급할 수 있을 테니까요.
학생 네, 문제없어요. 집에 가서 이메일로 보내드리겠습니다.

1 학생이 교수를 찾아간 이유는 무엇인가?
(A) 인턴제에 대한 교수의 충고를 청하기 위해
(B) 교수에게 추천서를 써달라고 부탁하기 위해
(C) Starmark 출판사에 대한 교수의 견해를 알아보기 위해
(D) 자신이 인턴제 일자리를 얻었다는 것을 교수에게 말하기 위해

해설 Starmark 출판사에 인턴사원으로 근무하려면 2가지 추천서가 필요하다. 학생은 그 중 하나를 영어 교수로부터 받기를 원한다.

2 교수가 Starmark의 규모를 언급한 이유는 무엇인가
(A) (취업을) 진지하게 생각하기에는 그 규모가 너무 작다는 것을 알려주기 위해서
(B) 직원이 너무 많다는 것을 알려주기 위해
(C) 일자리로는 비인간적인 장소일 수 있다는 것을 지적하기 위해
(D) 그녀가 졸업한 후에 (그 회사에서) 일자리를 제공할 수 있을 것임을 언급하기 위해

해설 규모가 큰 출판사이므로 학생이 인턴사원 과정을 잘 이수하고 또 본인이 원할 경우 정식 사원 자리를 내줄 수도 있다.

3 교수는 Starmark에 대해 어떻게 느끼고 있는가?
(A) 그녀가 경력 준비를 위해 일을 시작하기 좋은 회사라고 생각한다.
(B) 그 회사에 대한 정보가 많지 않다.
(C) 그 회사의 인턴제 프로그램에 대해 비판적이다.
(D) 규모가 큰 출판사 가운데 하나이기 때문에 다소 걱정스러워한다.

해설 출판사가 유명하고 규모가 커서 정식 사원으로 취직하기에도 좋을 거라고 했다. 이 출판사에 대한 평가가 긍정적임을 알 수 있다.

4 대화의 일부를 다시 들으시오.

P Okay. And you know what else would help me? A copy of your résumé, so I can mention some of your professional accomplishments, extra-curricular activities, that kind of thing.

교수가 다음과 같이 말한 이유는 무엇인가?

P Okay. And you know what else would help me?

(A) 학위 없이는 그녀의 경력이 쓸모없을 것이라고 충고하기 위해
(B) 그녀가 무엇을 원하고 있는지 잘 이해하고 있다는 확신을 주기 위해
(C) 그녀에 대한 정보가 필요하다는 것을 나타내기 위해
(D) 그녀가 전문 자격증을 가지고 있는 게 보다 이로울 것이라고 암시하기 위해

5 교수는 이메일을 받은 후 무엇을 할 것인가?
(A) 추천서를 쓸 것이다.
(B) 출판사로 그녀의 이력서를 발송할 것이다.
(C) 그녀가 추천서 양식을 가져올 때까지 기다릴 것이다.
(D) 그녀에게 좋은 경력이 될 만한 진로를 추천해 줄 것이다.

해설 학생이 보내는 이력서의 경력 및 기타 사항들을 확인하여 추천서를 쓸 것이다.

Dictation — Progress Test

Progress Test 5

① in attending and assisting with labor
② to attend their births
③ death in childbirth was a lot more common
④ it was less dangerous
⑤ they probably wanted less competition
⑥ related to the childbirth exclusively
⑦ the causes of disease
⑧ the leading causes of death in
⑨ sterilize instruments

⑩ on to midwives
⑪ the same effect for midwifery practices
⑫ in which scientific understanding increased

4 일반적으로 말해서, 사람들은 자신이 결정을 하는 것보다는 지시를 따르는 것을 선호한다.
5 6시에 고객과 약속이 있는 것을 잊으셨나요?

Progress Test 6

① I had an appointment with you
② I've decided to apply for an internship
③ Not only is it well-known
④ they will probably be able to
⑤ That's kind of what I'm hoping
⑥ to see if you would mind
⑦ it would be good to have one
⑧ Is there a form I need to fill out
⑨ I've got the hiring person's name and address
⑩ A copy of your résumé
⑪ your professional accomplishments

Vocabulary Review

다음 각 정의에 알맞은 단어를 골라 써 넣으시오.

1 midwife	2 childbirth	3 sterilize
4 internship	5 accomplishment	6 position
7 curricular	8 publishing	9 hiring
10 competitor		

1 아기의 출산을 돕는 일에 훈련된 여성
2 아이를 낳는 일
3 사물을 청결히 하고 세균을 완전히 없애다
4 교육 실습을 받는 기간
5 훈련을 통해 습득된 기술
6 회사나 조직 내의 일자리
7 학업의 교육 과정과 관련된
8 상점에서 팔게 될 책을 인쇄하는 것
9 당신을 위해 어떤 특정한 일을 할 사람을 고용하거나 그 사람에게 임금을 지불하는 것
10 당신의 경쟁 상대가 되어 당신이 물리치고 싶은 사람

다음 구문을 사용하여 문장을 완성하시오.

| 1 apply for | 2 filling out | 3 A number of |
| 4 rather than | 5 had an appointment | |

1 나는 어떤 회사에 지원할 건지 아직 결정하지 못했다.
2 이 주문서를 작성하시면 주문이 가능합니다.
3 나를 포함한 많은 사람들이 그 회의에 참석하기를 거부했다.

FINAL TEST

Final Test 1

1 - (B) 2 - (C) 3 - (A) (D) 4 - 번역참조 5 - (C)

P We're going to look at Piaget's cognitive development theory today. Now you've all read about this since it was on the syllabus. But, uh, even so I think it's better for me to have the list of the phases in sight so I can follow them.
The first is the uh... sensorimotor phase. Sounds odd, huh? But it makes sense given that kids learn totally through sensation and movement. So from birth to age 2, if you want to teach, appeal to the senses. Toy makers have the right idea by offering brightly colored, touchable toys.
Okay, next! Up to the age of about 7, is the preoperational stage. Here... kids personify certain objects. So a doll becomes basically, well, a real person. Time cannot be conceptualized. Using neutral words helps in learning, since kids cannot think abstractly in this phase.
Then, the child begins to think abstractly and make rational judgments in the concrete phase, which lasts until adolescence. So how can you teach kids in this phase? Let them ask questions. Also, have them explain things back to you.
All right, finally... the last phase is the formal operations stage. Here kids, er... adolescents begin to use deductive reasoning. So what'd be the best way to teach here? Well, I'd just lay out the facts, and let them figure out the rest. What's that mean for school curriculums? Well, uh...we should foster more creativity and require less memorizing of facts, a point which seems to have escaped the notice of educators.

교수 오늘은 피아제의 Cognitive Development(인지 발달) 이론에 관해 살펴보겠습니다. 강의 요강에 나왔으므로 이 자료에 관해서는 모두들 읽어보았을 줄 압니다. 그런데, 에, 그렇더라도 제가 각 단계를 따라가려면 각 단계의 목록을 가까이에 두는 게 좋을 것 같군요.
첫 단계는 에, Sensorimotor Phase(감각운동의 단계)입니다. 이상하게 들리나요? 하지만 어린이들이 자신들의 감각과 운동을 통해 학습한다는 점에서 보면 (이 표현은) 타당합니다. 그러니까 만약 여러분들이, 태어나서 2살까지의 아이들을 가르치고 싶다면 감각에 호소하세요. 장난감 제작자들이 밝은 색상의, 손으로 만질 수 있는 장난감들을 제공하는 것은 (이런 면에서) 좋은 아이디어라고 볼 수 있습니다.
좋아요, 다음을 봅시다! 7살이 될 때까지를 Preoperational Stage(전조작 단계)라고 합니다. 자, 아이들은 어떤 사물을 의인화합니다. 때문에 인형은 기본적으로, 그러니까, 진짜 사람인 겁니다. 시간은 개념화되어 있지 않습니다. 또한 이 단계의 아이들은 추상적으로 사고할 수 없기 때문에 중립적인 어휘들을 사용하는 것이 학습에 도움이 됩니다.
이제, 아이들은 사춘기까지 Concrete Phase(구체적 단계)에 놓이게 되며, 추상적으로 사고하고 합리적인 판단을 내릴 수 있게 됩니다. 그러면 이 단계에서는 아이들을 어떻게 가르쳐야 할까요? 아이들이 질문을 할 수 있도록 하세요. 그리고 그것을 다시 여러분에게 설명하도록 하는 겁니다.
좋아요, 이제 마지막 단계는 Formal Operations(형식 조작) 단계입니다. 이 단계의 아이들, 에, 사춘기 아이들은 연역적 추리를 하기 시작합니다. 그러면 이 단계에서 아이들을 가르치는 최상의 방법은 무엇이 될까요? 글쎄요, 그냥 사실을 던져놓고, 나머지는 아이들이 찾아내도록 하는 겁니다. 학교 수업 과정에서라면 어떤 것이 있을까요? 글쎄요, 음, 창조성을 더 많이 부여하고 사실들을 덜 암기하도록 해야 하지요. 교육자들은 관심 밖인 것 같아 보이지만요.

1 피아제의 이론 가운데 교수가 중점적으로 토론하고 있는 측면은 무엇인가?
(A) 처음 이론이 생성된 이후 어떻게 변화하였는가
(B) 학습 과정과 어떻게 관련이 있는가
(C) 수업 이론과 어떻게 비교할 수 있는가
(D) 피아제의 경험에 어떤 식으로 기초하고 있는가

해설 아이의 연령대에 따라 Sensorimotor Phase, Preoperational Stage, Concrete Phase, Formal Operations Stage로 구분하여 설명하고 있다.

2 교수가 Sensorimotor Phase(감각 운동 단계)에 관해 말한 것은 무엇인가?
(A) 이 단계는 2살에 시작된다.
(B) 감각들은 자극을 통해 학습된다.
(C) 감각을 통해 지식을 습득한다.
(D) 장난감 제작자들은 이 단계에 초점을 맞춘다.

해설 감각(sensation)과 운동(movement)을 통해 학습하는 연령이다.

3 다음 중 Concrete Phase(구체적 단계)의 특징은 무엇인가? 정답 두 개를 고르시오.

(A) 아이들이 합리적 사고 기술을 발달시킬 수 있다.
(B) 교사는 질문에 답함으로써 아이들을 도울 수 있다.
(C) 아이들은 스스로 문제를 이해하는 것을 좋아한다.
(D) 교사는 아이들이 질문을 하도록 장려해야 한다.

4 강의에서 교수는 피아제의 인지 발달 이론에 관해 얘기하고 있다. 다음 중 이 이론의 각 단계에 해당하는 박스에 체크하시오.

	Yes	No
아주 작은 변화에도 대단히 민감하다.		✓
장난감이나 인형을 자신들의 친구로 여긴다.	✓	
많은 질문들을 함으로써 배운다.	✓	
이론적인 질문에 추상적으로 답변한다.		✓
주어진 사실들 사이의 관계를 알고 이해한다.	✓	

5 교수가 다음과 같이 말하는 이유는 무엇인가?

> The first is the uh...sensorimotor phase. Sounds odd, huh? But it makes sense given that kids learn totally through sensation and movement.

(A) 이 용어가 부적절한 것이라고 설득하려고
(B) 이 날의 강의 주제를 밝히려고
(C) 이 단계의 이름이 갖는 의미를 설명하려고
(D) 일반적인 발달 장애를 강조하려고

해설 Sensorimotor가 Sensation과 Movement의 합성어임을 암시하고 있다.

Final Test 2

1 - (B) 2 - (A) 3 - (D) 4 - (C) 5 - (A)

교수와 학생의 대화를 듣고 물음에 답하시오.

S Good afternoon, Professor.
P Oh, hello Jack. Come in.
S Thanks. Did, uh, you notice I was absent today?
P Sure. The class is large, but I notice when students are absent.
S I caught that bug that's going around. Anyway, Debbie Rogers said you showed a short film on the South American Yanomami tribe.
P Right. You missed a good one.
S Well, the reason I'm here is that I looked through the textbook for info on them, but I came up short.
P Oh, don't even bother checking there. Can't you borrow Debbie's notes?
S I did, actually. But I feel I missed out by not seeing that film. Apparently it showed some religious rituals...
P It did. And there's a midterm soon. So I'll put it this way. That information shouldn't be overlooked. I guess you might even say it's vital.
S Yeah. I'd really like to see the film.
P Well, it wasn't actually a film. It was a DVD. Now you're a student, so you can't check out AV materials from the Anthro library, but well, with a note from me, I guess you could probably watch it over there. Want to give that a try?
S Oh, yes, thanks!
P Here, I'll write up a note now. I can't promise anything, but it's worth a try.

학생 안녕하세요, 교수님
교수 아, Jack, 안녕하신가. 들어와요.
학생 감사합니다. 저, 제가 오늘 결석한 거 알고 계세요?
교수 그럼요. 클래스가 크긴 하지만 학생들이 자리를 비우면 안답니다.
학생 제가 요즘 유행하고 있는 병에 걸렸었거든요. 그런데 Debbie Rogers가 말하기를 교수님께서 남미 Yanomami 부족에 관한 짧은 필름을 보여주셨다고 하던데요.
교수 그래요. 학생은 아주 좋은 자료를 놓쳤어요.
학생 저, 제가 오늘 여기 온 이유도, 그들에 관한 정보를 찾으려고 교재를 살펴봤는데 내용이 부족했기 때문입니다.
교수 아, 교재는 살펴볼 필요 없어요. Debbie의 노트를 빌리지 못하나요?
학생 실은, (벌써) 빌렸어요. 그런데 그 필름을 보지 못하는 바람에 제가 놓친 부분이 있는 것 같아서요. 어쨌든 분명히 그 필름에서는 몇 가지 종교적인 의식을 보여주고 있잖아요.
교수 그랬지요. 그리고 곧 중간고사도 있네요. 그래서 말인데, 이렇게 하죠. (그 필름에서 다루고 있는) 정보는 간과할 수 없는 부분이에요. 학생은 어쩌면 제일 중요하다고 할지도 모르겠군요.
학생 네. 정말 그 필름을 보고 싶습니다.
교수 저, 사실 그건 필름은 아니라 DVD랍니다. Jack은 학생이니까 인류학 도서관에서 시청각 자료를 빌릴 수는 없을 겁니다. 그렇지만 음, 내가 써 준 메모를 가져가면 거기서 아마 보게 해 줄 거예요. 그렇게 해볼래요?
학생 네, 그럼요. 감사합니다.
교수 자, 지금 메모를 써 줄게요. 장담은 못하겠지만 한번 시도해 볼 만은 할 겁니다.

1 남자가 교수를 찾아간 이유는 무엇인가?
(A) 수업시간의 교수 노트필기를 얻기 위해
(B) 다큐멘터리 시청에 관해 질문하기 위해
(C) 자신이 본 DVD에 관해 질문하기 위해

(D) 프로젝트에 관해 더 많은 정보를 구하기 위해

해설 남자는 몸이 아파 지난 수업 시간에 결석 했을 당시 교수는 남미 Yanomami 부족에 관한 영상물을 상영했다.

2 학생이 반 친구에게 부탁해서 필요한 정보를 얻지 않는 이유는 무엇인가?
  (A) 정보가 부족하다고 생각한다.
  (B) 교수의 노트가 더 낫다고 생각한다.
  (C) 그 학생의 공책을 얻을 수가 없었다.
  (D) 의식에 관한 정보가 잘못된 것이라고 생각한다.

해설 친구의 노트 필기가 영상물에서 보여준 남미 Yanomami 부족의 종교적 의식을 대신할 수는 없다.

3 교수가 다음과 같이 말할 때, 그 말의 의미는 무엇인가?

> And there's a midterm soon. So I'll put it this way. That information shouldn't be overlooked. I guess you might even say it's vital.

  (A) 그가 놓친 자료에 관해 보다 더 집중해야 한다.
  (B) 마감 기한을 대단히 중요하게 생각해야 한다.
  (C) 아직은 중간고사 시험에 대비해 공부할 시간이 있다.
  (D) 다큐멘터리에 실린 내용이 앞으로 있을 시험에 출제될 것이다.

해설 곧 다가올 중간고사에 출제될 것임을 암시하면서 주의 깊게 살펴보라고 (shouldn't be overlooked) 충고하고 있다.

4 대화의 일부를 다시 듣고 물음에 답하시오.

> Here, I'll write up a note now. I can't promise anything.

이 말을 통해 추론할 수 있는 것은 무엇인가?
  (A) 교수는 메모를 쓰지 않는 것이 더 낫다.
  (B) 교수는 그가 메모를 받을 수 있는지 확신하지 못한다.
  (C) 그 메모로는 교수가 의도한 바가 실행될 수 없을지도 모른다.
  (D) 그 메모는 정말 필요할 때에만 사용해야 한다.

해설 학생이 도서관에서 자료를 빌려볼 수 있도록 도서관 관리자에게 메모를 써 줄 수는 있지만, 그것이 효과가 있을지는 자신도 장담하지 못하고 있다.

5 학생이 다음에 할 행동으로 가장 알맞은 것은 무엇인가?
  (A) 다큐멘터리를 보기 위해 도서관에 간다.
  (B) Debbie를 만나기 위해 도서관에 간다.
  (C) Yanomami에 관한 책을 찾으러 간다.
  (D) DVD가 강의에서 (다 쓰고) 반환되었는지 확인하러 간다.

해설 교수가 써 준 메모를 가지고 도서관에 갈 것이다.

NEXUS makes your next day
www.nexusEDU.kr | 책에 대해 궁금한 사항은 넥서스에듀 홈페이지 1:1 고객상담 게시판을 이용하세요.

NEXUS TOEFL® *i*BT Listening Series의 특징

1. 단계별 기본 학습 훈련 장치 강조
2. 다양한 테마의 강의와 대화 체계적 분석
3. 체계적인 학습 스킬과 전략 구성
4. 어휘력 확장
5. *i*BT 실전에 맞춘 단계별 연습 문제

NEXUS TOEFL® *i*BT Series의 특징

Reading	Starter	Level 1	Level 2	Level 3
Listening	Starter	Level 1	Level 2	Level 3
Writing		Starter	Level 1	Level 2
Speaking		Starter	Level 1	Level 2

Listening

www.nexusEDU.kr
넥서스 초·중·고등 사이트

www.nexusON.com
넥서스 온라인 사이트

NEXUS makes your next day

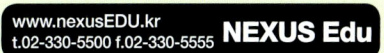

www.nexusEDU.kr
t.02-330-5500 f.02-330-5555
NEXUS Edu

단계적 학습으로
영어 읽기 끝장내기!

**영어로만 구성된 원서형 장문 독해 교재로 영어식 사고력과
독해 능력을 업그레이드시킨다!**

▶ 영어로만 구성된 원서형 독해 교재
▶ 다양한 주제의 지문을 통해 독해력 향상 및 폭넓은 배경지식 습득
▶ 요약, 주제 찾기, 어법, 어휘, 유추 등 다양한 문제로 각종 시험 대비
▶ 지문의 중요 단어가 일목요연하게 정리된 미니 어휘북 제공

THIS IS READING

Level 1 (2권) EDUCATION DESIGNERS 지음 | 210×290 | 142쪽 | 11,000원
Level 2 (2권) EDUCATION DESIGNERS 지음 | 210×290 | 142쪽 | 11,000원
Level 3 (2권) EDUCATION DESIGNERS 지음 | 210×290 | 142쪽 | 11,000원
Level 4 (2권) EDUCATION DESIGNERS 지음 | 210×290 | 142쪽 | 11,000원

NEXUS makes your next day

www.nexusEDU.kr
t.02-330-5500 f.02-330-5555
NEXUS Edu

뉴 토플의 중요한 학습 포커스는 논술의 기초 능력 배양입니다.
정보의 요지 파악, 요약 정리 능력이 논술의 기초이기 때문입니다.

- Global understanding을 강조한 정보 정리, 요약 훈련 강조 : text organization, summary, speed reading
- 다양한 테마별 · 수사학적 지문 구조 분석 강조
- 어휘력 확장, 나선형 · 반복형 학습 장치 강조

	Starter	Level 1	Level 2	Level 3	iBT TOEFL 실전모의고사 1 (LC / RC)
Reading	Vocab Workbook Starter	Vocab Workbook 1	Vocab Workbook 2	Vocab Workbook 3	
Listening	Starter	Level 1	Level 2	Level 3	
	Vocab Workbook Starter	Vocab Workbook 1	Vocab Workbook 2	Vocab Workbook 3	
Writing		Starter	Level 1	Level 2	
Speaking		Starter	Level 1	Level 2	

※ MP3 유료다운로드

Reading Starter - 13,500원
Reading Level 1 - 13,800원(CD 1개 포함)
Reading Level 2 - 14,000원
Reading Level 3 - 15,000원

Reading Starter Workbook - 3,500원
Reading Level 1 Workbook - 4,000원
Reading Level 2 Workbook - 4,000원
Reading Level 3 Workbook - 4,000원

Listening Starter - 13,000원
Listening Level 1 - 13,800원
Listening Level 2 - 13,500원
Listening Level 3 - 13,800원

Listening Starter Workbook - 3,000원
Listening Level 1 Workbook - 3,000원
Listening Level 2 Workbook - 3,000원
Listening Level 3 Workbook - 3,000원

Writing Starter - 13,800원(CD 1개 포함)
Writing Level 1 - 14,500원(CD 1개 포함)
Writing Level 2 - 14,500원(CD 1개 포함)

Speaking Starter - 13,500원(CD 1개
Speaking Level 1 - 15,000원(CD 2개
Speaking Level 2 - 15,000원(CD 2개